AN ANALYSIS OF EDUCATIONAL CHALLENGES IN THE NEW SOUTH AFRICA

Zandile P. Nkabinde

University Press of America, Inc.
Lanham • New York • Oxford

Copyright © 1997 by
University Press of America,® Inc.
4720 Boston Way
Lanham, Maryland 20706

12 Hid's Copse Rd.
Cummor Hill, Oxford OX2 9JJ

All rights reserved
Printed in the United States of America
British Library Cataloguing in Publication Information Available

Library of Congress Cataloging-in-Publication Data

Nkabinde, Zandile P.
An analysis of educational challenges in the new South Africa / by
Zandile P. Nkabinde.
p.   cm.
Includes bibliographical references.
1. Education--South Africa. 2. Blacks--Education--South Africa. 3.
Educational change--South Africa. I. Title.
LA1536.N53   1997   370'.968--dc21   96-51717 CIP

ISBN 0-7618-0657-1 (cloth: alk. ppr.)
ISBN 0-7618-0658-X (pbk: alk. ppr.)

⊖™ The paper used in this publication meets the minimum
requirements of American National Standard for information
Sciences—Permanence of Paper for Printed Library Materials,
ANSI Z39.48—1984

This book is dedicated to my late parents, Elka William and Thembekile Agnes Nkabinde (umaNgcobo), who always encouraged me to work hard and who instilled in me a sense of purpose.

Contents

List of Tables viii

Foreword x

Preface xii

Acknowledgments xv

Introduction xvi

Chapter 1 Educational Development For Black People In South Africa 1

   1.1 Introduction 1
   1.2 Historical Overview 2
   1.3 What Is Bantu Education? 5
   1.4 Plan for Nonracial Education 9
   1.5 Types of Schools Currently Available 13
   1.6 The Present Structure of Education 15
   1.7 Examinations 26
   1.8 Teachers 34

Chapter 2 Dropout Rates In Black Schools 49

2.1 Introduction 50
2.2 Prevalence 51
2.3 Potential Causes of Education Dropout Rates
    Among Blacks 52
2.4 Future Plans and Recommendations 57
2.5 Conclusion 61

Chapter 3 Adult Education 65

3.1 Introduction 65
3.2 Rationale for Adult Education 66
3.3 What Do Adults Need? 67
3.4 Workers' Education 71
3.5 Conclusion 74

Chapter 4 Special Education For Black South Africans 75

4.1 Introduction 75
4.2 Developments in Special Education 76
4.3 Brief History of Special Education in South Africa 77
4.4 Prevalence of People With Disabilities 78
4.5 Social Contributions To Disabilities Among Blacks 78
4.6 Early Childhood Special Education 81
4.7 Present Status: Residential and Special Day Schools ... 82
4.8 Training of Special Education Personnel 85
4.9 Curriculum 89
4.10 The Method of Special Education 90
4.11 Unique Challenges of Special Education in South Africa 92
4.12 Future Trends 93
4.13 Conclusion 96

Chapter 5 Language Policy In Postapartheid Education 99

5.1 Introduction 99
5.2 Current Language Policy 102
5.3 Can English Be a Medium of Instruction? 102
5.4 Arguments Against the Use of English as a
    Medium of Instruction 105

5.5 Rationale for Preserving Vernacular Languages 107
5.6 Recommendations 111
5.7 Conclusion 116

Chapter 6 Teaching And Learning In Black Universities ... 117

6.1 Introduction 117
6.2 Historical Background 118
6.3 Administration and Staff Composition 120
6.4 Curriculum 121
6.5 Teaching Methods 124
6.6 Academic Freedom 127
6.7 Recommendations 128
6.8 Conclusion 133

Chapter 7 Gender Issues In Education 135

7.1 Introduction 135
7.2 Historical Background 136
7.3 Problems Faced By Black Women of South Africa ... 138
7.4 Rationale for Educating Women 140
7.5 Empowering Black Women: A New Vision 141
7.6 Steps To Be Taken in Empowering Black Women ... 142
7.7 Conclusion 144

Chapter 8 Aims Of Education 147

8.1 Aims of Education in a Future South Africa 147
8.2 Curriculum Issues 150
8.3 Teaching Methods 153
8.4 Community Involvement 155
8.5 Teaching Diversity Issues in South Africa 157
8.6 Rationale for Teaching Diversity in Schools 158
8.7 Making Diversity a Learning Experience 159
8.8 Conclusion 162

Chapter 9 Beyond Bantu Education: Changes, Challenges, And Harsh Realities 165

9.1 Introduction 165
9.2 Will a Unitary Education System Achieve Anything? .. 167
9.3 Conclusion 170

Chapter 10 The Financing Of Education 173

10.1 Introduction 173
10.2 Historical Background 174
10.3 Current Educational Funding 175
10.4 Summary 180

Chapter 11 Africa's Lessons For South Africa 183

11.1 Introduction 183
11.2 The Case of Nigeria 185
11.3 The Case of Zimbabwe 192
11.4 The Case of Tanzania 199
11.5 Summary of the African Experience 202
11.6 Implications for South Africa 210
11.7 Legacies of Colonial Education 212
11.8 Conclusion 213
11.9 South Africa and the Future 216

Chronology 219

Clarification of Terminology 223

Selected Bibliography 229

Index 250

List of Tables

1.1 The Twelve-Year School Structure 16

1.2 The Thirteen-Year School Structure 17

1.3 Matriculation Results By Race 27

1.4 Underqualified African Teachers 41

1.5 Educational Expenditure for Different Groups 44

2.1 Percentage of Pupils Reaching Standard Four (Sixth Grade) and Standard Ten (Twelfth Grade) 52

3.1 Percentage of Adult Literacy Rate 67

4.1 Number of Hearing Impaired Children Receiving Educational Services 85

4.2 Number of Visually Impaired Children Receiving Educational Services 86

4.3 Number of Physically Handicapped Children Receiving Educational Services 87

4.4 Projected Number of Handicapped Children in the Year 2020 88

5.1 Languages Spoken in South Africa 100

6.1 Major Black Universities 120

6.2 Percentage of Lecturers at South African Black Universities 122

Foreword

May 10, 1994, was a triumphant moment in South African history, if not an equally momentous occasion in the annals of twentieth century history. On this day the entire world fixed its sights on the magisterial inauguration of Nelson Mandela as the first democratically elected president of South Africa. Remarkably, the transfer of power from the older order to a new one was not as calamitous as pundits had predicted.

While the end of the old apartheid order was an occasion for jubilation, it, sadly, bequeathed a ruinous legacy that will haunt generations to come. For the overwhelming majority of the South African population, the scourge of apartheid policies has left no aspect of human experience untouched: from racial discrimination, economic exploitation, social dislocation, cultural emasculation, and psychological impairment to educational deprivation. Much pain and disability have been suffered in each of these illustrative areas. Social scientists in all their variety will be engaged in investigating the effects of apartheid on its victims and its architects for the foreseeable future.

Not least among the broad spectra of fundamental human rights denied under apartheid has been some deliberate and systematic education policies whose undisguised intent was to withhold the one, and arguably, single-most important right to empower the individual and society: education. Human development, in its most democratic and inclusive sense, has not been an experience enjoyed equally by all South Africans regardless of race, class, and gender. The deleterious effects of segregated (and therefore inferior) education go far back into the history of colonial South Africa. These effects were further exacerbated by the imposition of the policy of Bantu education, which was passed into law in 1953. Assessing the effects of Bantu education in the 1960s, a South African educationist noted that it will take Africans, coloreds, and Indians sixty years to close the education gap.

Reconstruction of the structure and content of the South African education system is what consumes the energies of democratic educationists. Those with a vested interest in the racially exclusive rights and privileges of the past are waging fierce opposition to equity efforts. In this book, Zandile Nkabinde sets out to document the landscape, the faults in the topography, and the seismic traits of apartheid education. She eschews fixation in this gruesome past. The declared purpose of her book to "explore possible solutions to black education" furthermore calls for the active participation of those most disenfranchised from decision making during the old apartheid order. Not only is this consistent with the expectations of a democratic culture but, perhaps more fundamentally, authenticates the products of the reconstructed system, thus avoiding alienation. The added value of the book is its attempt to draw from relevant education experiences of other African countries.

The recovery of South Africa, as well as the restoration of sanity and stability, require a wholesale investment in human resources. Sixty years is unaffordable when we are poised on the precipice of another millennium. Current technological changes that are fundamentally affecting erstwhile traditions are expected to accelerate at a dizzying pace. If South Africa is to survive and secure for its people a dignified life in the twenty-first century, it must make herculean investments in human development for those who carry the ugly scourge of the past. The triumph of May 10, 1994, can be preserved for posterity only by a trenchant determination to guarantee education as a practical, not just theoretical, right to the overwhelming many who are still peering from the margins.

Mokubung Nkomo
New School for Social Research
March 9, 1996

Preface

The purpose of this book is to identify several educational challenges facing the "new" South Africa and the effect of Bantu education on black South Africans. I believe, therefore, that there should be a restructuring of the educational system in South Africa, with blacks taking an active role in formulating new educational policies in the postapartheid era. This book discusses current developments in black education in South Africa from the introduction of Bantu education to the beginning of the 1990s. During the period under discussion, improvements have been made in black education. These improvements are partly due to the significant political changes currently taking place in South Africa that are supposed to mark the end of apartheid. Despite these developments, much remains to be done in order to remedy the effects of Bantu education.

In particular, providing quality education in black schools will require innovative solutions. Proper planning, developing new teaching strategies, establishing practical educational goals, and identifying and using available resources must be controlled and harnessed to a new social order. Collaboration and coordination of all professionals, particularly blacks, will be a necessity. The process of change requires black participation in finding solutions to their educational problems; this is one of the major challenges facing postapartheid South Africa.

In the past, education has been planned for Africans without their participation. Too often, African aspirations and their way of life have been distorted or misrepresented. Now it is necessary to have Africans present their views in order to correct the record. I believe that with more written contributions from Africans that their history will be accurately written and that their past will be positively interpreted.

There are numerous reasons for writing this book. First, I will present an African perspective on educational issues. Too often the rich store of information from Africans is ignored. As a result, important work in the planning of education for Africans is formulated by others, whereas those it is designed to help remain marginalized. Meaningful changes in education for black South Africans will not occur without African participation. Black South Africans must take responsibility for mobilizing themselves to become active participants in improving the quality of their education. I believe that neither schools nor the government alone can help provide alternatives to Bantu education. The solution to move away from Bantu education lies in the involvement of people, particularly blacks, in all levels of education.

Therefore, in order to insure that education for blacks is designed in accordance with their immediate needs and aspirations, black professionals in all levels of education must make substantial contributions to education. This task will not be easy. It will require individual and collective input from all black students, as well as various professionals. Relevant books must be published and suitable programs must be designed for the black population in order for real social transformation in South Africa to be realized.

A more important purpose in writing this book is to explore possible solutions to problems in black education, thus contributing to the enrichment of popular debate. It is my hope that some of the issues discussed in this book will trigger interest for further exploration. Unless people who are victims of apartheid education take control of their lives no change will occur. Black South Africans must offer something in order to improve the quality of their education. They must take the initiative in educational change. Consequently, for black South Africans to reverse the legacy of apartheid, they must realize that the answers to their problems will come not from miracles but from themselves. Therefore, if black students are to achieve effective academic progress and if the effects of the apartheid system are to be completely eliminated, blacks cannot depend on grand designers of a system for their redemption.

The postapartheid era will present additional challenges. This book is, therefore, aimed at providing tentative alternative solutions to black education. This book also is intended for students in colleges of education, universities, and other institutions of higher learning. Even though I have looked forward to the postapartheid era, the impact of past apartheid also has been explored.

This book is not the answer to all problems currently facing black education in South Africa. South African scholars will find strengths, limitations, omissions, and personal emphases. However, I will be satisfied if this book provides insights and challenges in seeking alternatives to Bantu education. If the book encourages more Africans to seek solutions to their plight, it will have achieved its purpose.

Acknowledgments

This book is a product of various papers I have prepared for presentations and publications about education in South Africa. My academic career at the University of Utah occurred at the right time and in the right place. The academic environment at the university, complete with all the necessary resources, has made the task of writing a book more pleasant and rewarding.

I have borrowed heavily from the work of others, and I wish to make specific acknowledgment to all the authors whose work has inspired and encouraged me to compile my papers into a book.

I gratefully acknowledge proofreading and editing support from Carolyn P. Bennion who helped me shape my ideas, as well as improve on my writing style.

Special thanks to Humphrey Zukisani Magadla, my husband, for allowing me to use our meager family resources in order to bring this project to reality. A special thanks to my children, Siba, Samora, and Nandi Magadla, for their patience. I hope they will learn from it.

Introduction

The great majority of South Africa's population is African. Moreover, they have always been the consumers of an educational system designed for them without their active participation. For the first time in the history of South Africa, opportunities are emerging for Africans to participate directly or indirectly in the development of their education. The invitation to all stakeholders to take part in educational decisions in South Africa must be welcomed and encouraged. Comprehensive and diverse views from various experts in South African education are urgently needed if policymakers, planners, and the new government are to experiment with new policies aimed at replacing Bantu education.

Thus, the task of writing this book was undertaken in order to contribute to that pool of knowledge. Current educational challenges are discussed against a background of the past political system, as well as socioeconomic and cultural characteristics. An attempt was made to use the most recent and comprehensive available information on the subject, that is, to identify and discuss urgent priorities in education. However, the book is still an incomplete analysis of educational challenges in postapartheid South Africa.

Several chapters of this book are the product of various papers previously prepared for publications and presentations. Some of the key issues in black education likely to be the central theme of the transformation of education in South Africa are addressed. The purpose is to highlight, in a preliminary manner, some of the issues bound to be posed as new postapartheid education policies become eminent. These questions will help shape the direction of an alternative educational system for black South Africans.

The book begins with historical remarks about general education in South Africa. These remarks are aimed at providing the reader with a broader view regarding the previous government's policy of preserving Bantu education in South Africa. The foundations of Bantu education, the plan for nonracial education, the types of schools currently available, and the present structure of education are issues covered in Chapter 1. In addition, this chapter explores possible solutions to the dilemmas currently facing black education.

Chapter 2 explores dropout rates in black schools, focusing on the causes, as well as the social costs. Chapter 3 addresses adult education, problems currently faced by ill-educated, jobless adults whose education has been disrupted. The solution to these problems lies in providing skills and education. Allowing individuals a variety of choices is only one way to empower them with the skills needed to improve their lives. Therefore, adult education is essential for the rehabilitation of people currently excluded from the educational system.

Chapter 4 deals with special education from the past, to the present, and into the future. Attempts are made to define possible solutions in specific areas of special education that would contribute to the elimination of discrimination of persons with special needs.

Chapter 5 addresses the language policy in postapartheid education. Alternative forms of instruction are suggested. The importance of choice and how such an approach might contribute to social transformation constitute the theme of the chapter. This chapter shows, from different perspectives, the crucial roles of language. For example, Africans must relate their history using their languages. Through language, Africans can create and store their experiences, culture, rituals, religion, and traditions. The development of African languages into written form will provide many benefits. Schools, as well as the community at large, will benefit from rich stores of written information.

Chapter 6 discusses teaching and learning in black universities and concludes by giving recommendations for postapartheid South Africa. Chapter 7 discusses gender issues in education with an attempt to clarify gender inequalities connected to cultural attitudes and legal institutions. Thus, gender equality in education is not possible without changes in the customary traditions and laws that affect all aspects of life for women in South Africa.

Chapter 8 examines the aims of education that will incorporate curriculum changes, teaching methods, community involvement, and teaching diversity issues--all issues capable of addressing current educational problems.

Chapter 9 explores some of the difficulties of educational transition. In this chapter, I argue that educational transformation in South Africa will not be smooth because many inequalities cannot be solved quickly.

Chapter 10 surveys options in financing education. The purpose of this chapter is to offer realistic and financially sound innovative solutions to the educational system, which has had a negative impact on Africans for many years. The underlying assumption is that financing education in any society tends to have a decisive influence on the quality of education offered to its population. This chapter explores several funding options that educational experts of the new order might follow.

Chapter 11 provides an overview of Africa's experience since independence, and it discusses repeated efforts by specific African countries to reform their educational systems. These issues are examined against the background of each country's political, social, and economic development. The picture of Africa's educational development is designed to help readers gain a sense of how the new South Africa might avoid repeating mistakes made by other African countries.

The audience for this book is college students, South African scholars, South African policymakers, teacher training colleges in South Africa, and graduate students studying South Africa. The aim throughout is to identify, against an historical background, areas that address immediate attention in improving the quality of black education in postapartheid education. The treatment of different topics provides useful insights toward understanding educational disparities in South Africa. The identification and description of South African educational problems are meant to provide the audience with a sense of how the past has influenced the present as the country envisions the future. This book is a modest addition to the growing list of South African books dealing with education and the future. The text is meant to be a resource for South Africans seeking an alternative to Bantu education.

Chapter 1

Educational Development For Black People In South Africa

1.1 Introduction

As South Africa enters a new era, South Africans will have to realize that one of the most important aspects of the region's developmental challenges is that development depends on education (Barnard 1994). Education generates information, and informed people are capable of contributing to economic development. Black education continues to be a crucial issue as the country enters a new era. Years of neglect and inequality in black education will not disappear overnight; it will take countless years and a great commitment by the majority of South Africans to improve education. Lesage (1994) reported that, in order to establish parity between different groups, South Africa will need 33,000 new classrooms by the end of the decade and that the educational budget will have to increase from its current 19 percent of the national budget (already the highest in the world) to approximately 55 percent.

However, a question remains: What type of postapartheid education is needed in order to redress past inadequacies? Several facts are clear: Blacks themselves have responsibility for creatively changing the education system for the better. The postapartheid education system will be determined by historical, social, demographic, economic, political, and ideological factors. Whether postapartheid in black education remains a myth or reality depends on the joint effort of all South Africans, particularly those of black professionals, in the area of new programs. These programs must establish new developments in motion by generating a plan of action based on the educational and economic needs of the population. Comprehensive educational planning must be based on the transmission of knowledge, skills, and values necessary for the survival of a race. In South Africa, blacks are faced with two problems. First, the curriculum has been centrally designed for blacks without their input, allowing no flexibility. Thus, teachers operate on a tight schedule in which they must rush to cover the syllabus without trying innovative methods. Second, more emphasis is placed on examinations, promoting rote learning at the expense of problem solving and critical thinking. According to Thembela (1993), the moral skills of love, tolerance, and reconciliation are never taught. Values such as respect and honesty also are neglected. Therefore, cultural values that enable children to become useful and responsible citizens are not given the attention they deserve at school (Thembela 1993).

Education is a complex undertaking that has no ready-made solutions. Its design must be drawn on local needs, thus enabling people to acquire transferable skills, abilities, and aptitudes (Lesage 1994). Education is not stagnant but changes with time. Knowledge acquired at school must be usable in the real world. If education is inadequate, there will be insufficient skills. Without enough skills, the economy will not grow, and, without a growing economy, the basic necessities of life cannot be provided.

1.2 Historical Overview

South Africa's present educational needs for the black population should be viewed in the context of the population's lengthy experience with Bantu education and its particular aims. Therefore, in order to comprehend the present situation in black education in South Africa, it is important to have an historical overview of the general educational system. The education of black people in South Africa has progressed through several stages because of political forces within the country.

The indigenous system of education in South Africa, as elsewhere in Africa, is as old as the people themselves (McDowell 1980). Precolonial education for black South Africans was informal because

societal values were orally passed from generation-to-generation. Indigenous education included education about attitudes, values, behavior, religion, and economic matters (South African Bureau of Racial Affairs 1955). Like many other Africans in Africa, South Africans valued their indigenous education in precolonial times. The goals of the traditional education were to
1. Develop obedience for the elderly and authority figures
2. Develop certain survival skills such as farming, food gathering/preservation, and hunting
3. Preserve the culture through oral transmission and making of artifacts
4. Show respect for the environment and other living things
5. Foster communal values of sharing and protecting each other through family ties and extended families
6. Develop cognitive skills for practical purposes
7. Develop an understanding and respect of spiritual powers
8. Develop moral well-being of individuals and adherence to social fairness.

The goals of traditional African education in South Africa indicated that education was meant to enhance moral values, provide vocational training, inculcate codes of behavior, and give spiritual and cognitive foundations to individuals (Corby 1990). This type of education was designed to mold individual minds according to indigenous African community values. Despite its limitations, this type of traditional education proved to be successful in ensuring that families, as well as communities, were engaged in the education of their members.

Immediate family members, as well as communities, formed the cornerstone of education for black youths. Black children learned about their environment, work, and society from older members of the community (Christie 1985). Children learned by performing tasks for their families or communities. This type of education for blacks was continuous, that is, from childhood to adulthood. For example, there were "initiation schools," that is, certain rituals to mark certain stages of development that were part of people' s education (Christie 1985). Historical events, as well as important past traditions, were never recorded but were learned through songs, storytelling, and poems passed on orally (Christie 1985). Children were taught early in life to follow directions from their elders by observing and modeling of the adults. Trades or survival skills were taught by adults in same-sex groups. Boys were taught male-related skills such as hunting, fishing, weaving, constructing homes, farming, and woodworking (Avoke 1993). Girls were trained to be good mothers; consequently, housekeeping skills were important for them. For example, girls were taught child-rearing skills, cooking, making clothes, preserving food, and making baskets and pottery.

Nonformal education for black South Africans did not begin with the arrival of Europeans in 1652, rather it dates from before the first settlers arrived in the country. However, the type of education system that existed before the imposition of Western education was informal and aimed at preparing black people for life within their own environment. With the arrival of Europeans, the environment changed and was accompanied by a need to change education to meet new demands (South African Bureau of Racial Affairs 1955). Europeans introduced a formal education with its own particular methods of instruction and subject matter (Corby 1990).

Colonialism began in South Africa in 1652 with the arrival of the Dutch East India Company. The beginning of colonialism coincided with the reduced impact of traditional education among blacks and marked the beginning of European-style education in South Africa. Although this was a new chapter in the development of black education in South Africa, it unfortunately never considered the traditions or aspirations of the Africans it meant to help. Instead, the main aim of this new education was to civilize and evangelize the African. Geber and Newman (1980) explained that in the early years education for Africans was seen primarily in terms of the labor they would provide. Then it became logical not to allow blacks to have a say in the planning, structuring, and implementing of education (Molobi 1988).

Many blacks resented the fact that they were never consulted in the planning of their education. Since the beginning of colonial times through the takeover of the nationalist government in 1948, unequal education was unacceptable to black people. Molobi (1988) reported that as early as 1658 slaves at the Cape rejected the form of education offered. Later, according to Molobi, many African chiefs reacted by withholding their children from mission schools. As early as the 1920s and until the introduction of Bantu education in the 1950s, students adopted school boycotts and "stay-aways" as forms of protest.

Many schools for Africans were built during the first quarter of the nineteenth century throughout the Cape Colony. These schools were established and controlled by the missionary societies. The overseas missionary societies, primarily responsible for this undertaking, included the Moravian, London, Rhenish, Wesleyan, Berlin, Paris Evangelical, and Glasgow Missions, as well as the Church Missionary Society and the American Board Mission (Behr 1978). Prior to 1953, the types of schools blacks attended, as well as the content of what was taught, were different. These schools were mainly traditional missionary schools. In 1953, the Bantu education Act was introduced, and the South African government imposed a system known as "Bantu education." Simon (1991) reported that the introduction of Bantu education in South Africa marked the origin of the crisis in black education. This system was characterized by rote learning and a curriculum virtually unrelated to Africans' aspirations or practical job qualifications (Johnson and Devlin-Foltz 1993).

1.3 What Is Bantu Education?

The word "Bantu" in the Nguni group of languages such as Zulu, Xhosa, Ndebele, and others means "people" (Arnold 1981). Africans usually use the word "aBantu" to refer to people or the human race. However, the former South African government selected the term Bantu as an official term to refer to blacks. Thus, a phrase such as "Bantu education" refers to the type of education designed for blacks. The introduction of Bantu education in 1954 was aimed at providing separate and unequal education for different races of South Africa. Another motive of Bantu education was to inculcate in blacks a sense of inferiority (Arnold 1981). Hendrik Verwoerd, then Prime Minister, also stated that Bantu education's emphasis should be more practical, focusing mainly on technical skills. Arnold stated that the message was clear: Black carpenters, laborers, and artisans were to be trained for the white economy but not as professionals or thinkers who might threaten the status quo. Prior to the introduction and implementation of Bantu education, more than 70 percent of African schools were taught by missionaries of various denominations; the remainder were controlled by the state or the community (Pampallis 1991). The Bantu Education Act of 1953, implemented in 1955, permitted all African schools to be governed by a separate Department of Native Affairs. Thus, the missionaries and the community lost control over African schools. The system resulted in the control of curriculum, teaching methods, and teachers in return for continued state financial aid (Parsons 1993).

Bantu education, as described by Evans (1992), was a deliberately inferior form of basic education that trained blacks exclusively for employment in menial, low-wage positions in a racially structured economy. Education for other racial minorities prepared them for leadership positions, whereas Bantu education prepared blacks for subservient roles. Bantu education had its curriculum geared towards a "fit-for-blacks" emphasis, including the production of interpreters, messengers, porters, religious ministers, teachers, and nurses (Nkabinde 1993c). Given the narrow focus of the curriculum, its recipients were prepared for professions such as mine boys, bank tellers, plantation workers, construction workers, clerks, and other low-paying jobs. The limitation of Bantu education had the potential of making blacks feel inadequate and incompetent compared to other people. In addition, Bantu education was tailored towards producing certain types of black intellectuals, that is, intellectuals who were supposed to be passive and never question the status quo. Thus, such education was intended to silence the voice of government opponents, and it also was geared to provide certain skills commensurate with the needs of industry (Evans 1992).

The government' s interest was to educate more blacks to suit the needs of the economy. When Bantu education was legally introduced, it was meant to serve definite purposes, one of which was to prevent independence for blacks, including the freedom of expression. Blacks were prevented from owning themselves and, consequently, were controlled by others. Being controlled by others has led black South Africans to lose a sense of direction as to who they are and what they are capable of attaining. The inability to design their own education has done serious educational damage; it also debases self-image, destroys confidence, and lowers motivation.

Bantu education, as designed by the ruling elite, had the following intentions: (a) to provide some basic education for blacks, (b) to provide a system of education that enforced ethnicity, (c) to divide permanently the black population into manageable compartments, and (d) to provide a form of education that promoted technical training at the expense of critical thinking or education geared towards active participation in shaping one' s own life.

1.3.1 The Aim of Bantu Education

Bantu education was meant to replace the traditional missionary schools whose curriculum was criticized for creating inappropriate expectations in the natives, that is, expectations that clashed with life opportunities in the country (Moodie 1994). There was a belief that education available to blacks prior to 1953 was alienating them from their communities. Therefore, a new type of education was designed with the aim of training blacks for certain types of jobs, thus keeping them in their place or subordinating them in all ways to the ruling minority class. The medium of instruction included a change from English to the mother tongue. However, a large proportion of teachers, particularly in training colleges and universities, was ethnic minorities, particularly whites. The aim of Bantu education was well-articulated in a statement by the then Minister of Native Affairs:

> It is the policy of my department that (Bantu) education should have its roots entirely in the Native areas and in the Native environment and Native community. There Bantu education must be able to give itself complete expression and there it will have to perform its real service. The Bantu must be guided to serve his own community in all respects. There is no place for him in the European community above the level of certain forms of labor. Within his own community, however, all doors are open. For that reason it is of no avail for him to receive a training which has as its aim absorption in the European community while he cannot and will not be absorbed there. Up till now he has been subjected to a school system which drew him away from his own community and practically misled him by showing him the green pastures of the European but still did not allow him to graze there. This attitude is not only uneconomic because money is spent on education which has no specific aim, but it is even dishonest to continue with it. The effect on the Bantu community we find in the much-discussed frustration of educated Natives who can find no employment which is acceptable to them. It is abundantly clear that unplanned education creates many problems, disrupts the communal life of the Bantu, and endangers the communal life of the European. (Geber and Newman 1980, p. 62)

It is only logical, it was argued, to replace an education based on false assumptions with a segregated education aimed at developing a Bantu who is in touch with his or her destiny in a Bantu community (Moodie 1994). Henceforth, blacks would receive a more realistic education, with an emphasis on technical skills (Arnold 1981). However, one of the deep-seated intentions of this Bantu type of education, as described by Arnold (1981), was to produce black carpenters, laborers, and artisans who were needed by the white economy but not black philosophers or thinkers who might provide the political leadership to challenge the status quo. As a result, the curriculum in black schools was established by the ruling white minority in order to ensure control of the masses.

Nkomo (1990) cited the following objectives of Bantu education:

1. To produce a semi-skilled black labor force to minister to the needs of the capitalist economy at the lowest possible cost and earlier on; especially after the introduction of the Bantu Education Act, it was intended to blunt competition with white workers.
2. To socialize black students so that they can accept the social relations of apartheid as natural, that is, to accept the supposed superiority of whites and their own inferiority.
3. To forge a consciousness and identity accompanied by a sense of superiority among whites.
4. To promote the acceptance of racial or ethnic separation as the natural order of things or as an arrangement better suited for South Africa's complex problems of national minorities that can only be solved through the separation of the races or ethnic groups.
5. To promote black intellectual underdevelopment by minimizing the allocation of educational resources for blacks while maximizing them for whites. (p. 2)

The long-term aim of Bantu education was to deny its recipients intellectual independence, which would be a prerequisite to achieve economic, social, and political independence. Bantu education did not offer blacks the opportunity to develop intelligence in order to have control over their environment. Instead, Bantu education emphasized training black youths for the preparation of their role in uplifting their people and in their socioeconomic development (South African Bureau of Racial Affairs 1955). Consequently, the training of black youths was not geared towards benefiting humankind but restricted their own human background. This process was seen by many black people as negative social engineering. Evans (1992) described the aim of Bantu education as being the restriction of black mobility by placing real barriers on the chances of economic improvement. This view was supported by Cilliers, Botha, Capdevielle, Perkins, and van der Vyver (1994), who stated that Bantu education was unable to provide the intellectual development that is a vital prerequisite to effective and responsible economic, social, and political participation.

According to Herbstein (1992), Bantu education's aim of negative social engineering was designed to make black school graduates incapable of competing on equal terms with their white counterparts. As a result of this strategy of deliberate inequity, there are high illiteracy rates, overcrowded and poorly maintained classrooms, high pupil-teacher ratios, high failure rates, insufficient funding, and low teacher morale among the black population. Worse still, South Africa will need to employ 94,500 new teachers and to build 118,000 classrooms in order to implement compulsory free education for the black population (Sithole 1991). In order to move beyond Bantu education and to offer a better postapartheid education for blacks in South Africa, new curricula must be drawn, new textbooks must be written, and new schools must be staffed and equipped with relevant materials (Tygesen 1991).

Future education should be based on the skills the economy requires. In other words, there must be a relationship between the skills the economy requires and those produced by the education system (Lesage 1994). Technical and scientific subjects neglected in black schools must receive high priority. The serious mismatch between what black schools have produced and what is actually required by the economy have resulted in approximately 90,000 matriculants being unemployed per year. Lesage reported that, if this situation is permitted to continue, South Africa will have a surplus of more than nine million semiskilled and unskilled workers by the end of the century and a shortage of 200,000 skilled workers.

The destructive consequences of Bantu education still plague black schools in South Africa. Lesage (1994) summarized the underlying causes to the problem of skilled manpower:

--The poor quality of primary education offered to the majority of the people;
--Outdated concepts with respect to technical education;
--The generally low status of technical skills;
--A shortage of qualified science, mathematics, and technical teachers, as well as a lack of equipment and overcrowded classrooms. (p. 21)

1.4 Plan for Nonracial Education

In 1993, an Educational Renewal Strategy was released by government education experts. The report called for major changes in black education such as a nonracial education department for all

South African pupils ("Plan for Nonracial Education Unveiled" 1993). The proposal was supported by government officials such as Mr. Jack Rabie, Chairman of the Ministers' Council in the House of Representatives, who stated: "We are moving towards one education department." It was proposed that one new democratic, nonracial education system should be established, consisting of a central education authority and regional bodies having their own decision-making powers. This report was aimed at maintaining national unity while providing for particular religious, language, and cultural needs ("Plan for Nonracial Education Unveiled" 1993). Even though the report held a lot of promise in theory, in reality it meant the maintenance of the status quo. In resisting educational equity, some white schools have been transformed into private schools, charging fees prohibitive for most black South Africans.

Sithole (1991) explained that the suggested single education system, while geographically and nonracially based, also supported segregation based on language, religion, and culture. According to Sithole, accommodation of diversity in South African terms means that racial education will be accommodated in the future South Africa. This belief also was shared by the Director-General of the Department of National Education, Dr. Johan Garbers, who indicated that distinctive education will be possible in postapartheid education.

Obviously, regional control of education, designed to accommodate ethnic diversity, in practical terms, means that separate education departments will be maintained in the guise of serving a particular population group that shares the same culture, religion, and language. Sithole (1991) explained that whites, Indians, and coloreds (people of mixed races) of the same geographical region will have control of their education in order to preserve their cultures, religions, and languages. In reality, the report supported enforced ethnicity; that is, no change was recommended, except that in postapartheid education race will no longer be a factor of discrimination. Moreover, different communities will have the right not to allow people of other races to enter their schools based on the preservation of their culture, religion, or language (Sithole 1991). Admission tests for language and numeracy will be used to keep blacks away from certain schools. High fees also will prevent many blacks from attending racial minority schools.

The report did not address the issue of improving the quality of black education in postapartheid education. The real problems facing

postapartheid South Africa involve the need to provide educational assistance to the hundreds of thousands of blacks frozen out of the troubled school system and the ailing economy (Evans 1992). Forced integration will not be a viable option, especially because the privileged group is a minority. Improved conditions for black education will provide more positive solutions than limited integration.
Even though the proposal was promising, it had many shortcomings. For example, not one black educational organization took part in the initial discussions that resulted in writing this report. These black educational organizations included the Congress of South African Students (COSAS), various teacher organizations, and parent organizations. Some experts raised concerns about the report that contained only viewpoints rather than recommendations. Even though certain aspects of the proposal were criticized, they represented a great shift from discrimination in education, as well as a move towards a more equitable consideration for all ("Plan for Nonracial Education Unveiled" 1993). One of the positive recommendations mentioned in the report was the introduction of compulsory free education. The gradual implementation of this recommendation was to occur within the first nine years of schooling, with the state paying 95 percent of the expenses ("Plan for Nonracial Education Unveiled" 1993). According to the report, for the last three years parents would pay one fourth of the costs.
Even though some schools are desegregated, they serve only a fraction of black students. Chisholm and Fine (1994) reported that by the beginning of 1992 African pupils were estimated to comprise only 0.88 percent of the total enrollment of 904,403 in formerly white schools. Of this 0.88 percent, African pupils comprised 40 percent, colored pupils 43 percent, and Indian pupils 16 percent (Chisholm and Fine 1994, p. 240). The most desegregated schools in South Africa tend to serve black children from affluent families. The majority of poor black students remains the recipients of poor education. Thus, partial or restricted desegregation is formulated to benefit the small proportion of the existing black middle class. Yet, this exercise, when promoted, can be detrimental to the formulation of quality education for the majority of black students.
For example, black professionals can be caught in the commitment to design relevant programs in order to improve black education. Limited access to white schools provides a false impression that quick

and easy means of solving current educational problems, such as poor funding, inadequate teaching materials, curriculum changes, and poor teaching conditions, are possible. It also will provide an illusion of eliminating educational disparities. Partial integration can further perpetuate class division among blacks. The poor will continue to suffer the consequences of Bantu education with no sign of relief. The few rich black students, on the other hand, will benefit from limited integration. It also will be easy for black professionals, as well as the new government, to resist the temptation to look for quick results and shortcuts in meeting the educational needs of the majority.

Improving black education does not merely entail school integration. Allowing a handful of black students to attend private or selected white schools is not sufficient to address the current educational imbalances. The most important element in this changing situation is a major transformation of the socioeconomic and political infrastructure to ensure equal opportunities and access to educational opportunities (Johnson 1992). The provision of quality education requires careful planning and creativity. Upgrading black education also will be accomplished with the full participation and planning of black professionals.

Because integration in South Africa implies the inclusion of a majority group into an economically privileged minority culture, this may be unacceptable to the privileged class. One of the often-cited reasons for fear of integration is lowering standards. Another practical reason is that if all black children attend white schools, then all schools will be predominantly black. This situation raises concern among white South Africans about the preservation of their culture. While integration itself is good, it also can lead to the further neglect of the black schools. Professionals on both sides of the issue need to examine the merits of keeping neighborhood schools as well. Instead, the push towards quality education and equal access to information are to be encouraged in order to overcome major educational problems in black schools. Drastic changes in black education will occur if contributions are made by black scholars in areas of curriculum changes, improved facilities, adequate teaching, and sufficient funding.

Blacks need to understand that education is not a ready-made process but an evolving, self-generating cycle in which students are taught what they will need for the future. What is being taught at school must be relevant to the world outside the school. Therefore, education must change with the times in order to be considered meaningful. If black schools strive for quality, there will be no need for forced integration. However, the improvement of black schools requires a lot of money and committed manpower.

1.5 Types of Schools Currently Available

Within the new system of education, three models of schools for all pupils were recommended: (a) schools directly under state control, (b) state-supported schools under the control of a management council representative of the community, and (c) private schools that could exercise a high degree of autonomy ("Plan for Nonracial Education Unveiled" 1993).

In terms of the current legislation, all of South Africa' s students will be taught under a single educational system, regardless of race. That is, in practical terms, some public schools in South Africa currently are open to all racial groups. However, others are still segregated according to ethnicity, except where parents in a local school vote favorably to include children of other groups (Sithole 1991). Even when this type of decision is made by a local school, certain conditions still apply to children from other races and residential areas. These conditions ensure that there will be at least 47 pupils per class and that children from the townships will be bused into these schools if principals cannot fill their areas (Karamitas 1994).

Within the new education system in South Africa, government white schools consist of four models. Model A is composed of privately operated white schools subsidized by the state. These schools admit up to 50 percent of their children from other races provided they pass the entrance examination. Model B is composed of schools managed and funded by the state. Model C is composed of schools controlled by a managing body such as parents. The state pays only the staff, whereas other expenses are covered by parents of students. Model D and black schools are administered by the Department of Education and Training. These schools are governed by the Department of Education and Culture for the Department of Education and Training.

Colored and Indian schools are operated by the House of Representatives (colored) and the House of Delegates (Indian).

Even though these schools serve colored and Indian children, children of other races are permitted to attend. Entrance tests are administered for admission of other racial groups. Another type is private schools that are privately owned by private organizations or churches. These schools are partially subsidized by the state only (Mkhize 1993). In these schools, most of the expenses are covered by parents. Some of these schools are boarding schools.

There are still different departments of education with separate budgets and administrations, which is a waste of human and financial resources. Education has been declared compulsory and free for all racial groups to the end of secondary schooling. However, in many black schools throughout the country, compulsory and free education has been true only in theory, not in practice. The state spends approximately fifteen times as much on each white school child as it does on each black school child, with expenditures for colored and Asian children falling in between (Regehr 1979).

Chronic overcrowding is the most visible feature in black schools. The teacher-pupil ratio, for example, is approximately 1:15 for whites, whereas estimates for blacks range from 1:40 to 1:60 (Green 1991). The 1976 Soweto riots, which were triggered by an educational issue, focused on the inequality and the lack of quality in black education. At the end of 1976, the government announced changes in black education. For example, there was an increase in per-capita expenditure for black children (Regehr 1979). As the head of the South African Institute of Race Relations, John Kane-Berman, reported: "Between 1971-72 and 1987-88, state spending on African education went up by nearly 6,000 percent from 70 million rand to 4,097 million" (Green 1991, p. 12). Even though the government is currently spending more on black education, the gap between the races remains enormous at the same time that the black student population is exploding.

According to Bean (1994), of all the working people in South Africa, 30 percent have no formal education, 36 percent have only primary education, 31 percent have some secondary school education, and only 3 percent have university degrees or diplomas. Logically, no country or nation can enjoy peace and prosperity if the great majority of its citizens is not educated properly. White people, who represent less than one fifth of the total population, comprise 90 percent of all university graduates (Seedat 1984). Approximately only 10 percent of the college graduates are nonwhite (blacks, coloreds, and Indians).

1.6 The Present Structure of Education

Education in South Africa currently is experiencing social and political upheavals. Apartheid, which has dominated South Africa for decades and has imposed a deleterious effect on the educational system, is beginning to crumble. Nevertheless, the negative effects of apartheid and apartheid education are incalculable and will persist long after the demise of the system (Green 1991). At the beginning of 1995, the new government of national unity announced that South Africa's eighteen education departments were officially merged into a single educational system. In theory, this means that there are no separate departments for separate races, and, in reality, it means that separation of education structures is based on geographic locations. Director-generals of provincial education departments will be responsible for implementing educational policies in their respective provinces, that is, "the process of provincialization" ("Operation Date for Education Departments Set" 1994).

Each of the newly formed nine provinces is to take control of its education. These provinces are Pretoria-Witwatersrand-Vereeniging, Northern Transvaal, Eastern Transvaal, North West, Orange Free State, Natal, Eastern Cape, Northern Cape, and Western Cape. Schools will be divided into various categories, including primary, secondary, matriculation, teacher training, vocational training, and universities.

1.6.1 Primary School and Secondary Education

Prior to 1976, the school program for black South African students stretched over thirteen years from Substandard A to Form V. This trend changed after 1976 when the South African government changed basic education to twelve years, which currently exists. Table 1.1 shows the current structure of education.

Prior to 1976, the system was arranged as follows: 4 + 4 + 3 + 2, which is a thirteen-year structure of education for Africans. Later, it was replaced by a 4 + 3 + 3 + 2 (i.e., four years of lower primary school, three years of higher primary school, three years of junior secondary school, and two years of senior secondary school). This school structure applied to Africans only, which was meant to discourage African children from schooling. This group could not afford to keep its children in school for a long period of time. Table 1.2 shows the thirteen-year school structure before it was abolished.

Examinations are conducted at the end of each phase. These examinations usually are internal, except at the end of the second phase (higher primary school), in which an external examination is conducted. Another examination (known as the Junior Certificate) is conducted at the end of the third phase (junior secondary school). The end of phase four also is marked by an external examination. All examinations are designed and marked by representatives of the Department of Education and Training. The entire process gives African teachers no control over what they teach.

Table 1.1

The Twelve-Year School Structure

Class	Level	Duration
Substandard A	Lower primary	One year
Substandard B	Lower primary	One year
Standard I	Lower primary	One year
Standard II	Lower primary	One year
Standard III	Higher primary	One year
Standard IV	Higher primary	One year
Standard V	Higher primary	One year
Form I	Junior secondary	One year
Form II	Junior secondary	One year
Form III	Junior secondary	One year
Form IV	Senior secondary	One year
Form V	Senior secondary	One year

Table 1.2

The Thirteen-Year School Structure

Class	Level	Duration
Substandard A	Lower primary	One year
Substandard B	Lower primary	One year
Standard I	Lower primary	One year
Standard II	Lower primary	One year
Standard III	Higher primary	One year
Standard IV	Higher primary	One year
Standard V	Higher primary	One year
Standard VI	Higher primary	One year
Form I	Junior secondary	One year
Form II	Junior secondary	One year
Form III	Junior secondary	One year
Form IV	Senior secondary	One year
Form V	Senior secondary	One year

Students who successfully complete the Junior Certificate examination can pursue careers in teaching, nursing, or other technical training. Completion of the Senior Secondary Certificate (matriculation) provides admission to universities and other institutions of higher learning. Only African pupils are required to write three public examinations (at the completion of the primary school course and at the end of Forms III and V (Behr 1978). Historically, this procedure is followed to control the flow of African graduates at each phase of their schooling, not because they are obsessed with examinations and certificates, but because examinations are used to control the academic mobility of Africans.

1.6.2 Curricula

For South Africans, curriculum transformation might even be more important than issues of free education, class size, integration, and methods of instruction. At stake are the foundation and theoretical basis for the new educational system. The most urgent and pressing need is to rid the educational system of its apartheid past and anti-African character (Johnson and Devlin-Foltz 1993). The legacy of apartheid has meant that Africans are largely invisible in the current South African curriculum. Therefore, postapartheid curriculum is expected to be inclusive and to represent all inhabitants. Curriculum is a significant indicator of who has power in a given society. Development of a postapartheid curriculum will be a test of real change in the educational arena of black South Africans. Curriculum change will influence the content of what is currently taught in the schools, that is, a change in all subjects, as well as a revision of the entire syllabus. If curriculum change is possible, new textbooks must be printed.

Furthermore, major changes in the curriculum must be made by progressive scholars and communities in South Africa (Jansen 1990). For example, current textbooks are in desperate need of updating (Matloff 1996). Current events such as the end of the apartheid era, Mandela's role in political transformation, and the three-year transition period of intense negotiations between former white rulers and the blacks they jailed should be included in South African history books. School books still to be written also must address bitter realities in black communities such as poverty, unemployment, crime, and how communities can minimize these issues. Black professionals have the duty and responsibility to ensure that these pressing issues are addressed immediately. Teachers will continue to adhere to outdated syllabi unless something is done to correct the situation.

Bantu education and its legacy cannot disappear without an actual change in the curriculum; also, curriculum cannot change without major contributions and support from the society it represents and depicts. The development of a new curriculum will require a lot of money and hard work, but it, nevertheless, is the area that needs immediate change. Currently, the state assumes the responsibility for determining what curriculum is to be mastered. The departments of education, through the use of school inspectors, ensure that the content of education is given to teachers, and then they have the responsibility for imparting information to students (Peirce 1989). In "top-down" control, it is difficult for black teachers to explore innovative methods of teaching students. Because of external control, teachers in most black schools find themselves adhering to the syllabus regardless of its outdated nature or other perceived inadequacies. Curriculum change is necessary in postapartheid education, but policymakers will have to acknowledge the reality of the past before learning how to deal with the present. Therefore, it is necessary to discuss the current curriculum throughout all grade levels.

1.6.2.1. Preprimary-level curricula. Preprimary readiness or preparatory programs for black South Africans can be found, to a limited extent, in the cities. These programs are nonexistent, however, in rural areas, regardless of the large number of eligible children. Almost all of the African children attending rural primary schools have not participated in readiness programs (Baine and Mwamwenda 1994). The high dropout and failure rates among Africans are attributed to the shortage of preprimary school readiness programs. Baine and Mwamwenda reported that in South Africa, during the period 1987 to 1990, great attempts were made in providing preprimary programs for black children. However, as a result of social, political, and economic forces from within and outside the country, the entire school system deteriorated to a point that few of these programs actually functioned.

School readiness is crucial in laying a solid foundation in order to continue formal education. A poor beginning in school is believed to impact negatively education in the future. Because a child's background is an important component of the learning environment, it is important to make African parents aware of the importance of school readiness. Such attempts are ideal but are, nevertheless, realistic because many African parents are poor.

1.6.2.2. Primary-level curricula. In primary schools, the curriculum consists of language skills training, writing, arithmetic, and official languages. Africans are taught through the medium of their mother tongue until the end of higher primary education. In addition to their mother tongues, African children are required to learn English and Afrikaans (Behr 1978). Subjects such as social studies, physical education, environmental study, domestic science, health and hygiene, gardening, agriculture, and sewing also are commonly taught in most African schools at the primary level. However, very little time is allocated to these subjects. During the 1980s, only 6 percent of school time was devoted to teaching these topics (Baine and Mwamwenda 1994).

The apartheid legacy still influences current curriculum issues (Matloff 1996). During the apartheid era, curricula at the primary level for African children emphasized literacy and numeracy rather than an inculcation of the values and skills required to function effectively in their environments. According to Van Hook (1994), African young people studied England and Europe but learned almost nothing about their own country or that of their African neighbors, a lack that contributes to a higher dropout rate. Indeed, in 1983, it was estimated that out of all African children enrolled in Sub A (the first year of formal primary schooling) that at least 15 percent of them dropped out (Walker 1992). In South Africa, from 1987 to 1990, an increasing number of African children dropped out during the primary phase of schooling. Many of these students leave school without acquiring sufficient literacy skills.

1.6.2.3. Secondary-level curricula. In South Africa, the secondary-level curriculum is state controlled and white dominated (Baine and Mwamwenda 1994). The syllabi for secondary schools emphasize examinations and certificates, which encourage rote learning at the expense of stimulating critical thinking and analysis. At this level, students are never encouraged to acquire knowledge, skills, and attitudes through participation. Baine and Mwamwenda argued that the most common criticism of secondary schools is that they fail to prepare young people for the world of work and that the students fail to develop essential values, attitudes, and respect for self and others, as well as social and survival skills. The choice of subjects in black schools also is limited. Subjects such as history, geography, economics, mathematics, biology, and various languages are commonly taught at the secondary level. Science subjects are not taught in other schools in which there is a shortage of teachers of such subjects. Unfortunately, most students do not view technical education as worthwhile, which is usually associated with low-paying jobs. However, technical education is important and has proven to be of greater value to some students. Academic secondary education is necessary only for those students who intend to pursue studies at the university level. Training in academics only does not prepare the majority of black students for employment benefits.

Secondary education in South Africa was described by Baine and Mwamwenda (1994) as authoritarian, disciplinarian, teacher dominated, content oriented, and knowledge based. Usually teachers rely heavily on prescribed and recommended books; class notes are dictated; memorization is the order of the day; and students are never permitted to discuss and share their views. Interaction is rare, and active participation and projects involving "hands-on" activities do not occur. Therefore, the nature of the curriculum in black schools leads to memorization and cramming for examinations rather than comprehension and application of knowledge and skills.

Future education for black South Africans requires professionals to think from the point of view of the least advantaged, not of the privileged and those who have enjoyed power. Obviously, in order to improve black education, necessary curriculum changes are needed in order to address the staggering levels of unemployment and poor education, which is an enormous task that will require creative and innovative planning. Curriculum changes will require the eradication of race and gender inequalities. Future curriculum changes need to facilitate the incorporation of the unemployed. Rehabilitation of the unemployed through adult education and vocational training should be considered.

1.6.2.4. Secondary-level vocational education.

The development of vocational education programs at the secondary level in black schools can be employed as a way of overcoming unemployment and as an alternative to those who cannot benefit from academic schooling. In many cases, however, vocational education has been accorded a lower status for various reasons. Baine and Mwamwenda (1994) cited the following problems associated with vocational and agricultural educational programs:

--Because of the facilities and equipment required, they are more costly than regular education and their cost effectiveness is questionable.
--They are often associated with students perceived as cognitively deficient.
--They have a negative connotation because of their association with black education during colonial times.
--They are often not associated with increased employment opportunities or increased earnings.
--They are frequently rejected by both parents and students. (p. 118)

Baine and Mwamwenda argued that the failure of vocational education to enhance employment opportunities arises from a failure to conduct market needs assessments to determine what skills are and will be in demand in the marketplace; from an obvious mismatch between what education offers and what exists in the world of work; and from the fact that teachers lack sufficient knowledge and skills required for teaching vocational, agricultural, and technical skills.

In general, there is a feeling of alienation, a feeling that African students are taught skills that do not meet their demands or the needs and challenges of their daily lives. Some people fail to see the benefits of formal training when its recipients, regardless of passing examinations, still are unable to find employment. Therefore, education is regarded useless if it is not related to the circumstances, needs, and demands of a particular community in the dynamic, changing environment of today' s era (Duminy 1967).

Future education ought to prepare students for work, as well as for self-reliance. For instance, education that has a strong community orientation and also is based on the current needs of the community is likely to succeed. Therefore, postapartheid education has a challenge to equip students with the necessary skills that will enable them to obtain self-employment in urban and rural areas. While academic schools remain an option for many, vocational schools remain a viable alternative to those who cannot benefit from academic schools.

1.6.2.5. Curriculum recommendations. Other African countries in their search of relevant educational content concluded that four important curriculum aspects should be considered: (a) the African environment, (b) the African child' s development, (c) the African cultural heritage, and (d) the demands of technological progress and economic development (Yoloye 1986).

1.6.2.5.1. The African environment. In South Africa, the curriculum needs to address local needs. Historically, the state found it in its interest to keep African learners mainly as recipients of Western ideas rather than creators of ideas based on their African environment. Because the aim of Bantu education was to prevent Africans from controlling their environment, this is understandable.

Addressing local needs in the curriculum constitutes many different ways. For example, the emphasis in history lessons must cover Africa in-depth. Whereas, in literature, African authors such as Mphahlele, Nyembezi, Nxumalo, and Wole Soyinka must receive priority in African schools. The study of local plants and animals in biology, as well as the study of African art, drama, poetry, and folklore all enrich the curriculum. Even though the adaptation of curriculum to suit local needs does not mean complete exclusion of other foreign content, the African-based elements must be emphasized. In other parts of Africa, the localization of content has encouraged African authors to produce new books to fit the new demand (Yoloye 1986). African students who succeed socially and academically are those who are more secure about their African heritage and identity.

1.6.2.5.2. The African cultural heritage. Several strategies can be adopted to address cultural issues. One strategy is to establish libraries in which books and taped historical events are made available to the public. Cultural centers also can be established in different regions to promote education. Interviews with traditional elders will help provide oral history that can be stored for future use, which is one way of bringing the culture of the people into formal education (Yoloye 1986). In the past, Africans have been artificially defined by language and geographical demarcations, resulting from what is known as "divide and rule." These demarcations have further reinforced division among homogeneous groups, thus perpetuating hostilities. The strategy of racial division has helped to justify a false assumption that South Africa is a country of different minorities, that is, a white minority and black minorities (Jansen 1988). Thus, Africans need to define their identities and strive for unity. The use of schools to promote cultural survival, when attempted with a clear understanding of historical and political reality, will be of great benefit to society.

Currently, there has been a shift away from the obvious use of cultural heritage to justify apartheid. This shift has been replaced by protection of cultural identity and minority rights. Jansen (1988) explained this shift:

> The field of culture is exploited by the regime as a means of fostering division and discrimination. . . . Cultural variety amongst those who inhabit South Africa is falsely presented as involving the existence of groups with cultural traditions that are not only distinct but mutually incompatible. [This is then used as part of the whole rationale for physical segregation and "separate

development."] In turn, the educational system and the control of cultural activity are used to promote further division. (Jansen 1988, p. 383)

The end of apartheid must allow Africans to shake off artificial demarcations and to forge national unity through cultural activities that will unite them. Schools in South Africa are to become units of cultural revival by organizing cultural events of the arts among schools and the community at large (Yoloye 1986). Such events will help to change the image of the cultural traditions of Africans that have been suppressed during the apartheid era.

1.6.2.5.3. The needs of technological progress. The curriculum in South Africa must address the need for technological advancement and economic growth. Scientific advancement is a basic requirement for achieving economic, social, and, above all, political independence (Cilliers et al. 1994). At present, African schools are not keeping pace with the rate of change. If that trend is to be modified, then African schools need to teach students how to survive in a technological world. One way to address needs associated with technological progress in the new education system is the early introduction of applied science in the schools.

1.6.2.5.4. The science curriculum in formal school. Subjects such as home crafts, gardening, and health and hygiene (commonly taught in black schools) should be replaced by applied science, which will require the production of textbooks in African languages, teachers' manuals, and workbooks. There are many problems with this suggestion. First, there are few African teachers who have the appropriate training. Second, the supply of textbooks written in African languages will require a great commitment of resources. Teachers of science may be difficult to find among Africans. On the other hand, these problems do not mean that Africans should be complacent. Attempts must be made to bring awareness to the African community regarding the importance of science and technology. Through science, curriculum students can be encouraged to conduct more science projects. Schools can organize science fairs and competitions in order to stimulate scientific knowledge and appreciation. September (1990) explained the realities that future science education policymakers in South Africa will have to contend with: "Even now extreme dissatisfaction is expressed with the science curricula of South African schools on the grounds that they are too long, and too theoretical, and that too little time is left for practical work" (p. 482). Scientific knowledge is crucial for the development of any nation. The contributions of science in aiding humankind are evident worldwide. For this reason, postapartheid science curriculum must be transformed.

1.6.2.5.5. African child development. Early childhood education for Africans has been the responsibility of parents and the community (Eckstein 1994). Thus, research about African child development in South Africa remains limited. Recent studies on children have focused on violence and its psychological effect on them (Eckstein 1994; Norward 1994). According to Yoloye (1986), the curriculum should be adapted to characteristics of the child such as physical, intellectual, emotional, and social development in order to be effective.

Educators must recognize that regardless of a child's socioeconomic status, development needs must be nurtured equally. Children ought to be able to view themselves as being capable, worthwhile, loveable, and successful (Smith 1991). Therefore, understanding African child development can assist teachers in creating a positive learning environment. African teachers in training need more exposure to child development. More research must be pursued in the areas of psychology, counseling, and guidance. Currently, there are few black psychologists in the country (Waldman 1993). The growing number of street children from displaced families is one reason that counseling and well-structured rehabilitative services are necessary.

1.6.2.5.6. Curriculum development centers. An innovation in curriculum transformation that has been adopted by most African countries is establishing national curriculum development centers. These centers have been responsible for the preparation of many school-related materials such as textbooks, workbooks, teaching aids, learning guides, and audiovisual equipment for teachers' use (Yoloye 1986). In addition, the centers deal with the continuous evaluation and assessment of the curriculum.

South Africa is likely to benefit from the establishment of curriculum centers on a regional basis. Such centers will track what is taught in African schools, as well as ensuring that the educational content is current and relevant. Curriculum specialists, working together with subject heads from different colleges of education, can combine their efforts in operating such centers. Existing libraries, community centers, churches, and schools also can be used. The success of these centers will depend on the expertise, dedication, and sense of purpose of all those involved, which is an issue that policymakers need to look at as an option.

1.7 Examinations

External examinations in the black schools of South Africa are established and centrally controlled by the Department of Education and Training. Black pupils, unlike their counterparts from other racial groups, write three major external examinations during their school careers (Behr 1978). These examinations are written at the completion of the primary school level, at the end of junior high school (also known as Form III), and at the end of matriculation (Form V). These examinations limit the number of black pupils who enter the next level and, consequently, the job market. Therefore, these examinations are not given because of the particular importance that Africans attach to examinations and certificates (Behr 1978).

The common feature of African education is the low number of pupils completing high school. The pass rate of black students in high school has always been lower than that of other racial groups. Reasons for poor performance are varied. The language of instruction being foreign has made learning for blacks more difficult. Their learning environment at home and at school has been relatively poor. Table 1.3 shows the matriculation pass rates according to different racial groups.

Centralized external state examinations conducted in black schools have not been the method of choice, not because they establish normal standards for all students throughout the country, but because they provide a means by which the state controls the content of black education as well as the flow of graduates at each level. These examinations test only prescribed syllabi. Moreover, external examinations make success unattainable for rural children and others exposed to poor teaching and less academic stimulation. External examinations for the Junior Certificate and for matriculation remain controversial in South Africa. Several studies have shown that these examinations do not equip African students with the meaningful practical skills they require after graduation (King 1979; Nkomo 1990). Thus, time and educational resources are wasted to continue this type of evaluation. Perhaps other methods of evaluation must be considered.

Table 1.3

Matriculation Results By Race

Year	Group			
	Africans	Coloreds	Indians	Whites
1987	50.0%	66.0%	86.0%	90.0%
1989	42.0%	72.7%	93.6%	96.9%
1993	38.3%	86.0%	93.0%	98.0%

Sources: "Bad School or None," *The Economist* 302(7481) (1987):40; M. Skuy and H. Partington, "Special Education in South Africa," *International Journal of Disability* 37(2) (1990):149-57; L. I. Loxton, "Fewer Black South Africans Pass Key Examination," *The Chronicle of Higher Education* 11(28) (1994):A42.

The emphasis on examinations has resulted in teachers' obsession with preparing students for certificates and not for the development of general ability for independent thinking and judgment. Examinations controlled by the state and removed from important fields within society are meaningless. The ability to apply examination content in solving society' s ills makes education solid and transferable. Therefore, there must be a shift in examination management from state or external bodies to local and regional bodies. South Africa must consider internal examination control as an option for blacks. Through this type of control, teachers will be able to localize teaching materials and teaching methods (Maliyamkono 1980). Teachers are to be given an opportunity to select material to be taught, as well as suitable teaching methods. Motivation in shaping one' s work among black teachers is sometimes destroyed by force and exterior pressure (King 1979).

Recently, black schools experienced boycotts when students protested fees required to take external examinations. When parents cannot afford to pay these fees, students are rejected. This process results in resentment on the part of disadvantaged pupils who believe they are experiencing discrimination.

1.7.1 Reasons for Poor Performance

Several reasons can be found why black students perform poorly on external examinations. School-related factors such as language of instruction, lack of facilities, poor teaching, poor handling of examination papers, overcrowdedness, and school disruptions are among the most commonly mentioned reasons for school failure. Personal factors such as lack of motivation, poor study skills, and intellectual limitations, as well as emotional and physiological problems, are also reasons for poor school performance. In addition, family factors such as poverty, lack of parental support, and too many domestic demands are reported as reasons for poor performance among African students (Donald 1995).

1.7.2 School-Related Reasons

Among black South Africans, one of the reasons linked to poor matriculation results is language (Kachelhoffer 1995). For example, South African blacks face the challenge of learning in another language, as well as studying and writing examinations (Baine and Mwamwenda 1994). Being tested in a language in which they are not fluent can be disastrous for black students. Many black teachers in South Africa lack confidence in the use of English and, therefore, teach in their mother tongue. Thus, when an examination is given, many black students are at a substantial disadvantage when tested in English, which translates into dismal academic performance. Abstract intelligence associated with creativity and the ability to manipulate information in order to benefit the child cannot be developed by using a second language. Therefore, active teaching methods, that is, those that allow students to express thoughts, can be envisaged only in the linguistic context of the child' s mother tongue (Poth 1980).

External examinations also are designed in the absence of black teachers who are likely to understand the content on which their students should be tested. Black teachers in South African schools are expected to implement syllabi but are not involved in producing them. Such top-down prescriptions of what is being taught, along with a heavy focus on examinations, often result in what Woodhouse (1985) described as "diploma disease" (p. 6), that is, the act of acquiring certificates in which concepts or ideas become dead objects to be memorized for an examination but not pursued for their own sake (Woodhouse 1985). Too much emphasis on the examinations also creates a dubious conflation of certificates and competence. Such certificates sometimes trigger unrealistic expectations for those who acquire them. Schoeman (1981) explained that the attainment of certificates becomes a short-term ambition unrelated to the true relations among qualifications, experience, and productivity. According to Schoeman, holders of such certificates might use them as status symbols without reflecting upon the marketability of the skills acquired. The true purpose of examinations is to equip students with lifelong knowledge rather than testing them for insignificant knowledge. In South Africa, many blacks have no control over what they learn; thus, the true meaning of education continues to elude many. While education is liberating, it is not a cure for all socioeconomic ills. Consequently, examinations must be linked to realistic goals.

The lack of facilities and equipment such as teaching materials, libraries, electricity, computers, laboratories, and scientific apparatus has been well-documented (Simon 1991; Slammert 1991) as contributing factors to poor academic performance in schools. Poor teaching in black schools has contributed to the academic failure of many black students. Kachelhoffer (1995) stated that, especially in the natural sciences, the majority of African teachers who have taught these subjects has no formal training. Similarly, overcrowding, a common feature in most black schools, makes effective teaching difficult. The pupil-teacher ratio at some black schools ranges from the astronomical (50:1) to the absurd (70:1) (Simon 1991). In practical terms, no teacher can control a class of fifty or more students without contributing to declining standards. Simon maintained that black schools in South Africa continue to be plagued by inadequate library facilities, a poor supply of textbooks, and poorly trained teachers.

Another contributing factor to the high failure rate among black students is the mishandling of examination papers and dishonesty in the grading system. Reports have been made of the poor handling of scripts by markers (Simon 1991). In other cases, among the people being used to mark the matriculation scripts are student teachers who reportedly are ignorant of the syllabus and of the subjects marked (Baine and Mwamwenda 1994). Sometimes sharp contrasts are found between what has been taught to students during the year and what the external examiners ask. Such practices result in many errors and failure among students who might not otherwise fail.

In order to reverse this situation, a positive school climate must be created. The language of instruction must be reviewed and examinations must not be centrally controlled. Instead, schools and regions are to establish their own standards of testing students. Teachers who deal with students in their daily learning are to be given an option to prepare examinations. African teachers must consider establishing clubs and/or education support networks. These networks will provide a place to which schools and teachers may turn. One major examination will be sufficient at the completion of high school for all students rather than several external examinations that currently are prevalent in black schools. The education department must incorporate a continuous assessment policy as an evaluation strategy for the schools, colleges, and universities of South Africa. Mishandling of examination papers will be reduced when black teachers take full responsibility for the preparation of examinations. African students and teachers resent the imposition of examinations that determine how and what is taught without their input (Baine and Mwamwenda 1994).

1.7.3 Other Factors

Sometimes black students contribute to their own failure through absenteeism or disruption of classes. For example, in September 1994, it was reported that schooling was collapsing in many parts of Soweto ("Soweto Schools Chaos" 1994), which is when end-of-the-year matriculation examinations are written, a crucial time for teachers and students. According to the report, students roamed the streets as principals stayed away from schools after eviction by members of the South African Democratic Teachers' Union (SADTU). Even though such protests are sometimes justified, they affect students the most. In some instances, lack of discipline in black schools, coupled with violence, have been major factors in poor performance. Often a great deal of learning time is lost because of student and teacher protests. This time is never recovered, and usually it is the students who suffer the consequences of such activities.

Protests and/or school boycotts by students, as a way of airing their grievances, must be replaced with more democratic ways. For example, channels of communication ought to become readily available to black students, and student representatives must be permitted in all schools. Unless open communication is established between students and authorities at all levels, protests and school boycotts will continue because they are the easiest and quickest way of gaining official attention ("The Business Day" 1994).

Loss of motivation and negative self-concept are personal factors that account for poor school performance. Repeated failure enhances a sense of helplessness among African students. Inappropriate study skills due to a lack of self-motivation or study facilities also affect performance.

In addition, lack of counseling facilities in African schools places students with emotional problems in a difficult position. Emotional problems often result in poor achievement, lack of motivation, an invitation for punishment, and victimization of students by school authorities (Donald 1995). Unless these problems are dealt with effectively, they will continue to plague the educational system.

1.7.4 Family Factors

Family roles and participation in education are important for various reasons. First, children whose parents take active roles in their education are likely to recognize virtue in academic achievement. In such families, children will not lack academic facilities and support, and they will be encouraged to further their education. Second, children whose home backgrounds provide a culture of learning will have a successful school life. Many African students come from deprived socioeconomic backgrounds in which educational support services are limited. Some African students live in overcrowded conditions in which study opportunities are not available. Thus, poverty, trauma, and domestic responsibilities placed on children by families are seen to contribute substantially to school failure (Donald 1995). On the other hand, home experiences and family values brought into the schools by pupils play a central role in determining academic achievement (Morris 1986).

1.7.5 Recommendations

The following recommendations address two themes of education: (a) encouraging all stakeholders in education to play a determining role and (b) placing more emphasis on quality of education. Because opportunities in education are emerging, Africans must take advantage of them. Experimenting with innovative ideas and testing them at the local level can be a beginning. Teachers, students, policymakers, and parents are to adopt new attitudes if change is to materialize. Educational decisions should be made by local school districts, where appropriate. Provinces ought to be free to decide on educational matters as long as their decisions are in the best interests of their citizens.

Permitting local control in education gives voice to the people, and diversity of educational opinions enriches communities rather than deprives them. Local control in postapartheid South Africa should be viewed in that background. If teachers are given the opportunity to participate fully in the decision making and operation of the schools, there will be less hostility. Local control allows schools to meet the needs of their students. The establishment of curriculum centers at local levels is one way to solve creatively local problems. These centers could assist in the assessment of syllabi, as well as the content and quality of textbooks, that are delivered annually at black schools (Scheepers 1991). A group of concerned academicians in the black community could offer their talent in operating such centers, and teaching methods could be evaluated in order to reverse the trend of passivity used in black schools towards teaching strategies that foster understanding. Teaching students to transfer knowledge to other settings and to life outside school is more essential than rote learning.

African parents, students, community leaders, and academicians also are sources who must inform curriculum change. Africans cannot expect the founders of Bantu education to bring substantial changes in black education. According to Scheepers (1991), Bantu education has been maintained and supported for years by many people, and it has become "big business." Thus, discarding Bantu education would be putting the nation out of business (p. 6). The evidence of Bantu education being big business in South Africa is pervasive from textbooks to teaching experts. Curriculum change is no guarantee of social change. Jansen (1990) described curriculum change as more a reflector than a generator of social change or development. McDowell (1980), in describing postcolonial education in Nigeria, said:

> The assumptions made by government that the school system alone can accomplish the multifaceted tasks of teaching skills and appropriate attitudes, develop useful character, provide in-service education for school leavers and all workers, produce literacy for all, eradicate regional disparities, regulate indigenous and private educational institutions, reform teacher methods, and provide for free lifelong education, all, "as soon as possible," are challenged. It could be challenged in any country. Admirable as these long-term goals might be, inherent weaknesses in the educational system and society, including the ability to finance these programs, will prevent their attainment in the foreseeable future. (p. 61)

If the above statement is true for broad educational reform, then it is widely applicable to curriculum change, which is an element of the former (Jansen 1990). Other causes of school failure do not originate from education; rather they are socioeconomic in origin, requiring multifaceted approaches such as social welfare, health, psychology, guidance, counseling, and general socioeconomic development (Donald 1995).

According to Donald (1995), the success of the present government' s reconstruction and development program will depend upon its reduction of poverty, trauma, domestic responsibility, and transport reasons for underachievement. On the other hand, school-related problems for academic failure, such as inadequate facilities, language medium, underqualified and unmotivated teachers, and the curriculum, are all educational components that require direct attention of an education department. According to Donald, school-related factors for academic failure are preventable, requiring immediate attention from the new education ministry. African teachers sometimes find themselves overwhelmed because of a lack of support, poor working conditions, and the pressures of survival under demanding circumstances. Teachers who work under poor conditions usually lack the skills to influence the learning of their students. The needs of learners are as crucial as the needs of teachers in understanding what is required for future education in

South Africa. The government must recognize this need.

1.8 Teachers

Well-trained teachers are a central component in the educational process. Thus, all proposals for improving education are to go hand-in-hand with high-quality teacher development in order to enhance that process. Unfortunately, in South Africa, many black teachers are unqualified. Baine and Mwamwenda (1994) reported in 1988 that 17 percent of South African primary school teachers in black schools outside the homelands and 28 percent in the nonindependent homelands were not qualified. They further observed, in the then homeland of Transkei, that approximately 51 percent of the teachers in the senior secondary schools and 63 percent of the teachers in the junior secondary schools were given roles beyond their qualifications, even though a majority had been qualified to teach at lower levels. These teachers were not qualified to teach at the secondary level, and they were not qualified to teach specialized subjects (Baine and Mwamwenda 1994) such as mathematics, science, and technical skills.

Little focus has been directed to improve black teacher training. The problem of teacher training has been complicated by an education system separated under apartheid according to different racial lines. Education also was funded on an unequal basis; that is, the least amount of money was allocated to blacks.

1.8.1 Training of Black Teachers

Teacher education is an essential component in any strategy for human development. Teachers are faced with the enormous task of promoting the potential of children by motivating them to learn in a challenging and stimulating environment and by providing guidance in which they can unlock their talents. Not all teachers have the ability to inspire students to utilize their potential. Some teachers should be trained to become aware of their responsibility, whereas others with sufficient teaching experience will develop the necessary skills. Training black teachers must be enhanced to match the challenges and needs of a changing South African society. In other words, teacher education must adopt a new approach to education that will address the practical problems of society. For example, according to Nxumalo (1990), in order to serve changing communities displaying cumulative sets of values, norms, and beliefs, teachers must be adequately equipped. Teachers must be empowered to contribute towards community uplifting and directed towards nation-building projects. Historically, teacher education for black South Africans has failed to address the pressing needs of black communities. That is, teachers at all levels of education have been operating with a top-down, centrally prescribed syllabus that has been inappropriate and largely irrelevant to the practical needs of black communities (Gray 1995). Another reason is that black training colleges generally are staffed by poorly trained teachers who are the products of Bantu education.

1.8.2 Historical Analysis in Teacher Training

When the first teacher certificate was introduced for black South Africans, two years of teacher training were allowed for primary school teaching for candidates with a Standard Six Certificate. Primary school teachers qualified for the Lower Primary Teacher Certificate. In order to teach at a secondary or high school level, the teacher must complete at least a Standard Eight Certificate or obtain a Junior Certificate before qualifying for the Junior Primary Teacher Certificate. For completion, the training requires two years. Other advanced teacher diplomas include the Junior Secondary Teacher Diploma, which requires the candidate to have a matriculation certificate. This course also requires two years to complete. An additional advanced diploma is a Secondary Teacher Diploma, which requires two years after completion of certification of matriculation, whereas the Senior Secondary Teacher Diploma requires three years.

Beginning in the early 1980s, the level of entry requirements for courses in primary schools was raised (Johnson 1992). All prospective teachers were required to have at least a Senior Secondary Teacher Diploma in order to qualify for training for a Primary Teacher Certificate. Training black teachers is perceived to be inferior to that of other racial groups. For example, African teachers have fewer academic credentials than their white counterparts. Kachelhoffer (1995) explained that the majority of black teachers is trained according to a three-year curriculum at teacher colleges for primary and secondary education. Their white counterparts are trained at teacher colleges for primary education and at universities for secondary education; both programs are offered over a four-year period. This type of training gives white teachers an advantage over their African counterparts. According to Kachelhoffer, currently very few white teachers are below category D (four years of postmatriculation training), which is normally an acceptable qualification for the adequately trained teacher. However, approximately 45 percent of black teachers have less than three years of training after matriculation certification (Kachelhoffer 1995). The poor qualifications of black teachers affect not only the quality of instruction students receive, but they also prevent intellectual curiosity that makes learning self-rewarding for students. Therefore, while raising the standards of teacher training is a positive step, it has not improved the quality of teaching in black schools. More focus must be given on what and how black teachers should be prepared for their new roles in an apartheid-free South Africa. Teachers exposed to quality training will be able to subject their students to quality instruction as well.

1.8.3 Curriculum

The Department of Education and Training determines how and what are being taught in black training colleges. This practice has left black colleges with little innovative work and thinking, stifling the development of critical, creative, and innovative teachers capable of taking the initiative (Gray 1995). Therefore, changes in the form and content of teacher education are crucial in accomplishing real progress in black education. Teacher training must be more practical, with less emphasis on theory. Black teachers must be exposed to practical research and useful projects. This exposure is crucial if teachers are to develop skills that will enable them to participate in the planning and evaluation of educational programs, and it is necessary if black teachers are to help students reach full potential.

Teacher training colleges for blacks, like many other educational institutions, do not permit flexibility for students. Instructors take an authoritarian approach towards how and what are taught. Instructors tend to be regarded as the keepers of knowledge, whereas students are the consumers. Usually a strict code of compliance is imposed upon black students. Such treatment is likely to be modelled by students after completion of their training. New attitudes in teaching and learning should be cultivated. Teacher training colleges need to encourage and nourish critical/analytical thought among students. Situations in which community links with teacher training colleges are poor or inadequate should be encouraged or established if students are to gain practical experience. Attempts aimed at addressing issues such as the root causes of illiteracy, poverty, and unemployment in the curriculum are important because of the overwhelming effect they have had on the African population. If teachers are to develop a meaningful understanding of the problems facing their communities, they need to develop projects that address those problems. In almost all black teacher training colleges, current teaching methods involve rote learning and the amassing of information. This method hinders creativity and imagination on the part of students. Attempts to change the trend are encouraged.

1.8.4 Methods of Teaching

For a variety of reasons, many African teachers are unable to employ innovative methods of teaching, which is partly because of their educational experiences in teacher colleges. Walker (1992) described black teachers as being influenced by the educational process in training colleges, which is dominated by transmission teaching. Thus, they lack models of quality practice. To expect black teachers to produce curious, analytic pupils unless they are teachers of the first rank is not fair. South Africa is in need of improving teacher preparation and in sharpening the skills of teachers currently employed. Poor training of teachers affects their creativity, motivation, and the effective use of talents.

As a result of poor training, many black teachers cannot devise teaching aids and materials to fit the conditions found in their schools. Consequently, they rely heavily on prescribed textbooks. The teaching process in most black schools emphasizes chalk-and-talk methods, inevitably leading to reliance on rote learning (Donald and Hlongwane 1989). That is, black schools are forced to neglect the development of mental abilities, promotion of reasoning and problem-solving powers, or creative imagination.

In many instances, black teachers are ill-prepared for the actual problems that confront them in their classrooms. These problems are compounded by the fact that, for the most part, black teachers receive little or no support from education authorities. Tight external control also has made it difficult for black teachers to move away from rigid and outdated methods of teaching. There is always a need to comply and adhere to what is prescribed by the syllabus. Lack of exposure to more current innovative teaching methods also affects teaching methods in black schools. In order to explore creative teaching methods that will encourage development of the original mind require wide knowledge, a trained sensibility, the habit of reading, and the opportunity to travel, few of which the black teacher has experienced (Hey 1961). Reading for pleasure is not a common practice among many black teachers, which is due, in part, to their upbringing, as well as a limited means to develop the habit. Because many black teachers do not read for pleasure, they also lack the ability to read quickly or widely (Hey 1961).

Teaching in a language other than one's own can be problematic. The black teachers' training has meant the acquisition of Western values, the manipulation of English, and the habit of Western thought at the expense of their African values (Hey 1961). Teachers in black schools consistently require their students to demonstrate the value of an acquired knowledge that has nothing to do with real-life situations. Black students are drilled through simplistic tests that require no creative ability and little analytic thought other than the manipulation of syllabi.

The use of a foreign language such as English generally is limiting to most black teachers not proficient in it. Moreover, their creativity is likely to be affected by this limitation. The language used for teaching determines the quality of methods to be employed in all school situations. Even though the use of English may seem convenient, it is detrimental to the survival of African culture overall. Effective communication between teacher and child also is affected when a foreign language is used for teaching purposes. Concept formulation is affected in day-to-day teaching when instruction is not conducted through the mother tongue. In similar fashion to the language conflict, there is a cultural conflict as well. Traditionally, South Africa has been biased against African cultures, which transmits conflicting messages to children. For example, black children are taught to value Western ways of life, while indirectly encouraged to look down upon African life. Black teachers have not been trained to study their own culture that, in turn, impacts the minds of their students. Moreover, none of the teaching materials used in black schools is designed by Africans. Content in all of the books is foreign, which helps to foster a sense of inferiority among

African teachers and students (Hey 1961). Black teachers in South Africa have never been given the opportunity to think independently or to discover for themselves, which translates to teaching methods they adopt as teachers in the classroom. Most black teachers have never developed a critical awareness of the world (Christie 1985). This lack of awareness implies that they, in turn, cannot instill the same values in their pupils. Because of their limited frame of reference, black teachers do not know what they can or cannot do to change circumstances, resulting in an education that has no purpose or direction. Christie referred to this limitation as education for domestication. If meaningful changes are to occur in black education, new forms of education with improved teaching methods must be developed. Black education in the new South Africa needs direction and purpose. New teaching methods in black schools need to be interactive, which will result in teachers and students becoming active participants in the learning process. By the same token, more opportunity needs to be given to African teachers in order to become critical thinkers and to question their authorities in educational matters. However, if teachers are not critical thinkers willing to challenge the system within which they operate, they are less likely to encourage students to become critical thinkers and creative problem solvers (Dreyer 1994).

1.8.5 Professional Morale

Perhaps the most serious issue related to inadequate teaching methods is the lack of professional morale among teachers in schools in which the culture of teaching and learning is broken down (Gray 1995). Lack of support from other peers with regard to teaching strategies and curriculum thinking also contribute to poor teaching methods. Black teachers, by and large, work in academic isolation, even within the same school (Gray 1995). The situation is complicated further by the fact that only in rare circumstances do teachers in the same school teach the same subject. Staff meetings, in general, address administrative or extracurricular concerns rather than professional issues. Teachers have been subjected to passive roles in which permission is given for teacher-based initiatives, which has a negative impact on teachers who have the skills and determination to try new and effective teaching methods.

Professionalism refers to teachers' commitment to the concept of teaching and learning, as well as teachers who have great allegiance to authorities and the teaching profession in general. Professionalism in teaching consists of teachers who always do their best under changing conditions, including the desire for ongoing professional growth and being involved in teacher forums and research. Professionalism tends to be weak among South African teachers. That is, they neither exercise control over the services offered or over training and work standards of their members nor do they have autonomy in the workplace (Sonn 1994). Professionalism also concerns professional qualifications and higher professional status. Generally, African teachers' status and prestige are low because of their poor working conditions and poor qualifications.

In conclusion, many teachers in South African schools lack the expertise, skill, and experience to be regarded as professionals. This description helps to explain the statistics in Table 1.4. The relatively poor qualifications of black teachers also affect the quality of student performance. Even though students are partly responsible for their own learning, it is the motivation and imaginative quality of teachers that spark students' meaningful learning.

1.8.6 Lack of Motivation

An unmotivated teacher cannot be the best teacher. Why do some teachers perform better in their teaching methods than others? This question is rarely investigated. A variety of factors contributes to this state of affairs, all of which impact on the quality of teaching methods. Nxumalo (1990) cited the following reasons why some students choose the teaching profession:

(i) The program appeared to be less demanding than what was available for the students at a given time.
(ii) There was some relative security of tenure since, under normal circumstances, governments have absolute faith in compulsory education.
(iii) It was cheaper to pursue teacher education than other diplomas.
(iv) Parents attached more status to teaching than to other professions.
(v) The student had failed to attain promotional grades to degrees or diplomas that had been chosen at the beginning. (pp. 33-34)

Table 1.4

Underqualified African Teachers

Year	Percentage
1987	89
1989	71
1990	45

Sources: D. Everatt, *Creating a Future: Youth Policy for South Africa* (Johannesburg, South Africa, Ravan Press, 1994), 36-66; P. M. Kachelhoffer, "Teacher Enrichment Programs in Kwa-Ndebele, South Africa," *Higher Education Policy* 8(2) (1995):19-22; E. Unterhalter, H. Wolpe, and T. Botha, *Education in a Future South Africa: Policy Issues for Transformation* (Trenton, New Jersey: Africa World Press, 1992), 200-20.

Given the reasons why people enter the teaching profession, it is not surprising that few excellent and innovative teachers are produced by the system.

1.8.7 Problems Related To the Teacher Shortage

Education for blacks was deliberately neglected during apartheid. This neglect was aimed at restricting access to schooling. The philosophy of apartheid was initially directed at educating blacks in line with their supposedly limited cognitive abilities and with a view of equipping them for what was seen as their role in society (Skuy and Partington 1990). In short, it was aimed at producing docile people who would never challenge the political status quo. Thus, little was done to improve the quality of black teachers.

There has always been a lack of qualified black teachers to meet the needs of the growing student body. This teacher shortage has resulted in hiring untrained teachers in most black schools. According to Bean (1994), the South African population is expected to increase from its estimated 35 million to approximately 70 million in the year 2020; this rapid increase will further impact the black school population. With the growth of the black population, the employment of unqualified teachers in black schools also will continue unless the quality of black teachers is raised.

Baine and Mwamwenda (1994) contended that the employment of unqualified teachers perpetuates the vicious cycle of poor teachers, producing poor students, resulting in high failure rates. Insufficient training facilities have always contributed to this shortage. For example, in 1991, black teacher colleges turned away ten applicants for each one accepted (Johnson 1992). This action was further compounded by the high failure rate in some teacher training colleges. For example, Baine and Mwamwenda reported that, in Transkei (now Eastern Cape), the failure rate among teachers-in-training in 1990 was 58 percent for primary school teachers, whereas 66 percent of the secondary teachers-in-training obtained less than 50 percent on their examinations.

Some teachers are driven away from the teaching profession because of poor working conditions, low pay, lack of accommodations, an inadequate supply of school materials, and overcrowded classrooms. As a result, it is difficult to attract and retain highly qualified teachers. In some instances, persons with suitable educational qualifications have opted for better paying jobs rather than teaching. Providing teachers varies from region-to-region. For example, urban schools tend to attract more teachers than rural schools because conditions are slightly better in urban than in rural areas. Yet, rural and farm schools are currently the largest category of black schools, comprising 73 percent of all African schools (Christie and Gaganakis 1989).

Centralized design and planning of curriculum without the participation of teachers is another aspect of the problem. Black teachers in South Africa usually are passive receivers of the curriculum designed by the Department of Education and Training. This practice leaves many talented and innovative black teachers with little or no room for flexibility. On the other hand, participation of black teachers in the curriculum planning process enables them to control the process of teaching and learning on their own terms.

1.8.8 Student-Teacher Ratio

Black schools continue to be plagued by shortages of facilities such as classrooms and inadequate funding. Textbooks, library facilities, and other teaching materials remain in short supply. These factors, combined with poor qualifications of black teachers, have led to high teacher-student ratios (Baine and Mwamwenda 1994). The teacher-pupil ratio ranges from 1:50 to an absurd 1:70 (Simon 1991). The situation is even worse for rural schools, including farm schools and former homeland schools. The average ratio in Transkei, as reported by Baine and Mwamwenda (1994), is as follows:

> Junior primary: average = 73:1, range = 39:1 to 142:1
> Senior primary: average = 51:1, range = 30:1 to 86:1
> Junior secondary: average = 22:1, range = 10:1 to 31:1
> Senior secondary: average = 26:1, range = 19:1 to 34:1. (p. 120)

Based on 1994 statistics, Lesage (1994) estimated that in order to reduce the teacher-pupil ratio to an acceptable level, an additional 33,000 new classrooms would be required by the end of the decade. Marcum (1982) reported:

> The government's new (1981) policy of progressively introducing compulsory primary education for blacks is expected if and when fully implemented by the year 2000, [and it] will require annual expenditure of roughly 4 billion and a cadre of 320,000 teachers. This translates into 11,000 new teachers and 10,000 new classrooms per year. (p. 17)

Ironically, the unavailability of classrooms and the shortage of qualified black teachers in South Africa are occurring at a time when many white schools are closing because of poor enrollment (Sithole 1991). White teachers are retrenching, whereas training colleges for whites are lacking a student body (Baine and Mwamwenda 1994). It has been difficult to convince authorities to make these vacant schools available to those who need them. This fact has changed with the new political dispensation, but the location of the schools always determines availability.

The 1994 elections and a new political dispensation marked a fresh beginning in education. Funding black education has been very poor. Just before the elections, the government announced changes in black education. For example, compulsory schooling of nine years from the age of six or seven years to the age of fifteen or sixteen has been placed in the South African constitution ("New Schools Scheme" 1992).

There also has been an increase of per-capita expenditure on black children (Nkabinde 1993b). Baine and Mwamwenda (1994) reported that the relationship between white-and-black-per-capita costs improved from 15.1 in 1972 to approximately 10.1 in 1980 and approximately 5.1 in 1990. The government currently spends more on black education, but the gap between the races remains enormous; that is, the black student population is exploding. This notion was supported by Davies (1985). He explained that, even though expenditures on urban black education have increased, little has changed in the overall quality and content of black education. Table 1.5 shows per-capita expenditure on various racial groups.

Table 1.5

Educational Expenditure for Different Groups

	Group			
Year	Africans	Coloreds	Indians	Whites
1984	R234	R569	R1,088	R1,654
1989	R927	R2,115	R2,645	R3,575
1991	R930	R1,983	R2,659	R3,739
1993	R1,659	R2,902	R3,702	R4,372

Sources: A. Penny, S. Appel, J. Gultig, K. Harley, and R. Muir, "Just Sort of Fumbling in the Dark: A Case Study of the Advent of Racial Integration in South African Schools," *Comparative Education Review* 37(4) (1993):412-33; E. Sithole, "Education in the New South Africa," *SASPOST* 2(4) (1991):1-7; L. Slammert, "Rethinking Mathematical Knowledge: The Quest for People's Mathematics in South Africa," in J. D. Jansen (Ed.), *Knowledge and Power in South Africa: Critical Perspectives Across the Disciplines*, Johannesburg, South Africa: Skottaville (1991): pp. 203-12; R. Watson, J. Contreras, and J. Hammer, "Black Power," *Newsweek Magazine* (1994, May 9):34-39.

Additional problems associated with providing adequate funding for black South Africans are (a) the sheer numbers of school-age children because of the rapidly growing black population; (b) the lack of full, free, and compulsory schooling for Africans, which translates into a lack of uniformity in terms of age for starting school; (c) the lack of control by blacks over their own education, resulting in a lack of control over funding; and (d) poor facilities, poorly qualified teachers, and many children from disadvantaged backgrounds. These factors alone do not sufficiently explain centuries of neglect of black education. Simon (1991) noted that South Africa has always had the financial means to upgrade black education, and it has the resources with which to build a successful future because of its vast mineral wealth. Simon also noted that the nation ranks number one in the world in the production of platinum-group metals, gold vanadium, and gem diamonds. He further stated that South Africa ranks number two in the production of chrome and manganese ores and number three for industrial diamonds and asbestos. Its foreign debt at the end of 1993 was only R87,6 billion or 23 percent of the gross domestic product. These statistics are in line with international standards ("R30bn in Reserves Needed" 1994). However, South Africa's remarkable wealth has been used to benefit only the privileged minority and to suppress the majority.

New developments in the education system must be focused on the integration of the previously fragmented system. The new policy of education must be directed towards equal opportunity and quality, and the standards and relevance to the changing educational needs of South Africa also must be addressed (Collins and Gillespie 1984). Funding for black schools must receive attention in a new government of national unity. Eliminating inequalities due to years of apartheid will require a massive intervention. Just as apartheid education was implemented over the years, redressing its harmful consequences also will take years of hard work and dedication on the part of educators. Year-by-year objectives need to be established, and all forces at the nation's disposal must be harnessed to achieve them ("R30bn in Reserves Needed" 1994). Teachers, parents, students, and other community leaders must join forces to make this new education a reality. Full use of expertise of all community members will make a great impact on the education of children. Ending racially segmented education has been proposed but will provide no solutions unless those who are or who have been affected by poor education find answers to their problems. Furthermore, upgrading facilities and teaching materials will not be sufficient without changing the content. Meaningful changes are those that affect curriculum, teaching methods, and scope. Valid changes will start at the foundation, at the very core of learning.

1.8.9 Recommendations

In South Africa, there is a need for reform in teacher education for blacks. Raising the quality of black teachers is crucial in providing quality classroom instruction. Black teachers should be given more input. Their roles must expand from that of syllabus implementers to that of creators of content such as tests, questions, and even teaching materials within the context of their classrooms. Rather than being passive recipients of teaching materials designed for them, they need to be active participants in the educational dialogue. Historically, policy discussions regarding educational planning for black South Africans frequently have been conducted in the absence of the three groups most likely to understand issues: (a) parents, (b) students, and (c) teachers. The central government has always designed educational policies, whereas black teachers have been expected to implement them. Many of the conflicts in black schools are a result of not having a voice. Allowing black teachers to have control over what is taught in the schools is one way to a new education system that will be acceptable to the majority.

African teachers who are on the receiving end in terms of curriculum, teaching materials, and teaching methods are not learning analytical skills or critical capacity. They do not know what it takes to design their own education. How can they analyze and make contributions to the country's new educational system if they do not have the skills or the practice? Teachers' experience and educational reasoning are crucial tools in educational transformation. Therefore, if black education in South Africa is to be changed, black teachers' input will be the driving force. That is, black teachers' concerns, ideas, and their needs are essential in the planning of educational reforms. Participation of black teachers in the planning process will give them the opportunity to control the process of teaching on their terms. Incorporating black teachers in policymaking will be beneficial in the long run. Moreover, such teacher networks have always proven to be a key asset for administrators in any educational planning endeavors. Teachers in black schools must be able to exchange activities and procedures in order to enhance their teaching methods. The development of teachers' manuals at local levels ought to be encouraged as a way to create dialogue among classroom teachers. These manuals will give black teachers a place to turn, as well as to provide them with an avenue for creativity.

Organized seminars and conferences increase teachers' knowledge and keep them informed about new teaching strategies being explored, and, most importantly, they give them an opportunity to share their successes and struggles in the field with other teachers from different backgrounds. Local journals, when fully utilized, are another avenue for teachers to remain current.

Educational change cannot occur without shaping this work force such as recruitment, adequate training, in-service education, and career structures of teachers in black schools (Connell 1994). The crisis of black schooling is largely a crisis of staffing. According to MacKenzie (1993), 87 percent of black teachers are not adequately certified. He also indicated that the need to improve black teachers through in-service training is an enormous task requiring much funding and many long-term solutions. Years may pass before its benefits penetrate significantly into the school system. In addition, distance education, as a way of training more black teachers, has been recommended as another option (Johnson 1992).

Ongoing training is important for teachers at all levels. International conferences are always helpful in providing teachers with new strategies and innovative methods. However, it is extremely expensive for black teachers in South Africa to attend conferences. Sending teachers to regional conferences to keep abreast of new developments in the field is helpful. Another alternative is in-service training. In South Africa, pre-service and in-service teacher education has been fragmented. Insufficient connection is often found between what African teachers learn in training colleges and the actual experiences they encounter in the classrooms. This limitation needs improvement by making teacher training colleges more connected to what actually occurs outside the colleges. One alternative is to engage those who are training to become teachers in community projects. Maintaining a continuous link between training colleges and community projects can be beneficial over time.

Quality education, if it becomes a reality for all people in South Africa, also will translate into quality teacher training. Curriculum changes at all levels need to focus on practical implications rather than abstractions. Teacher training curricula ought to be reevaluated and modified with the purpose of designing a more current training model based on the new demands of a postapartheid South Africa. Black teachers need to play a key role in the improvement of black education; thus, democratic practice and community empowerment will guide the educational practice and conception of a new era beyond Bantu education.

1.8.10 Conclusion

Educational change in South Africa must rely on changes in the way teachers are trained and socialized. Teachers trained under apartheid are more likely to teach the way they were taught. Consequently, a vicious circle of poor teaching will continue. A new mode of teaching and a change of attitudes are required in order to reverse the trend of Bantu education. The task of retraining teachers is complex because old behaviors do not die quickly, and teachers alone cannot carry the responsibility of educating children. Parents of black children need to be empowered and encouraged to participate in the responsibility of preparing their children for school. Black teachers must learn to cope with the environment and to modify their teaching methods in accordance with the changing times by building up their knowledge of the world and expanding the horizons of their students. These skills are achieved by teachers who are willing to explore new paths and by being widely read themselves. Teachers need to be accepting of new ways to teach and to remember that learning does not mean "book learning" alone.

Chapter 2

Dropout Rates In Black Schools

This chapter investigates a continuing problem in South African black education, that is, the significant numbers of black students who drop out of school before they have attained functional literacy. For example, Baine and Mwamwenda (1994) reported that in South Africa at least 300,000 young black people had joined the ranks of the unemployed and unemployable. This chapter covers three general aspects of the dropout phenomenon: (a) the prevalence among African youth, (b) the potential causes of this problem, and (c) future plans and recommendations aimed at reducing the incidence of dropping out among black South Africans.

Some of the underlying causes of the high dropout rate among Africans have been neglected in existing theory and research. The purpose of this chapter is to offer tentative proposals and suggestions to guide program development, implementation, and evaluation for dropout prevention.

Historically, black students and their parents in South African schools have had little or no part in the schooling of their children. This practice has left many students and their parents disconnected from the educational system designed for them. As recently as 1995, compulsory school attendance laws have just been introduced to black schools.

This chapter attempts to provide a clear view of dropout characteristics in a South African context. The importance of involving all persons who work closely with students in preventing dropout rates also is covered.

2.1 Introduction

During the past decades, South Africa has witnessed a rapid increase of education dropout rates among Africans. The incidence of the high dropout rate among Africans is not a new concept. Recently, renewed public attention has been focused on this issue, in part, because of its threat and the need for action. For example, Green (1991) reported that increasing numbers of South African leaders, both black and white, are referring in despair and in fear to the current generation of youth from the black townships as the "lost generation." That is, there are hundreds of thousands of young blacks who lack the education, skills, and work habits to participate constructively in the South African economy and society.

The rising number of school dropouts in South Africa must be addressed as it relates to the economic well-being of the country. Even though school enrollment for a majority of black students has improved significantly, providing compulsory education, as well as other appropriate educational services, remain promises yet to be realized. In 1950, slightly more than one third of black children of all ages attended school; currently, the figure is approximately 80 percent (Green 1991). This progress, however, tends to deteriorate at the secondary level, which has a high black dropout rate.

There are various reasons for the high incidence of school dropout among black South Africans. For example, blacks experienced poor teaching by teachers who are themselves the product of Bantu education, inadequate facilities, the lowest per-student expenditures, and the highest pupil-teacher ratios (Herbstein 1993). Harsh conditions exist in most South African black schools, forcing many students to leave school early. Excessive use of corporal punishment also has been reported as a source of dropping out (Simon 1991).

Corporal punishment is viewed as a cruel disciplinary measure, but teachers in black South African schools have learned these practices as part of their existence. Consequently, this practice becomes a vicious circle. A new generation of teachers must be taught various ways of humane disciplinary measures. Communication and negotiation could replace corporal punishment. Several other factors also contribute to the school dropout rate. These factors include being taught in a foreign language, lack of school readiness training, financial constraints, uneducated parents, lack of motivation, and poor school attendance. In order to comprehend the current problems of the education dropout rate among Africans, it is important to have an overview of the prevalence, followed by a discussion of some of the contributing factors.

2.2 Prevalence

Determining prevalence (the exact number of pupils dropping out of school) is difficult to establish, in part, because there has been no compulsory education for blacks in decades. Of all black children who commence schooling in Substandard A (kindergarten), only 54 percent complete four years of lower primary education; 28 percent complete the higher primary course; approximately 7 percent attain a Junior Certificate level; and only 1 percent receives the Senior or Matriculation Certificate (Behr 1978, p. 182). This finding leads me to believe that approximately half of the school entrants drop out before they attain functional literacy, and only 1 out of every 100 completes the entire school program.

For every 100 black pupils who begin school, only 10 complete the final examination ("Bad School or None" 1987). Of these, only 50 percent pass compared with more than 90 percent for whites, nearly 86 percent for Indians, and approximately 66 percent for coloreds or people of mixed race. Baine and Mwamwenda (1994) cited the following statistics regarding those who reach Standard Ten (matriculation) in South Africa: whites = 69 percent, Indians = 43 percent, coloreds = 11 percent, and blacks = 4 percent. Usually, the incidence of dropout is higher among girls than boys.

Despite the recent changes and general improvement in black education during the 1990s, the dropout phenomenon is an area of concern for black South Africans. Approximately 1.6 million black children are receiving no education ("One,6-M Black Children Not in School" 1994). In understanding this educational problem, it is important to identify potential causes of school dropout among black South Africans. The dropout trend in South African education for various racial groups is shown in Table 2.1.

Table 2.1

Percentage of Pupils Reaching Standard Four (Sixth Grade) and Standard Ten (Twelfth Grade)

Group	1973		1984	
	Standard Four	Standard Ten	Standard Four	Standard Ten
Asians	83	25	100	58
Africans	43	4	55	16
Coloreds	56	5	74	22
Whites	88	56	95	73

Source: R. C. Jones, "Large-Scale Implementation of a Computer-Based Education Program for Disadvantaged High School Pupils at Matriculation Level," Unpublished M.Ed. Thesis, University of the Western Cape, South Africa (1986):18.

2.3 Potential Causes of Education Dropout Rates Among Blacks

South African blacks drop out of school for various reasons. One of the major reasons is alienation, which results in lack of hope and a sense of purpose. Many factors play a role in enhancing school alienation such as unfavorable learning environment, absenteeism, discipline problems, repeated failure, poverty, and family.

2.3.1 Unfavorable Learning Environment

The subject matter in black schools does not focus on practical implications of the curriculum; rather, it focuses on abstract and remote emphasis. For example, in the subject of geography, African children must learn about the landscape of England rather than the landscape of Africa and South Africa. Land distribution and its impact on the black population have been avoided in the curriculum. Therefore, the curriculum is viewed by many black pupils as irrelevant, something that does not reflect their needs, aspirations, and interests (Jansen 1990). Many students drop out of school if they feel excluded or undervalued. Black students continuously exposed to a learning environment that provides negative feedback tend to leave school early. The learning experience needs to occur in a warm, positive, and stimulating atmosphere. Schools should not be a place that pupils fear or resent but a desired place for students. Black students exposed to racist syllabi tend to develop low self-esteem (Herbstein 1993).

Problems facing the South African black youth are further compounded by underqualified teachers who have poor morale because of low pay and unsafe working conditions. A 1979 study reported that only 20 percent of the teachers in African schools had completed high school and only 2.6 percent held university degrees (Dempster 1982). An investigation by Ka Choeu (1991) suggested that teachers in South Africa are caught in the vortex of the education crisis. Youth accuse teachers of not performing their duties sufficiently, whereas parents label them incompetent (Ka Choeu 1991).

There is a reasonable solution to teacher-related problems. The involvement of black teachers in all aspects of education such as identifying their teaching needs, planning, decision making, priority setting, and implementation and evaluation of services will help reduce the dropout problem. This exercise ensures that teachers and students get a sense of ownership and control over what is being taught.

Parents need to be drawn in as partners in the education of their children. This strategy works to prevent truancy among black youth and also to reduce tension that sometimes exists between parents and teachers.

2.3.2 Absenteeism and School Disruptions

Violence and school disruptions are additional indicators of problems experienced by black students in most South African schools. Therefore, it is not surprising that black students faced with life-threatening circumstances would seek to leave such a negative environment. In some areas, there has been a complete breakdown of discipline, which has further compounded the problems. After the elections in 1994, violence in most parts of South Africa decreased tremendously. Yet, black schools still face many challenges in postapartheid South Africa.

2.3.3 Discipline Problems

Another reason associated with dropping out of school is the application of harsh disciplinary measures, including excessive use of corporal punishment and other aversive procedures. Use of the cane and other punitive objects to mete out corporal punishment is widespread in South African schools (McFadden 1990). This type of punishment is cruel and has long-lasting psychological effects, and it is regarded by many as an extension of the repressive state apparatus. Fear prevents children from realizing their maximum potential, and it also suppresses their inner capacity containing talents.

More humane and effective strategies such as isolation and denial of privileges are rarely applied in black schools. Some teachers in black schools abuse and misuse punishment, resulting in various conflicts with their students. In some instances, what begins as a disciplinary measure ends as being dangerous and harmful to students. In a violent society like South Africa, corporal punishment tends to encourage violence among black youth. Teachers in black schools have failed to realize that harsh and unusual punishment is more likely to instigate additional aggression or hostility than treatment perceived as fair or just.

2.3.4 Student-Related Problems

School repetition for poor achievers is a common practice in many South African schools. This practice is said to compound further the problem of overcrowdedness, and it also stretches to the limit scarce educational resources. Mosha (1988) proved that repetition does not lead to better performance; rather, individual attention, coupled with other methods, enhance performance for students.

Repeated failure encourages students to drop out of school and contributes to a sense of worthlessness or low self-esteem among affected students. Repeated failure also cannot be expected to provide motivation for parents to continue spending money on children who could be out of school and working.

In black schools throughout South Africa, learning disabilities are not assessed or treated. Therefore, disabled black pupils tend to be ignored or regarded as unmotivated, lazy, or even stupid. Students with mild disabilities, such as an inability to succeed and achieve, find themselves discarded by learning institutions. Poor academic performance, truancy, early marriage, and pregnancy for girls are strong predictors of leaving school early for black youth in South Africa.

2.3.5 Teenage Pregnancy

Early and repeated pregnancy among African girls is a leading cause of school dropout. Teenage pregnancy contributes to early deprivation and poverty of children because of a lack of material care. King (1979) determined that early and repeated pregnancy reduces the chances of developing talent. In an African community, unmarried mothers are sometimes viewed negatively. Therefore, pregnant girls or teenage mothers are less likely to receive the support from their families to complete schooling.

2.3.6 Family Factors

The term "school dropout" usually refers to students, not their parents. Parents, however, are as guilty as their students. For example, parents who fail to stay involved in their children's education indirectly contribute to them leaving school early. Parents also must share the responsibility of their children's failure. Sometimes lack of support from families occurs as a result of poor education of parents and/or a lack of means.

Research studies consistently indicate that students whose families remain involved in school activities perform better academically ("Homework for Parents" 1994). Family-school connections are rarely encouraged in black schools because of the previous structure of education that denied Africans the freedom to direct their schools. Thus, black parents have never believed that they were "owners" of the schools. The gap between home and school has contributed to many problems students encounter at school.

Children learning in the home are enhanced by a rich environment. Parents who are available to monitor their children and to help them with homework reduce the chances of failure, which is a contributing factor to school dropout. Many black parents cannot afford the luxury of books. Involving parents as a way of helping students not to drop out is an important undertaking that has to be encouraged.

Blacks have been the only people in South Africa who have had to pay in full for their education, which has compounded the problem of school dropout. Most parents have found it difficult to keep their children in school because of financial limitations. Therefore, school experiences, family circumstances, and economic factors have determined how long students remain in school.

In some rural areas, children are required to walk long distances to school, which, in part, is due to the lack of transportation and the absence of neighborhood schools. Lack of school lunches also forces children from poor backgrounds to drop out of school. A hungry and tired child is expected to learn just like any other student. For some children, that type of life becomes unbearable; thus, they are encouraged to leave school early. School lunches were introduced in 1995. Children who could not afford lunch are now benefiting from this new undertaking.

2.3.7 Poverty

Studies have shown that dropout rates are common in poorer countries, especially affecting lower income groups such as girls and those in rural areas (Bray, Clarke, and Stephens 1986). Poverty is the underlying factor behind a child' s decision to leave school early. For example, some children are not involved in school because their parents cannot afford to pay the required fees. Books, uniforms, examination fees, exercises, and pens are major expenses for many families. Since the government of national unity has just recommended free and compulsory education for all its citizens, there is renewed hope that all children will have an opportunity to attend school regardless of their economic backgrounds.

Some parents in rural areas have had their children leave school early to work on the farm in order to supplement the family' s income. Girls have been required to perform domestic duties because their parents are concerned that they will become pregnant at school (Bray et al. 1986). Poor conditions prevail in rural schools. That is, facilities are in short supply and learning opportunities are scarce, resulting in high dropout rates. Teachers attracted to work in rural areas, in general, are poorly trained; thus, pupils are more likely to be bored with school (Bray et al. 1986). In addition, rural pupils have fewer out-of-school programs and no libraries, which makes learning more challenging. In the absence of national government commitment to black education and its funding, any effective dropout program will remain an unattainable ideal. The government alone cannot eliminate all the problems in black schools. Therefore, money spent on education will have long-term benefits to the economy.

2.4 Future Plans and Recommendations

Plans to reduce the dropout rate among black youth in South Africa reflect an understanding of the history of the interrelationship between the educational system and the political economy of the country. The willingness of a new government to restructure society, as well as the educational system, will benefit all children. Matabane (1990) argued that the appalling dropout rate for blacks points to the devastating effects of Bantu education.

In addressing the education dropout problem, the causes of school dropout must be identified in order to move forward. It is recommended that quality education be made attainable for all citizens in South Africa regardless of race, religion, or social class. Safety and security at school also ought to be guaranteed for all students, encouraging them to become successful within the school system. Parental involvement in the education of children must be encouraged. Black communities, with the government's support, must become full participants in helping their children to remain in school.

School facilities and teaching materials need to be upgraded in black schools. Teachers in these schools must be encouraged to develop materials commensurate with their needs. Each member of the community needs to acknowledge the value assigned to education. More neighborhood schools must be built to prevent students from walking long distances in search of education.

There is a possibility of reducing the shortage of school buildings by allowing full use of vacant schools previously owned by other racial groups. Renting out such spaces or buying the buildings is an option for the new government. Some white schools closed because they could not enroll sufficient numbers of pupils, and some schools have been allowed to organize as private nonracial schools. Equal spending per student should be a right for each child, not a privilege for a selected few.

The introduction of compulsory education, currently underway, will reduce the dropout rate among black South Africans (Behr 1978). This program needs to be accompanied by a strong commitment of the state and parents to ensure that children enrolled in school attend regularly. Another incentive to keep children in school is the introduction of school meals.

In addition, when students are given an opportunity to voice their concerns in educational matters without being victimized and when learners have a sense of control over the subject matter, alienation is greatly reduced. A school that gives its student body a voice, a sense of safety, a sense of self-worth, and a feeling of belonging is more likely to retain its students. Respectable role models from the black community, when used to instill pride and self-confidence among its youth, provide incentives and a desire to learn or compete. Teachers in black schools must help students build their self-esteem rather than contribute to its destruction.

Schools are expected to care about children' s dreams, hopes, and aspirations. Schools are places in which children learn through experience and growth, and they are places in which joy in learning are to take place. According to Baine and Mwamwenda (1994), many teaching practices in African schools are not pleasurable for students; thus, learning is boring and discouraging. Ineffective teaching includes (a) experiencing long periods of lecturing and rote recitation, (b) having students copy from the blackboard, (c) giving students few opportunities to ask questions or participate in active learning, (d) having students memorize texts with few opportunities for hands-on involvement, and (e) providing little ongoing monitoring and feedback related to student learning. Improving teaching methods by exposing black teachers to innovative methods is needed in order to form the foundation of educational transformation in South Africa.

Another area of emphasis in a new South Africa is school readiness training, which would afford each child a rich beginning. Early stimulation of intellectual skills is crucial in the mastery of academics. A relationship between school readiness training and student achievement has been established in the literature. Against this background, school readiness training is recommended as a way to prevent school failure, which, consequently, leads to school dropout.

Implementation of a dropout prevention program requires commitment on the part of parents, the black community, professionals, students, and institutions of higher education in addressing pressing educational problems. These problems include improving black students' motivation levels, attracting students who have dropped out of school because of social problems in the education system, and organizing schools in ways that motivate black students to learn. Individual and family counseling also help to decrease adverse family problems that contribute to school dropout.

Parental involvement is needed, including, but not limited to, sharing students' progress and areas of concern in order to establish healthy relationships. This process opens communications between teachers and parents. A supportive home and school environment is more likely to prevent dropout rates. Furthermore, research has indicated that working with parents is an effective way to bring about positive behavioral changes and improvement in student achievement (Warner 1974). The benefits of increased parental involvement include improved student attendance, decreased dropout rates, more positive parent-student communication, and increased parent-community support of the school.

School-community support is another component that is vital in combating the dropout rate, including provisions for after-school programs. The use of school buildings, church buildings, and recreational halls is to be encouraged in order to benefit students who cannot study at home because of overcrowdedness and other related circumstances. Responsible adults from the community, such as retired professionals, can assist in supervising and monitoring these facilities when in use. Providing recreational facilities makes school more exciting for students who are at risk of dropping out. The government's support to fund these programs is required, as well as the community's contributions when necessary.

Black institutions of higher learning must take the initiative by involving faculty and students in the educational reform movement. For example, black faculty members can serve on the planning teams of a new educational dispensation at the national and local level, whereas others can serve as advisors to teachers in local schools and families of children at risk. Giving children a meaningful life and a second chance help decrease some of the social ills that feed on ignorance and lack of education. In this regard, a safe environment is a prerequisite for blacks to take the initiative.

Additional support is warranted for black pupils who have dropped out of school. This support includes evening classes, adult education, correspondence classes with regular teacher support, and/or special tutoring for pupils too old to attend elementary or secondary schools. This practice reduces the embarrassment of being an older student. These programs will be too costly, but it benefits all when more people are educated properly.

The state, with the help of the private sector, must make financial commitments to prevent school dropout. The state, however, needs to assume a greater portion of the burden in establishing programs and ensuring that, through legislation, such programs are implemented. Vocational schools are to be encouraged for students who cannot attend college.

Over time, programs will be less costly and more beneficial for individuals and the state. Black students must be informed or made to realize that unless they attend school that future generations will be robbed of leadership throughout all professions. Moreover, education is not only a right but a responsibility. Thus, all individuals have a duty to improve themselves by utilizing knowledge made available.

A successful education dropout prevention program includes the following components: (a) improving teacher performance, (b) providing adequate textbooks, (c) ensuring relevance of language and content of learning materials, (d) improving school and system management and supervision, (e) making basic education accountable to parents and the community, and (f) effectively evaluating what is happening.

Teachers need to have more control over the curriculum in order to prevent high failure rates among black students. This process can be accomplished only by allowing all African teachers to plan and implement programs with the establishment of a single ministry of education in which all racial groups are equally represented. However, as long as one racial group dominates and controls the educational administration, cheating and bias toward the controlled group will not cease.

All structures in education that alienate black youth need to be abolished. Corporal punishment must be replaced by mild and more effective disciplinary measures. Replacing books that are demeaning and humiliating to blacks is recommended. Education needs to be responsive to the needs of all children regardless of color or creed. Schools must ensure relevance of the curriculum by making the everyday experience of students the content of lessons, preserving the dignity of each pupil and stressing realistic practical work skills.

Research studies have indicated that family life education and the use of contraceptives have a positive effect on unintended pregnancies (Helge 1989; Williams 1995). Thus, education seems to be a preventative measure of teenage pregnancy. Providing counseling facilities in schools will help teenagers find needed help. Youth clubs and churches must consider offering counseling to teenagers who do not attend school (Williams 1995). Inclusion of sex education in the school curriculum remains optional.

Sex education in schools is viewed by parents as an unacceptable infringement of their privacy and moral obligation to teach their children. However, the reality of sexually transmitted diseases and the spread of AIDS (acquired immunodeficiency syndrome) in South Africa might alter attitudes about sex education. Education and the prevention of early pregnancies must assume a high priority if the cycle of poverty is to be broken. The spread of contagious diseases such as AIDS also can be reduced through education.

2.5 Conclusion

The obligation of any government is to invest in the education of future generations. Until services and programs for the dropout population are developed and implemented, neither the government nor society at large will enjoy the peace and prosperity needed for economic progress in South Africa. However, reclaiming the lost generation of South African youth to the classroom requires addressing a whole set of related social problems.

West (1991) suggested that if a dropout program is to succeed that the response of educators at the local level to the characteristics of their students and to the social, economic, and political dynamics of the immediate community is of primary importance. In a situation such as South Africa's, more than the creation of dropout programs is necessary. Future policymakers, comprised of all South African racial groups organized on democratic principles, will need to consider an extensive restructuring of education throughout the country. Research studies have indicated that substantive changes in education occur only when people are equally represented at all levels in the educational governing body. Currently, this process is underway in South Africa.

West (1991) cited various components responsible in successful dropout prevention programs. These programs reconnected at-risk youth to the demands and opportunities of education, provided more opportunity for success than failure, and made students feel accepted by the school system and their teachers. These components could be helpful in South Africa. Instructional practices are meaningful and exciting for students. Finally, these programs could create places where students want to be, as well as create enjoyable places for teachers (West 1991).

Removing blame from black teachers, who also are victims of circumstances, includes allowing them in the national and local decision making, planning, implementation, and evaluation of education programs. For example, black teachers need to understand new proposals for educational change, and they must participate in changes likely to impact their lives and those of their students. They also must be given an opportunity to become creators of information rather than receivers of ready-made information as in the past. The process of neglecting their educational input has disconnected many black teachers from the content, thus creating lack of motivation and low morale.

Teachers, who are part of educational planning and implementation of programs, are more likely to be responsible for what is right or wrong in the educational system. Such practices eliminate blame and/or finger pointing because all concerned parties are responsible. There is a greater need for effective training of teachers when they take on new roles for which they have not been trained.

Research implies that the dropout rate among black South Africans, for the most part, is caused by the denial of educational opportunities, poverty, lack of school facilities, and violence, as well as many environmental factors that are not responsive to the pupils' needs. Attempts to remedy the dropout problem with dropout preventative programs will not succeed without proper attention to the underlying causes of the educational dropout rate problems. On the other hand, it would be unfair to expect black communities to "pull themselves up by their bootstraps" without financial assistance from the state.

Development of a well-articulated educational policy in which all racial groups are equally represented will help create a stable society. A variety of effective programs and curricular changes to prevent dropout rates becomes a reality only when education, as well as all other social structures, are restructured on democratic principles. Black youth must be made aware that they are the next generation and the future leaders of the nation; it also makes it easier to exploit them economically when they do not possess the necessary skills. Their failure to be educated means the failure of the next generation. The youth of today occupy an important place in society; therefore, their needs are a critical priority. Parental support for formal education is believed to have a tremendous effect in reducing school dropout among black youth. Such support remains crucial.

At the other end of the dropout problem, students who have not participated in formal education must be given a second chance. In order to encourage these young adults, new programs of nonformal education are to be encouraged. These programs are to take the form of technical training and/or adult education.

Chapter 3

Adult Education

3.1 Introduction

Several studies have confirmed the benefits of literacy on society (Johnston 1990; Kundu 1984; Mushi 1991). According to Johnston (1990), societies with a high level of literacy are materially better off than those with a low level, and the presence of widespread literacy skills substantially affects society's culture, relationships, power structure, and economy (p. 83). Literacy, in any form, is an important measure of progress.

Adult education should not be regarded as a luxury; it is a necessity. In South Africa, ignorance and poverty are widespread among blacks. Kundu (1984) contended that there is a definite correlation between illiteracy and poverty. In light of the claim that ignorance is directly related to illiteracy and the fact that illiteracy breeds poverty (Kundu 1984), it can be said that adult education becomes a necessity.

Adult education in South Africa is designed to serve those who left school early. The aim of adult education is to improve the quality of life of the adult population. Adult education aims at eliminating illiteracy, ignorance, and exploitation of any person by another.

In Africa, many people live under the constraints of poverty, disease, ignorance, hunger, and miserable living conditions, which are seen by ordinary people as a situation that cannot be changed (Mushi 1991). Adult education equips people with the knowledge on how to take charge of their lives. Making people aware of their circumstances through literacy decreases a sense of helplessness and cultivates in them the desire to transform their circumstances.

South Africa needs adult education that has a solid theoretical foundation, as well as practical implications. In a postapartheid South Africa, educators and practitioners are challenged to design and implement effective and quality programs for adult education. The primary goal of adult education in postapartheid South Africa is to help those adult individuals who have been silenced because of illiteracy.

On the other hand, if adult education in South Africa is to be effective, the following questions should be asked: Why adult education? What do adults need? Is there a connection between participants' needs and programs to be designed? What curriculum will adult education adopt? What methods of teaching will be most effective for an adult population?

3.2 Rationale for Adult Education

South Africa cannot afford to sustain all of its people unless they have minimum skills enabling them to be self-sufficient and independent. Levels of illiteracy among Africans perhaps justify a need for adult education. Table 3.1 gives a picture of illiteracy in South Africa.

Bhola (1984) argued that illiterates put less into, and get less out of, the environment. Whereas high literacy rates of approximately 75 percent are related to low fertility rates, low infant mortality, and improved health standards (Bhola 1984). Illiteracy in the workplace also is associated with lower productivity, even in simple occupations such as peasant farming, construction, and handicraft (Bhola 1984). Considering the growing use of modern technology, literacy has become a requirement.

Adult literacy in South Africa is aimed at dealing with content related to the participants' occupations. However, such education is not to be limited to individual occupations. Teaching literacy to adults must be flexible and broad. In other words, adult learners must be free to read whatever they choose if adult education is meant to be liberating. Young people of South Africa need literate adults as role models.

Table 3.1

Percentage of Adult Literacy Rate

Year	Group			
	Africans	Coloreds	Indians	Whites
1995	52.0	68.0	79.0	97.0
1993	54.0	66.0	84.0	99.0
1986	66.5	84.1	91.7	99.2

Sources: L. Chisholm and B. Fine, "Context and Contest in South African Education Policy: Comment On Curtin," *African Affairs* 93(371) (1994):233-48; International Labour Office, *Special Report of the Director-General on the Application of the Declaration Concerning the Policy of Apartheid in South Africa*, Geneva, Switzerland: International Labour Office (1988):50; D. Krige, S. Cairns, M. Makalima, and D. Scott, "Mapping Education: The Education Foundation," *Indicator: South Africa* 12(2) (1995):76-80.

3.3 What Do Adults Need?

Adult education in South Africa ought to begin with the learner' s needs and then be upgraded continually (Kerfoot 1993). Adults' needs vary based on unique circumstances. Therefore, a needs assessment exercise will have to be conducted to determine community needs. Such an exercise is necessary in order to prevent a clash of interests between the community' s needs and actual programs. Because most people are inclined to participate in programs that address personal needs, mutual agreement on learning priorities is crucial between adults and policymakers (Mushi 1991).

Adult learners require adult education as a tool to manage their environment, not necessarily by learning the English language but by acquiring lifelong skills. These skills include being able to perform tasks with their hands such as sewing, pottery, embroidery, and basketry. Such skills help adults become economically independent, and, for some, it gives them a sense of worth, freeing them from a sense of hopelessness and/or helplessness associated with illiteracy.

Another factor determining what adult learners need is their level of literacy. Some adults have had limited schooling as children, whereas others may not have had an opportunity to attend school. For such learners, different approaches are needed. Some learners require basic living skills such as being able to read prescriptions, taking care of finances, writing letters to relatives, reading newspapers and letters from friends, and taking care of family affairs, whereas others require advanced skills in reading and writing. A variety of needs is important for curriculum planners to understand such complexities.

3.3.1 Curriculum

Curriculum for adult education is a product of broad consensus among key players in Africa, as well as those experiencing it (Kerfoot 1993). In this case, adult education is forced to adopt a different curriculum based on adult aspirations and guided by practical needs (Kunene and Mokae 1990). Adult education can be academic or nonacademic. For example, nonacademic curriculum incorporates matters such as health, daily living skills, political participation, conflict resolution, and current affairs.

The themes for curriculum are a crucial aspect drawn from various sources and/or organizations such as parent groups, women' s organizations, trade union groups, and domestic workers' unions. The core curriculum can incorporate issues from various fields of study. The content of adult education must be learner centered rather than imposed from above; then it does not need to be fixed but is dynamic and changes with time. Adult learners are to generate content issues based on need rather than a prespecified series of topics (Gillespie 1993).

In a learner-directed curriculum, learners generate themes separated into component parts that, in turn, form the foundation for a series of curriculum topics. Thus, handouts, notes, and manuals developed using learners' knowledge as a guide are useful. This approach provides an appropriate learning environment for adults and allows them to be part of the learning process.

Adult education draws learners from diverse backgrounds, which presents a challenge to providers of such education. Therefore, teachers are likely to be challenged to meet the educational needs of all learners.

Environmental issues must be part of the curriculum as far as they relate to learners. In this context, curriculum ought to be flexible and subject to change. Adult learners are to be free to make choices regarding the content of what they learn because adults, unlike young learners, no longer have time to learn what they do not need. The aim of adult education is to expose individuals to change, as well as to allow adults to adjust to change.

3.3.2 Language of Instruction

A policy of empowering adults through literacy, if it is to be effective, needs to take the language that adults know as the starting point. Phillipson (1992) explained that self-reliance presupposes an adult educational system without waste and then allows the development of life skills and access to knowledge through language spoken by the learners.

If the aim of adult education is to accommodate realities (e.g., everyday life), as well as job prospects of the adult learner, then the use of a well-known language by learners is a necessity. This is, of course, essential in order to avoid wasting educational resources, as well as excluding the majority from effectively participating in political proceedings and in promoting their development and that of their communities ("Affirmative Education" 1994).

Therefore, the choice of language in adult education is often directed by the practical implications it has for its users, as well as the benefits it renders. If use of the mother tongue in adult education is to become an important vehicle for reaching learners' personal goals, then attempts to encourage its use are necessary.

Use of the mother tongue in adult education has practical and cultural importance in South Africa. Language embodies the experiences and life situations of African adults. Therefore, African adults must view literacy in terms of being able to do for themselves rather than vague goals of mastering a foreign tongue. Mastering concepts in a first language is viewed as a stepping stone in learning a second language (Klassen and Burnaby 1993).

Learning the mother tongue is a powerful vehicle for controlling one' s environment and learning strategies that can be transferred to a variety of contexts (Kerfoot 1993). Kerfoot also explained that engaging learners in discussion and critical analysis in their first language accelerates the acquisition of unfamiliar concepts and new learning skills, thus ensuring that learning the English language is contextualized and used purposefully.

The only way to allow the silent voices of the majority to be heard is to allow learners to use their first languages. This enormous task will be achieved by encouraging African professionals to create and write most of the language teaching materials for adult learners. By using the words of Peirce (1989), teaching adults to use their first language can be reconceptualized as a pedagogy that opens possibilities for students and teachers of these languages in terms of material advancement and in terms of the way they perceive themselves, their role in society, and the potential for change in society.

The suggestion of using the mother tongue for adult learners sounds too ambitious, but it is realistic and provides a new trend in African language development of a new social order. Denying other languages the opportunity to grow is "information apartheid." If adult education is meant to empower learners, then influencing what they believe of themselves and the world around them is accomplished better through their languages.

Peirce (1989) described empowerment as follows:

> To empower is to enable those who have been silenced to speak. It is to enable the self-affirming expression of experiences mediated by one's history, language, and traditions. It is to enable those who have been marginalized economically and culturally to claim, in both respects, a status as full participating members of a community. (p. 408)

"Empowerment" is a term that carries more meaning when using the African languages in teaching; it is about giving individuals the skill to take charge of their lives. Empowerment is taking responsibility for success in learning. Success is measured in many ways such as in the application of knowledge in solving one's life problems.

3.3.3 Recruitment of Teaching Staff

Adult teachers need at least minimum training in teaching adult learners. Not all teachers have the capacity or skill to teach adult learners. Therefore, adult educators require specific training in order to be equipped with the knowledge and skills required to deal with adult learners (Mushi 1991). Training can take various forms, that is, from academics to technical skills. Efforts to attract voluntary teachers are recommended because adult education cannot survive without such personnel. Retired teachers, university students, and retired professionals are possibilities in which adult teachers can be found. Monetary compensation is a good incentive to attract those who volunteer expertise and time to teach adults, allowing a variety of people with different expertise to participate. Adult education cannot depend on volunteers alone, but attempts must be made to train specialists in the field.

Bamgbose (1991) argued that, if community effort is tapped, adult education could be linked to community development projects such as South Africa through the Reconstruction Development Program. Illiteracy, as a threat to the political and economic development in Africa, has been acknowledged. The commitment to reduce illiteracy ought to be matched by a greater commitment in the form of increased funding of adult literacy programs (Bamgbose 1991).

3.3.4 Teaching Methods

Teaching adults requires different approaches. Mushi (1991) asserted that adults do not learn by compulsion but by what they believe is significant for their purposes. Methods such as dramatization, storytelling, group projects, and/or demonstrations are to be selected, whereas television, radio, and tape-recorded lessons provide alternative methods for others.

Addressing current problems with the view to help adults solve their problems can be meaningful. Adult education must be functional, that is, dealing with the immediate needs of the community. Local history will have to be taught and developed by interviewing the elderly and documenting events. Pictures, press cuttings, and slides, where possible, could be sources of information.

3.4 Workers' Education

If the African people are to become self-reliant, adult literacy levels in disadvantaged communities must increase drastically; in fact, private-sector companies should not underestimate their contribution in achieving this objective ("Literacy Education for Community Upliftment" 1995). Workers' education is defined as "on-the-job literacy training." The aim of such training is to enable workers to perform their jobs properly. Workplace literacy programs usually occur on site in order to provide specific job-related skills to improve the job performance of employees (Gillespie 1993). Workplace literacy programs, in general, are geared toward a company's needs and expectations. For example, the content of such programs includes aspects of the company's work ethics, being able to read instructions on how to operate heavy machinery, recording of work hours, understanding the company's benefits, and other job-related matters. Workplace literacy programs, thus, vary from company-to-company. The content is likely to differ in quality and will reflect the company's objectives. Some employers may be hesitant to offer training to employees because they may seek better opportunities elsewhere. However, when adult training is offered, employees need to take advantage of such an offer. A worker who is well-informed and knows what is expected is likely to take his or her job more seriously. Job-related accidents such as exposure to chemicals and/or radiation, incorrect operation of heavy machinery, and exposure to any health hazards are reduced when employees are literate.

Employers who can afford to train workers are likely to benefit by having productive employees. However, some studies have shown that workplace literacy programs, often funded by the employer, are constrained by the agendas of the employer who funds the program (Gillespie 1993; "Literacy Education for Community Upliftment" 1995). For employers interested in productivity and quality products, the focus is on specific products manufactured by the company.

3.4.1 Literate Environment

Literate environment is exposure to extensive reading materials. The development of literacy requires easy access to information, as well as encouragement to engage in reading for pleasure and acquiring knowledge. Thus, completion of a literacy program demands a literate environment. The new literates usually require a supply of supplementary reading material in order to use their newly acquired skills. Thus, libraries, newspapers, television, radio, and film education are tools that facilitate permanent literacy.

3.4.2 Rural Libraries

In South Africa, public libraries are located in towns and large cities, with only the urban population having access to them. True commitment to eliminate illiteracy will be the establishment of libraries in rural areas. A culture of learning is nourished by the existence of libraries. Volunteers and retired teachers are to be used as librarians, and, where possible, professional librarians must be hired. Book groups, when encouraged among adult learners, will give them an opportunity to share their thoughts. This practice, if well-structured, encourages reading for pleasure among participants. The establishment of rural libraries is costly, but the long-term benefits will be great.

3.4.3 Rural Newspaper

Numerous newspapers are printed in South Africa primarily for the consumption of urban readers. The majority of rural people is illiterate. However, establishing rural newspapers with regional news will encourage people to read more and maybe even to make contributions. Newspapers will have to be written in the local language in order not to limit their readers. Newspaper production is costly, but small-scale productions is one way to begin. Loans and government subsidies are to provide initial support unless the government wants to own such undertakings.

3.4.4 Television Education

Mass media such as television and televised instruction are excellent in providing information, but how many people can be reached and benefit from such instruction? Can they reach the most needy adult learners in the remote areas of South Africa? The use of television instruction to support a literacy program is limited to those who have access to electricity. Many rural people do not have the means to access such learning. Whereas television, when used, does provide continuous literacy support services for adult education. Continuous exposure to information helps adult learners in maintaining their literacy skills.

3.4.5 Radio and Film Education

Radio and film education plays an important role in the dissemination of educational information. The use of local languages in such media also helps to make the content more meaningful. However, critics of such media argue that it is a one-way communication; that is, the audience cannot interact, ask questions, engage in a discussion, and share views with such a media. Therefore, the use of radio and film education is limiting; for example, adults become passive recipients of information.

The advantages of radio and film education are that many people are reached at the same time. Different topics of interest to adult learners can be shared with the public. Contributions on topics of interest, when encouraged, add to the rich information broadcasted. Allowing adults to select topics increases their interest and support of such media.

3.5 Conclusion

Adult education makes a great contribution towards community upliftment; it provides adult learners with essential skills that can be applied in specific situations; and it promotes individual and community development. The overall contribution of a literate population on the economic growth rate in any country is prevalent. Adult education is likely to give learners a taste for reading and writing. Literacy is not only good for the mind but it also allows people to explore the world around them. Fussell (1996) explained that, as a community improves its ability to acquire knowledge, life choices are expanded and the potential for advances in the quality of life is enhanced. Education is a tool that enables communities to provide solutions to their daily problems. Thus, acquiring knowledge is beneficial only when people are able to apply it to meet believed needs. Adult education is necessary to communities for their economic and social benefits. Local knowledge and community experiences form the foundation of adult education.

Chapter 4

Special Education For Black South Africans

4.1 Introduction

This chapter discusses the development and current status of special education for black South Africans. In addition, the chapter provides an historical background of South Africa's special education services and highlights the theory underlying special education for Africans in South Africa. This chapter looks at what has been done in the past and what is being done currently regarding services for children with various disabilities, teacher training, and the future. Finally, the chapter provides tentative solutions to identified problems.

The changing nature of South Africa requires the redistribution of all human, physical, and educational resources. The establishment of the new order demands fresh visions and offers the opportunity for innovative changes. Thus, this chapter focuses on the redistribution of special education services. Special education for blacks has been neglected. South Africa, like many other countries, has been plagued with stereotypes that promoted discrimination against people with special needs, making them invisible and nonessential.

4.2 Developments in Special Education

As is the case with many developing countries, special education for blacks is a recent development in South Africa's educational system. Historically, special education programs in South Africa for black children with disabilities have been neglected. This neglect is not because of a lack of need for special services but because divided and unequal education systems exist. Black students with special needs are seldom considered. Behr (1978) explained that special education in South Africa was introduced in 1863 by philanthropic organizations and religious groups such as the Irish Dominican Sisters. The first schools of this type served individuals with hearing and visual impairments.

The first special schools also were divided according to two racial lines; that is, one served white children and the other served colored children. According to Behr (1978), 100 years later there were nine schools for handicapped African children. These schools served children with hearing and visual impairments, cerebral palsy, and physical disabilities. The former South African government has been slow in funding special education for blacks in South Africa.

Several existing special schools for black South Africans were established by Western missionaries. Currently, there are many special schools throughout the country as a result of community and state initiatives. However, the need for more schools remains a problem. Because most black South Africans live in poor environmental conditions, they are more vulnerable to mild/moderate disabilities. Therefore, the development of special education for blacks in South Africa demands immediate attention.

According to De Lange (1981), by the year 2020, 8,536 African children will have hearing impairments, 3,916 will have visual impairments, 5,389 will have physical disabilities, 9,703 will have cerebral palsy, 4,336 will have epilepsy, 10,616 will have a specific learning disability, 456 will have autism, 21,710 will have mental retardation, and 16,748 will have severe emotional disorders. Therefore, it is the duty of all professionals in South Africa to design a plan providing special service delivery for large numbers of children. What challenges are facing South Africa in this field? What are the prospects for providing special education for black South Africans? This chapter highlights a brief history of special education in South Africa and then attempts to address the questions raised above.

4.3 Brief History of Special Education in South Africa

The beginnings of special education in South Africa date as far back as 1863 when the first school for the visually and hearing impaired was established by the initiative of six Dominican sisters (Behr 1978). The school was located at Cape Town, and it was divided into two sections. One part of the school served white students and the other parts served colored students or people of mixed races. One hundred years later nine special schools were established. These schools catered to African children with visual and hearing impairments, cerebral palsy, and physical disabilities (Behr 1978). Special education in South Africa was introduced by philanthropic organizations and/or religious groups. Apparently, their motive was to fulfill God' s commandment of helping the helpless/hopeless and the poor.

Behr (1978) explained that the first special education school was purely a charitable undertaking with no state support. As years advanced, some special schools were subsidized by the state, but they were managed by missions such as the Lutheran, Presbyterian, Catholic, and Dutch Reformed churches. In 1969, a survey was conducted in the Transvaal area to determine the incidence of deafness and blindness among certain groups of Africans. The intention was to provide ordinary schools for these pupils (Behr 1978). According to Behr, in 1976, provision was made for 1 out of 500 pupils with various disabilities.

Even though African people with disabilities have never been protected by law in South Africa, the public' s attitude towards these people showed its low regard of such persons, at times even their abuse and exploitation. Africans sometimes view the handicapped as a curse from angry ancestors and unworthy (Possi 1994), as well as unpredictable, dangerous, stupid, and incapable. Some Africans believe that albinism is a result of angry ancestral spirits, reincarnation, or a bad omen (Possi 1994). Some believe that albinos never die but simply vanish.

Parents are sometimes blamed for having a child with an obvious disability. This state of affairs is tragic because, in general, Africans are more vulnerable to handicapping conditions, particularly those associated with poverty such as poor prenatal care, malnutrition and undernutrition, disease, and accidents (Kriegler and Farman 1994). Unfortunately, poor perception, as well as negative and unhelpful attitudes, are evident at all levels, including administrators, teachers, parents, and the public at large.

4.4 Prevalence of People With Disabilities

Approximately 15 percent of the South African school-age population are in need of special education (De Lange 1981). According to statistics of the Human Sciences Research Council, 120,000 South African children have disabilities. Of these, only 26,000 are receiving specialized education (Hlatshwayo 1992). Actual figures for all racial groups in South Africa are difficult to establish because of the history of a separate and unequal education system. Based on a conservative estimate of 10 percent incidence of disabilities in the school-age population, there are 600,000 African children with special needs currently not attending school or struggling without additional help in ordinary classrooms (Skuy and Partington 1990). Kriegler (1989) predicted that because of the current increase in the number of persons with disabilities, approximately .75 million African children will be diagnosed with learning disabilities in the near future.

Because there was no compulsory and free education for Africans until recently, accurate figures on disabilities are not known. No statistical data are available on the prevalence of various disabilities for Africans in South Africa, which, in part, is due to the absence of adaptive behavior and intelligence tests developed and normed for Africans (Gwalla-Ogisi 1990). Therefore, assessment and diagnosis of people with disabilities are nonexistent in African schools. The hospitals also do not maintain records on African children born with handicapping conditions.

4.5 Social Contributions To Disabilities Among Blacks

The connection between poverty and poor health has been well-documented in several studies (Asbury, Maholmes, and Walker 1993;

Wilson and Ramphele 1989). Over the past few years, literature reviews have continued to support the idea that poor environmental conditions have interfered with all aspects of the child's development, that is, physical, intellectual, and social (Gelfand, Jenson, and Drew 1982). These conditions have temporary or lifelong harmful effects (Gelfand et al. 1982). In South Africa, a majority of black children is born and raised in poverty, which contributes to mild/moderate disabilities. Jacobs (1991) suggested that the lack of health and welfare services, early childhood education, child care, and community facilities, as well as conditions of extreme poverty and social disruptions, is the cause of horrendous levels of child abuse that range from death by malnutrition and poverty-related disease to psychological trauma, physical abuse, and tragic levels of human development in South Africa.

More than twice as many South African children die from preventable causes before the age of five than expected in a country with its level of income ("Too Many Infants Die in South Africa-UNICEF" 1994). South Africa was reported to have 70 deaths per 1,000 live births. That is, the country's infant mortality rate is double the average of 34 deaths per 1,000 expected for its U.S. dollar 2,670 gross national product per capita ("Too Many Infants Die in South Africa-UNICEF" 1994).

The standard of living for Africans in South Africa is low. For example, millions of people in South Africa live without toilets, clean drinking water, or access to basic health care ("Millions Lack Basic Facilities 1994). According to this report:

> 31 percent of South Africans could not afford to feed their children under the age of five. Among blacks, 12 percent (2.1 million) in rural areas and 7 percent (1.5 million) in informal settlements had no toilets at all, neither pit latrines nor bucket toilets. Only 10 percent of blacks had flush toilets inside their homes. About 33 percent of blacks had regular refuse removal and 44 percent had to fetch water from outside their yards. The study also found that 11 percent of blacks had medical aid coverage as opposed to 83 percent whites. This meant that 28 million blacks had no medical coverage. (pp. 6-7)

Because many black people live in extreme poverty, they are likely to be exposed to certain types of disabilities associated with poverty such as blindness, paralysis, and loss of extremities (Asbury et al. 1993). Violence, urbanization, disease, accidents, and other social problems continue to make disability an ongoing problem in South

Africa. Unhygienic environments associated with poverty contribute to various forms of disabilities. This finding suggests that improving living conditions, including adequate sanitation facilities, safe drinking water, and clean spacious houses, is the single most important issue for reducing preventable disabilities. Birth traumas and other related accidents also are considered a cause of mental retardation. Such causes can be reduced to a minimum by improving health care, including maternal and neonatal care for black South Africans.

According to Gwalla-Ogisi (1990), poverty among Africans persists to adult life, given the circumstances prevalent in South Africa in which there are staggering economic inequities in income. Seedat (1984) reported that figures for average per-capita incomes show even greater discrepancies. For example, for the year 1974-75, the numbers were as follows: white = R2,534, Indian = R584, colored or people of mixed races = R496, and Africans = R237. Because of poverty, most black South Africans do not enjoy easy access to physicians and other qualified health personnel.

According to Asbury and colleagues (1993), lack of adequate parental education regarding proper nutrition and health care predisposes children to the likelihood of acquiring a developmental or congenital disability even before they are born. Consequently, because of inadequate prenatal care, poor African pregnant women likely will have children with mild disabilities. For example, it is estimated that the doctor-patient ratio is 1:330 for whites, 1:730 for Indians, 1:12,000 for coloreds, and 1:91,000 for Africans (Seedat 1984). Considering the high rate of unemployment among blacks, poor black people also are more likely to be without health insurance, enabling them to practice preventive medical care and to seek immediate assistance when physical and/or mental illness is obvious or suspected.

Exposure to hazardous health environments also causes certain types of disabilities. Because most Africans lack education, they are likely to work in low-level employment, thus exposing themselves to physical harm that leads to disability. Occupations at risk are mining, construction, factory work, and handling heavy sophisticated machines. Some neurological disorders have been associated to exposure of certain toxic wastes ("Occupational Hazards" 1994).

Even though no one can confirm the actual causes of many childhood problems, it is known that the greater the number of adverse factors, the greater the child's chances of developing intellectual or behavior problems (Gelfand et al. 1982). Therefore, prevention efforts must center around the provision of good health care measures, maintenance of safe environmental conditions, legislation of appropriate policies, and increased awareness of disabilities and their causes.

Many disabilities have no single cause. However, Asbury and colleagues (1993) found that education, in general, is preventive medicine that decreases the likelihood of different types of disabilities and degenerative conditions among those most at risk. Well-educated people are likely to seek medical help that reduces the risk of poor health. Good health habits associated with longevity are more likely to be followed by the well-educated than less-educated counterparts.

4.6 Early Childhood Special Education

The importance of early detection and intervention for children with disabilities has been widely documented in professional literature (Eckstein 1994). In South Africa, early childhood special education services for blacks is the most urgent need. Eckstein (1994) reported that less than 1 percent of the total education budget from 1991 to 1993 was spent on preprimary education. Eckstein also found that more than 50 percent of the preprimary teachers in Natal lost their jobs in 1991 because of reductions in preprimary expenditure.

Such financial cutbacks are likely to affect children with disabilities even more. This population needs early intervention in terms of sensory, educational, and intellectual stimulation. Depriving them of early childhood education is detrimental to the entire country.

Another dilemma facing early childhood special education for blacks is the lack of appropriate tools for early identification, as well as lack of facilities. Lower expectations, as well as lack of awareness of the importance of school readiness skills for children with disabilities, are also common problems among black parents. Many South Africans believe that the responsibility for early childhood education remains with the parents and community (Eckstein 1994). Parents are the first teachers of their children. Therefore, school readiness skills also can be taught through formal preschools. According to Eckstein (1994), for many South Africans early childhood schooling is an unattainable luxury.

However, for those working mothers, at-risk families, and single parents who cannot be with their young children, day-care has been the viable option in giving them safety, security, good nutrition, and opportunities for social and intellectual development (Eckstein 1994). The greatest challenge is investing in children, even those who have disabilities. Currently, black parents are suffering from lack of employment, access to resources, and the knowledge and skill in dealing with their disabled children.

Children are the leaders of tomorrow and, thus, deserve to be better prepared for challenges. Education and knowledge are the key components to their success. As South Africa embarks on a new era, much will change, including the early education of children with disabilities. However, prevailing conditions can be overcome with proper planning, a clear definition of what is to be done, goals and objectives to be achieved, and coordination and collaboration among professionals (Peresuh 1994). Training and providing teachers at the preprimary level must be promoted.

4.7 Present Status: Residential and Special Day Schools

Special education services currently available for black South Africans are residential schools or special day schools. These services cater primarily to the severely handicapped, whereas those with mild disabilities are served by regular education. Special schools focus mainly on vocational training. Even though major attempts have been made in providing educational facilities for people with disabilities in South Africa, they have been challenged. Service delivery has been adequate for minority racial groups, whereas services and resources for Africans have been inadequate and nonexistent in some areas (Kriegler and Farman 1994). Because there is no specific special education legislation in place to ensure the rights of African students with disabilities, little commitment has been made to provide services for those school-aged children encountering problems in traditional classes. The lack of special education programs and facilities has led a large percentage of the special needs Africans to drop out of school early.

Children whose handicapping condition is obvious at birth such as brain injury or visual impairment and/or hearing impairment are classified as disabled. These children are not served in regular schools because the common belief is that they are uneducable. Clinics, provincial hospitals, and residential institutions are limited that cater to the needs of these children. Children whose parents have abandoned them often are housed in state hospitals and orphanages in which they receive little or no education. Facilities exist for significantly handicapped African children. However, such facilities are inadequate because there are still many African children with special needs who are not receiving services. There is also a lack of basic equipment and materials in schools such as textbooks in Braille script, audiotapes, hearing aids, and large print books. These items are needed for self-reliant and independent living for people with disabilities.

African children with mild to moderate disabilities attend regular schools, whereas those with severe disabilities are served by institutions under the guidance of the Department of National Education. The department maintains residential and day-school facilities for black South Africans (Gwalla-Ogisi 1990). However, such facilities are inadequate to meet the growing needs of this population and are segregated from the regular school population. Such facilities and schools are care related and/or focus on vocationally directed education with little, if any, functional academics (Nkabinde 1993a). Among Africans it is common to equate special education with visual and/or hearing impairments, as well as severe mental retardation and physical disability. Disabilities that are not obvious are disregarded.

Children who are hearing or visually impaired attend specialized schools, whereas no services exist for children with speech impairments, behavioral disorders, and learning disabilities. Limited services exist for children who have physical disabilities; in fact, some have been integrated into regular school settings. Attempts are being made to organize classes for slow learners within regular schools, but the process is slow. Currently, no attempts are being made to address the needs of severely or profoundly impaired children in regular schools (Nkabinde 1993a). Segregated schooling remains the default option for many.

In South Africa, most formal special education facilities are concentrated in large cities. For example, the Efata School for the Deaf and Blind is located in the Eastern Cape (Umtata); St. Thomas School for the Deaf is located in King William's Town; Bosele

School for the Deaf and Blind is located in Middleburg; Helena Franz School for the Physically Impaired is located in Bochum; Entokozweni School for the Severely Mentally Handicapped is located in Pietermaritzburg; and Tshilidzini School for the Deaf, Blind, and Physically Handicapped is located in Louis Trichardt. Additional new special schools for blacks exist throughout South Africa. Some of the schools are described in Tables 4.1, 4.2, and 4.3. These tables do not include schools located in former black homelands. Even though residential facilities for children with severe disabilities are increasing in South Africa, currently there are several schools throughout the country serving African children with severe mental retardation.

Certain community resources are being introduced such as the Panel for Identification, Diagnosis, and Assistance (PIDA) scheme and the Remedial Advisory System whose specialists diagnose and provide assistance to children with special needs (Skuy and Partington 1990). The sustainability of such an undertaking is always in question, however, because of the lack of specially trained educators and the lack of materials and appropriate instruments needed for nonbiased diagnosis.

At present, many African children with mild disabilities have no choice except to receive what is offered at a regular school or to leave school early and risk not being educated. Lack of early screening and identification of disabilities in African children also compounds the problem of minimizing or preventing certain disabilities. In residential schools for the profoundly handicapped, whatever learning occurs is not individualized. In fact, all students are taught only one subject: vocational skills. Vocational training does not support a transition to community life because many employers are hesitant to hire single-skilled individuals who may remain institutionalized for the remainder of their lives (Nkabinde 1993b).

Many different forms of disabilities will continue to plague communities unless preventative measures are actively pursued. Educating the public about various forms of disabilities, as well as possible causes of disabilities, will help to reduce these ailments. Many black people hold negative views and beliefs about disabled persons. In some instances, causes of certain types of disabilities are associated with bad luck or being bewitched. Such attitudes must be changed in order to help the disabled and the public. Efforts directed at helping people with disabilities will be costly, but the long-term gains far outweigh the costs. The De Lange (1981) investigation revealed projections regarding the number of disabled children in specific categories (see Table 4.4).

Table 4.1

Number of Hearing Impaired Children Receiving Educational Services

School	Students	Type
Dominican	270	Hostel
Indaleni	130	Hostel
Katlehong	210	Day/hostel
KwaDingane	0	Day
KwaThintwa	270	Hostel
Noluthando	90	Day
Reuben Birin	90	Day/hostel
Sizanani	60	Day/hostel
Sizwile	180	Day
St. Martins	210	Hostel
Total	1,510	

Source: Department of Education and Training, *Special Education Information for Schools in the Republic of South Africa*, Pretoria, South Africa: Department of Education and Training (1994-95).

4.8 Training of Special Education Personnel

The overwhelming majority of teachers of children with disabilities in South African black schools has had no formal training in special education. Teacher preparation commonly takes the form of short-term training and/or on-the-job training (Skuy and Partington 1990).

Table 4.2

Number of Visually Impaired Children Receiving Educational Services

School	Students	Type
Ethembeni	100	Hostel
Khanyisa	130	Day/hostel
Sibonile	60	Day/hostel
Siloe	300	Hostel
Total	590	

Source: Department of Education and Training, *Special Education Information for Schools in the Republic of South Africa*, Pretoria, South Africa: Department of Education and Training (1994-95).

For example, a one-year diploma is offered, through correspondence, by the University of South Africa to prospective teachers holding any bachelor' s degree or teacher' s diploma. Whereas secondary school teachers are trained at universities, some universities cooperate with teachers' colleges for specific subjects that lead to special education certification (Heyns 1987-88). In the past few years, more and more of the white universities in South Africa have opened their doors to students from all racial, ethnic, cultural, religious, socioeconomic, and language groups (Goodey 1987).

All fourteen white universities offer higher specialization degree and diploma programs in different areas of special education, including learning disabilities, mental retardation, visual handicaps, and behavior disorders (Skuy and Partington 1990). For those Africans admitted to white institutions, there is an opportunity for them to take advantage of specialized training. Part-time studies in the form of in-service training also are available to most African teachers.

Historical black universities in South Africa should embark on an intensive effort to provide different training for special educators. A shortage of black special education personnel in South Africa currently exists. The new dispensation in education must address this need. Introducing special education courses at all levels of teacher training is one way to address the problem. Staff development can be met through distance education or televised instruction, where possible. Research opportunities must be made available through institutions of higher learning.

Table 4.3

Number of Physically Handicapped Children Receiving Educational Services

School	Students	Type
Ethembeni	210	Hostel
Ezibeleni	180	Day/hostel
Harding	120	Hostel
JC Merkin	190	Day/hostel
Kwazamokuhle	90	Day/hostel
Lonwabo	90	Day/hostel
Philip Kushlick	220	Day/hostel
Reunion	80	Day
Tembalethu	110	Day
Tswellang	150	Day/hostel
Total	1,520	

Source: Department of Education and Training, *Special Education Information for Schools in the Republic of South Africa*, Pretoria, South Africa: Department of Education and Training (1994-95).

Promoting research in the field of special education will reduce some of the myths about disabilities. Unfounded misconceptions and superstitious beliefs about the etiology of disabilities that ought to lead to unfair treatment of such individuals can be supported by valid findings of research. Peresuh (1994) argued that if wrong perceptions, negative attitudes toward, and ill treatment of people with disabilities, embraced by many Africans, are based on ignorance regarding causality of disability, then appropriate ways of dislodging these beliefs must be found. One method is through research in which the expertise of social scientists in the university and other institutions of higher learning is needed.

Table 4.4

Projected Number of Handicapped Children in the Year 2020

Conditions	Group			
	Whites	Coloreds	Indians	Africans
Auditory	850	773	237	8,536
Visual	398	362	96	3,916
Physical	552	498	152	5,389
Cerebral palsy	987	775	275	9,703
Epilepsy	441	401	123	4,336
Specific learning disabled	1,080	982	361	10,616
Autism	46	42	12	456
Mental handicap	2,210	2,008	616	21,710
Committed (severe/emotional disturbance)	1,703	1,549	465	16,748

Source: J. P. De Lange, *Provision of Education in the Republic of South Africa: Report of the National Investigation Into Education,* Pretoria, South Africa: Human Sciences Research Council (1981).

According to Peresuh (1994), research confirms or disputes unfounded beliefs, thus benefiting the public. Conducting research on various categories of special education will give the impetus to search for ways of teaching this population effectively. Many black teachers are not equipped to teach children with special needs. Development of appropriate curriculum and teaching materials for special education will require a scientific study by educators, educational psychologists, special educators, and other related experts from institutions of higher learning (Peresuh 1994).

4.9 Curriculum

A clear need for social, communication, and vocational skills, as well as other important abilities, must be included in the curriculum of black disabled persons. These tools will equip them with the skills needed for growth and development. Basic skills in math, reading, and writing ought to form the core of the curriculum at the elementary level. Basic self-management and physical skills must form part of the curriculum in order to address the needs of the severely handicapped. Secondary school curriculum needs to be a preparation phase for work. For adolescent students with disabilities, vocational training is essential in their curriculum.

In particular, special educators should promote development among black persons with disabilities for the desire to be independent and self-reliant. These goals are important in making persons with disabilities productive members of society, as well as society' s belief that these individuals are nonessential. Peresuh (1994) stated that black professionals need to study the African culture, noting its strengths and values and then designing cocurricular and extracurricular activities that will best fit the African disabled child.

Therefore, the content to be taught for special education in South Africa must be practical and realistic for those who are to benefit. Local materials should be used in the development of adaptive equipment such as prosthetics, wheelchairs, and canes for the blind. Communication devices for black people with visual and hearing impairments in African languages are needed. Braille codes and sign languages, developed in African languages, will be more meaningful and functional. Universities that experiment with ideas in the development of teaching materials will bring many benefits to special education. Such an endeavor will benefit all children, and the public will learn to be self-sufficient.

4.10 The Method of Special Education

Groups of professionals should be employed to assess needs and to plan for intervention. These professionals will help to determine approaches that must be taken to ensure the best possible means of education for black children with disabilities. This practice can be associated with what is known as the "related services in the special education system of the United States." If South Africa is to provide special services worthy of being considered significant, such facilities must be staffed by professionals with a variety of specialized abilities such as speech pathologists, audiologists, psychologists, social workers, physical and occupational therapists, recreation and medical specialists, and counselors. Regular education teachers, students, and parents will play a role in planning and implementing special education programs. Special education will not succeed without a "teamwork approach."

Parents of disabled children must be consulted at all times regarding the education of their children. Due to the lack of education and the lack of access to knowledge, many African parents have been excluded in the decision-making process or planning of the education of their children. Thus, they have not advocated for the education of their handicapped children. Parental involvement in special education is crucial because children cannot adequately fight for themselves; the parent is the ultimate advocate for the child. Without parental knowledge, concern, participation, or direct communication, any unusual home situation such as divorce or death may hamper the child's educational progress. Also, in order for interventions to succeed, parents need to play their roles in implementation. Therefore, in implementing special education programs for blacks in South Africa, open communication must be present among parents, professionals, and disabled students.

The black community must be informed about human exceptionalities. Ignorance and superstitious beliefs about various handicapping conditions among blacks in South Africa currently exist (Gwalla-Ogisi 1990). Such influences create problems in the implementation of special education programs. Information about children with disabilities includes educating the community that these people are able to learn even though they may be slower than other members of the class. With adequate and appropriate training, children with disabilities are able to care for themselves and lead independent lifestyles. Such information also helps in preventative measures crucial in reducing preventable disabilities.

Children with mild-to-moderate disabilities are to be taught in regular classes whenever possible. Students in all categories ought to be placed in a traditional class if they adapt well and can benefit from such classes. However, educating children with severe disabilities in separate classes or facilities is sometimes justified, especially when integrating them does not benefit or facilitate learning.

In implementing special education programs, a critical question is language. For example, having many dialects among Africans, is it possible to develop programs in each language? Special education programs must be developed in African languages, as economically possible, so that all students have a fair chance to develop their maximum potential. The development of programs based on the needs of the African learner is necessary. For example, culturally relevant tests developed by Africans will prevent the importation of ready-made programs likely to fail in an African context.

Historically, the government's language policy in education favored those students whose home language was Afrikaans or English (Alexander 1992). In order to prevent such practices, textbooks used for special education ought to be written in all major languages spoken in South Africa (Alexander 1992). This expensive and time-consuming task is to be initiated by black professionals at all levels of education, with funding from the central government or the private sector.

Hence, it is even more imperative that Africans produce their own teaching materials in order to lessen their dependency on others. If people with disabilities are to have easy access to all available information, they need educational information in a language they understand and in a form they can relate to their situation (Barnard 1994). Assessment instruments for screening and identification purposes, especially in the areas of intellectual and cognitive domains, are currently being researched by African professionals in their languages.

4.11 Unique Challenges of Special Education in South Africa

Given the educational and other problems currently facing South Africa, developing special programs for Africans with disabilities is not an easy task; it will require dedication and cooperation among professionals. Current political changes must bring greater economic support, and financial resources should be distributed fairly for all racial groups in South Africa. Services for Africans are still concentrated among the significantly handicapped, whereas mild disabilities such as learning, behavioral, and speech receive little or no attention. More services are needed in areas currently not receiving attention.

Special education services are offered in segregated settings such as clinics, hospitals, residential homes, or day schools. There are few, if any, specialists, remedial teachers, and/or school psychologists. Overcrowdedness in regular schools makes it difficult for teachers to provide assistance to slow students. Little knowledge is available among African teachers and parents on human exceptionality, which complicates the situation for students with disabilities. Lack of suitable assessment materials and practices makes early screening and identification of disabilities in African children almost impossible.

No research has been conducted on issues dealing with special education among Africans. This deficiency is attributed, in part, to the lack of qualified African personnel in the field of special education. African professionals must develop their own research base in special education that will address the needs of persons with disabilities and practices appropriate to their needs and culture. Historical institutions of higher learning can be pioneers in this task of research. Moreover, the traditional role of universities is research, promoting scholarship, teaching and training, being a storehouse of information, and disseminating information and ideas (Peresuh 1994).

Lack of specific special education legislation regarding the provision of special services for African students with disabilities makes it impossible to provide them with sufficient quality education and training. Public attitudes toward individuals with disabilities make it even more difficult to advocate for such a population. African parents are not well-informed about human exceptionality and, therefore, cannot advocate for their children with disabilities.

African parents need encouragement in taking the initiative to advocate for their children. The formation of parent support systems of children with disabilities is needed in order to help African parents in sharing their experiences. The public' s low regard of people with disabilities limits their life opportunities.

The absence of indigenous and cultural relevant test materials and referral agencies that would help schools with the identification and remediation of special needs in children (Peresuh 1994) makes the implementation of special education in black schools difficult. Unless an attempt is made by African researchers to develop tests in African languages, black children will remain unserved and/or misclassified.

4.12 Future Trends

Factors associated with causation of various disabilities are too numerous to list. Seipel (1994) argued that epidemiologists have asserted that major gaps exist in data and the knowledge about risks associated with disability. However, research studies have suggested that primary prevention efforts are tied to factors that decrease the risk of certain disabilities and guarantee good health. Therefore, good health care, education, and policies protecting the rights of the disabled form the basis for prevention efforts.

First, because there is a strong relationship between good health care and the reduction of some disabilities such as mental retardation, illness, and diseases related to malnutrition, it is important to make good health care programs easily accessible to all South Africans. Several studies have suggested that much disability can be prevented if careful health care measures are followed (Seipel 1994). Good prenatal care can protect unborn children from acquiring preventable diseases, especially among those at risk of problem pregnancies. Qirbi (1993) stated that, with good health care services, the occurrence of visual and auditory disabilities, resulting from infections and sometimes inadequate medical care, could decrease.

Good eating habits at an early age prevent malnutrition, and immunization helps maintain good health. Polio has been eradicated from developed and developing worlds, as well as many other childhood diseases. Immunization has been helpful in reducing disabilities associated with childhood diseases such as polio or leprosy in South Africa. However, the low standards of health services among Africans and the shortage of physicians (an average of 1 per 91,000 people) are alarming (Seedat 1984). Most physicians reside in major cities, with few living in rural areas populated by approximately 68 percent of the people (Christie and Gaganakis 1989).

Good health care also includes the existence of a clean environment. The absence of effective environmental policies, coupled with the inept application of such policies, lead to disease. According to Seipel (1994), safe drinking water and adequate sanitation facilities are attributed to good health, whereas deprivation of these basic needs leads to illness and even death. Water pollution (such as dumping of toxic wastes and other poisonous materials into waterways) must be avoided. Developing policies aimed at controlling water and air pollution reduces diseases related to such abuses.

Work-related accidents and disabilities are common occurrences in South Africa ("Occupational Hazards" 1994). Increasing evidence has been found that many black workers in South Africa are exposed to occupational hazards, including deadly chemicals, sophisticated machinery, and unsafe working conditions. According to the magazine, the black work force usually is not informed about how to handle high-risk substances. Moreover, precautionary measures are often overlooked by employers. In fact, the government has failed to enforce laws in order to ensure safety in the work place.

Lack of specific special education legislation, aimed at promoting the rights of black children with disabilities, is affecting the education of these children. The absence of any legislative mandate to specify the rights of the handicapped makes it more difficult for parents and professionals to advocate for them. Negative public attitudes about people with disabilities exist among many South Africans. Superstitious beliefs also make it difficult to plan any meaningful intervention programs. There also is limited knowledge among many Africans about disabilities.

Assessment tools normed on Africans must be developed in order to decrease reliance on assessment materials produced for Western consumers. A multitude of documentation is available on the failure of imported assessment materials used in Africa (Igbalajobi 1984). Moreover, foreign assessment instruments often lead to misdiagnosis and misclassification. The lack of assessment tools in South Africa has contributed to the difficult identification of black children with disabilities. Black South Africans have not yet embarked on the development of testing, as well as assessment tools, that easily identify black children with disabilities of school age. Availability of assessment tools will help in the early detection and intervention for children with disabilities.

Many African parents cannot advocate for their children with disabilities because of their lack of knowledge. Some parents of children with disabilities have lower expectations. A stigma also is associated with having a disabled child. Negative attitudes regarding handicapping conditions include reasons such as ancestral curse, bad omen, witchcraft, supernatural causes, and evil spirits (Possi 1994). Such superstitious beliefs have an impact in providing education for the handicapped. Parents of these children feel helpless, frustrated, and often do not seek better opportunities for their disabled children.

Well-informed parents are able, in turn, to teach their disabled children self-advocacy skills, decision-making skills, assertiveness skills, and many other social skills required for survival. Even though not all children with disabilities benefit from formal education, some can be trained to become contributing members of their communities. When supported by their families and communities, children with disabilities are able to voice their concerns on various issues.

Another major problem in South Africa is the inadequate training opportunities for black teachers of children with disabilities. This situation has led to the employment of black teachers who have no formal training in special education. On several occasions, teacher preparation takes the form of "on-the-job training" (Skuy and Partington 1990). This training is inadequate in meeting the needs of children with disabilities. Therefore, existing training facilities for special educators must be expanded; that is, all prospective teachers must have a basic knowledge in special education. Special educators in black schools should be exposed to pre-service and in-service training programs organized locally and abroad (Igbalajobi 1984).

All children with or without a disability should have their learning partially supported by the state. Empowering parents of children with disabilities helps them to be advocates in the education of their children. Community support systems for parents provide necessary information, material support, and emotional support (Kriegler and Farman 1994). These community support systems include, but are not limited to, day-care centers, community-based rehabilitation for the profoundly handicapped, and community recreational centers. More research in the field of special education is needed to assist African professionals in properly planning for the disabled. Education or training of people with disabilities helps them to become productive members of society and to enhance their self-confidence. Training special education personnel in different categories of human exceptionality should receive first priority. Including people with disabilities in positions of power helps present a positive aspect of them to the public, as well as alter negative attitudes. Segregated facilities for people with disabilities must remain a viable option only when no other alternatives exist.

4.13 Conclusion

Predicting the trend in the development of special education for the black population in South Africa is difficult to determine. However, the future seems likely to involve "education for all," including people with disabilities. If educational reform in South Africa becomes a reality for all students, a more tolerant society will be evident in which the contribution of the strong and the weak, the disabled and the nondisabled, will be valued. South Africa has embarked on a democratic society in which all citizens will be granted respect and assured dignity, as well as the right to contribute to the development of the country. In this context, it is hoped that the goal of education will be equal access for all children with or without disabilities.

As South Africa enters a crucial phase, it has many challenges such as providing quality education for all its citizens and compulsory free education for all its students. Socioeconomic improvements are to be achieved in the background of limited resources, as well as the lack of qualified personnel in various fields, including special education. The necessary improvement in the South African education system will be accomplished only with the full participation of black South Africans. However, if necessary, outside help, support, and guidance should be sought in dealing with educational problems only after a well-formulated plan is in place.

In order to attain the highest goal in providing special education in South Africa, all sectors of society, including the government, private sector, education-related institutions, parents, and students, are to join hands and become involved in a combined effort (Barnard 1993). At the same time, all professionals, particularly black Africans, must support the development of special education in South Africa. Programs that address the needs of black children with disabilities must be developed. Emphasis on early intervention, as well as early assessment, should be promoted. Black parents must be empowered to become active advocates for children with disabilities. Moreover, the talents of all South Africans, with or without a disability, are to be utilized. Human potential need not be wasted, which is the most important challenge of a new South Africa and one that holds the key to the future.

Institutions of higher learning are to play their role in the development of programs aimed at benefiting their communities. These institutions are regarded as research bases in which data banks of ideas are stored (Peresuh 1994). Research about special education needs to begin at the university level. Then research findings can be shared with the public through conferences, workshops, scholarly publications, books, pamphlets, or direct and practical demonstrations (Peresuh 1994). According to Peresuh, disabilities and handicaps pose educational and social problems that universities must help solve by providing practical solutions.

Equal access to quality education is necessary in order to prepare South Africa' s children to function as contributing, full participants in a dynamic, diverse, and multicultural society. All children, with or without disabilities, need the necessary skills in order to contribute in the economic development of the country. People with disabilities need skills for survival in ever-changing environments.

Chapter 5

Language Policy In Postapartheid Education

5.1 Introduction

South Africa is a country of multilingualism with more than twenty spoken languages (Desai 1992). In a population of thirty-five million people, 75 percent speak any of the African languages and the remainder speak English or Afrikaans. Of the languages most spoken by black South Africans, the following are common: Zulu, Xhosa, Sotho, Tswana, Tsonga, Swazi, Venda, Shangaan, and Ndebele. Zulu is the mother tongue of more than one fourth of all South Africans. Of those who understand the language, the Zulu-speaking portion escalates to more than one third ("In Your Language or Mine?" 1994).

In a white population of approximately five million people, there are more Afrikaans speakers than English speakers. Approximately 60 percent of white people are Afrikaans speaking, and 40 percent are English speaking (("In Your Language or Mine?" 1994). A majority of colored (people of mixed races) people also speak Afrikaans as their first language.

English remains popular in spite of the fact that more citizens presently speak Afrikaans than English (Eastman 1990). The difference between the two languages is that English is associated with economic opportunities and Afrikaans is associated with discrimination and denial of opportunities. Table 5.1 describes the different spoken languages in South Africa. African languages are spoken by more than half of the South African population. However, these languages are not accorded the political, social, and economic status of English. According to Bamgbose (1991), "A language is like a currency; the more it buys, the greater value it has" (p. 74). In short, the perceptions of people, coupled with its perceived status, have brought the English language to the forefront (Eastman 1990). English continues to play an important role in postapartheid South Africa.

Table 5.1

Languages Spoken in South Africa

Group	Language	Percentage
Zulu	Zulu	26.0
Afrikaans	Afrikaans	18.0
Northern Sotho	Sotho	11.0
English	English	11.0
Xhosa	Xhosa	9.0
Southern Sotho	Sotho	6.0
Tswana	Tswana	5.0
Tsonga	Tsonga	5.0
Swazi	Swazi	4.0
Ndebele	Ndebele	3.0
Venda	Venda	2.0

Source: Modified from "In Your Language or Mine?," *The Economist* 332(7881) (1994):48.

Currently, there is a need for dedicated and creative writers and journalists to promote the revival of African languages (Maake 1991). Perhaps the most damaging obstacle in raising the status of African languages in South Africa is the low prestige attached to them. African languages have been regarded as insignificant and, consequently, have not been viewed as official. This view is likely to change with the new South African language policy, which recommends all eleven major South African languages as official (Desai and McLean 1994).

Historically, all black school children were forced to learn English and Afrikaans in addition to their vernacular languages. The language imposition in schools was seen by blacks as a way of stripping them of their heritage (Twala 1994). The resistance of language imposition resulted in the 1976 student uprisings in which black students protested against the use of Afrikaans as a medium of instruction. The language plan of using Afrikaans in black schools never materialized because of the uprisings.

African teachers, parents, and students are opposed to the use of Afrikaans as a medium of instruction because it is viewed as the language of a former hostile government.. English, on the other hand, is viewed positively by blacks and is regarded by many as the passport to information, success, work, and the outside world.

The prestige of the English language is supported by Van Dyken (1990). In order for Africans to obtain prestigious positions in the government, they must learn the language of the colonial powers. Unfortunately, throughout Africa, foreign languages are still valued more than the local or indigenous languages. According to Van Dyken, those who saw the value of the mother tongue seem to be outnumbered and overpowered by the imbalance of opportunities. That is, money, personnel, and materials relatively abounded in the colonial language but scarcely existed in the mother tongue.

Several studies have indicated that existing school systems in Third World countries have served only to train elites to govern a bureaucracy and the modern sector of an economy but have neglected the training of human resources capable of stimulating production in areas essential to welfare of the majority of the population (Bamgbose 1991; Maliyamkono 1980; Mbaku 1994; Sure, 1991-92; Weiss 1994). The only way to reduce illiteracy in Africa, as well as to prevent education from being a mechanism for elitist differentiation, is to encourage the use of the mother tongue.

5.2 Current Language Policy

South Africa continues to encourage the use of the mother tongue as a medium of instruction in the primary classes (Substandard A to Standard 4) (Behr 1978). Then, after six years of primary schooling, English becomes the medium of instruction and the mother tongue is retained as a school subject (Baine and Mwamwenda 1994). The educational process in any society ought to be conducted through a language that the learner and the teacher command well. In a South African context, most African teachers are not proficient in the English language. This situation creates a barrier for any minimum communication to occur in a teaching and learning setting. Therefore, for any meaningful learning to take place, children must be taught in the language accessible to them.

Black South African learners encounter English only at school. In order to bring about language equality in the schools, all children at the primary level must be granted an option to be taught in their mother tongue. For education to be meaningful, it must relate to people' s lives, their environment, and their history; also, the books they read must portray vivid pictures of their surroundings and/or way of life. Great ideas, sound expressions, and fresh and spontaneous enthusiasm for creative works are nurtured through use of the mother tongue.

Teaching children in their mother tongue brings education closer to the environment (Dakin, Tiffen, and Widdowson 1968). Bringing the status of indigenous languages to an equal footing with other minority languages in South Africa will be difficult. African languages have been undermined for decades, if not centuries. This low regard of African languages is viewed as the languages of an inferior people (Satyo 1988). Therefore, the development of such languages have been regarded as a meaningless and fruitless activity. Convincing black South Africans about the importance of developing their languages will involve creativity and commitment.

5.3 Can English Be a Medium of Instruction?

> The forces of conservation and change [may] have to be reconciled, and stability achieved, by deliberate policy decisions. It might, for example, be decided to have the mother tongue used as a medium of instruction in the primary school so as to ensure that the child' s educational development is

rooted in his [her] own cultural heritage, and then transfer to a foreign language as the medium for secondary education. (Trappes-Lomax 1990, p. 94)

The situation described by Trappes-Lomax (1990) represents what has occurred in black South African schools from the beginning of Western education, except that English has always been accorded a higher status in black schools than the mother tongue. Thus, spoken and written indigenous languages were heard less and less in the schools. However, despite the low status accorded indigenous languages, there is accumulating evidence that these languages have survived extinction and can be developed if a language plan is undertaken.

One of the reasons that English is popular as a medium of instruction in black schools is that it is regarded as the main language of industry and commerce and, hence, beneficial to "school-leavers" seeking work (Desai 1992). English also is perceived as politically neutral, commercially useful, and, in its American version, fashionable with young blacks ("In Your Language or Mine?" 1994).

In support of English as a medium of instruction in black schools, Desai (1992) cited the following reasons:

> English is an international language, spoken by some 750 million people around the world. It is the medium for 80 percent of the information stored in the world's computers. In South Africa, it is claimed, it is the language most spoken in business, industry, and educational institutions, and it is the language of education for most pupils who study beyond primary school. There are powerful financial reasons associated with the use of the English language. (p. 117)

The use of English to access information and as a means to interact with one another is important. However, black South Africans must be careful never to view English as a substitute for their own languages. For example, Ngugi (1993) described two crucial aspects of all languages: (a) communicating for survival and (b) preserving the history and culture of a particular group of people. According to Ngugi, the meeting of languages is based on terms of independence and equality, as well as dependence and inequality among nations.

In South Africa, blacks use their mother tongue and also must learn two additional languages (English and Afrikaans) (Baine and Mwamwenda 1994). This exercise not only robs black children of their heritage but it forces them to learn and compete in a foreign language. Thus, according to Baine and Mwamwenda, black children are always at a disadvantage when competing with white students. Ngugi (1993) explained that, when nations meet on terms of dependence and inequality, their languages cannot experience equal status. For example, in South Africa, blacks are compelled to use languages other than their own.

When nations meet on equal footing, there is no imposition of language over the other. For example, the Japanese, Germans, French, Scandinavians, and other non-English-speaking nations use English as a communication tool and a language of trade and commerce (Ngugi 1993). English for these people is not used in their countries to continue national cultures, store information, or define values and beliefs. However, it is a tool that enables them to work and conduct business together.

Given the practical and financial role English plays in the lives of many in South Africa, it remains the majority choice. However, the question of whether or not English becomes a national language in a new South Africa remains unanswered. The new South African language policy recognizes all eleven major South African languages (Desai and McLean 1994).

The authenticity of the language policy is yet to be tested. The symbolic achievement of the language policy will be translated to reality only when the African language speakers implement the policy based on informed decisions. Central to the choice of national language policy is the question of what type of educational transformation black people envision. Do they want to follow what is created for them, or do they want to create their future using their languages for the enrichment and maintenance of their cultural survival?

Therefore, the pros and cons of abandoning one's language ought to be stated clearly; then people can make solid judgments regarding the choice of language in school. If the aim of a new South Africa is equal access to information, political participation, and educational and social settings, then the type of language policy selected has to address those issues. Language is a powerful tool that gives people a voice. By voicing their opinions, people have power to change their life circumstances, to direct and shape their futures, to make solid contributions, and to live productive lives. The new language policy in South Africa must avoid silencing the voiceless, particularly those who have been excluded politically and economically. A language policy that favors a foreign language such as English, at the expense of indigenous languages, will continue to reinforce the advantages of the privileged classes and to perpetuate the exclusion of the poor. Language policy in South Africa is highly relevant to the prospects for positive race relations. True democracy, based on a nonracist, nonsexist, and nonexploitative society, will be determined by the maximum flexibility and imagination of the new language policy. Many black South Africans have opted to use English as a medium of instruction in senior primary and secondary schools (Baine and Mwamwenda 1994), but there are opponents who argue against this measure.

5.4 Arguments Against the Use of English as a Medium of Instruction

Phillipson (1992) argued that the export of English to formerly colonized countries has not paved the way to modernity and prosperity, as was foreseen by some planners in the post-World War II era. According to Phillipson, the study of English has impeded literacy in mother-tongue languages, has thwarted social and economic progress for those who do not learn it, and generally has not been functional for the needs of ordinary people in their day-to-day or future lives.

Opponents of developing English as a national language in South Africa argue that this could perpetuate class division. This argument is not without foundation because the majority of people in South Africa cannot speak English. For example, it is estimated that only 11 percent of South Africans speak English at home ("In Your Language Or Mine?" 1994).

Furthermore, Rubagumya (1990) argued that European languages in former colonial Africa and Asia, with their elitist status, have remained the languages of an educated elite, thus enhancing the subordination of the uneducated and the poor. For example, many African people who cannot communicate in English are likely to feel excluded. These people include the uneducated, as well as those in remote rural areas. Newspapers, television, and other forms of information dissemination do not easily reach rural people who are mostly illiterate.

The arguments against the use of English as a national language also point out that it is capable of holding captive black cultures, their values, and, hence, their minds (Ngugi 1993). A fear also exists that the use of English will marginalize the languages of others. Language empowers and disempowers, validates and invalidates, represents and misrepresents different social groups, as well as their knowledge and identities. For instance, in South Africa, where English and Afrikaans are highly valued languages, experiences and practices of these language groups are validated and well-represented in the literature, whereas those of other groups are marginalized (Ngugi 1993).

Information defined by representatives of a different language group is likely to be inaccurate or to exclude or deauthorize the knowledge and experience of the other or to incorporate them on terms that suit the dominant language group. Defining one's identity in a language other than one's own is the worst of nightmares. To understand concepts in a foreign language is difficult; in fact, the entire practice makes learning a demanding task. Many black students in South African schools do not understand English sufficiently to learn effectively through it. The shortage of English teachers, combined with poor use of the language by students, results in high failure rates in black schools (Baine and Mwamwenda 1994).

Other opponents of the use of English as a national language argue that the culture and history carried by African languages may be forgotten and, consequently, lost, which may have a lasting negative impact on future generations. Whatever language policy South Africa adopts, the country must ensure that as few people as possible are disadvantaged (Desai 1992). Thus, the language used at school needs to be accessible to the majority of people, and the community has to be able to participate actively in the language of its choice. The repetition of past language policy has to be avoided.

Because English is not a language that has been mastered by masses of people in South Africa, it can prevent access to information. If the English language is imposed on people, it leads to alienation and self-hatred on the part of those who are unable to master it (Sure 1991-92). The use of English also helps to maintain the status quo by working in favor of privileged groups whose children have sufficient language support at home and at school (Sure 1991-92). Consequently, it creates a division between the educated black elite who have access to economic, political, and social advantages and the uneducated masses who have no access. English alone is not a source of division, but it perpetuates social division by giving access to information to the educated and the black elite. Therefore, it is important for language planners to ensure maximum participation at all levels for all people. This process can be achieved by adopting a consistent policy that will promote political, cultural, and linguistic pluralism.

Most people agree that English has served the political, cultural, and economic interests of the principal colonial powers at the expense of local and national development in Third World countries (Phillipson 1992). The high status of English in education in South Africa will serve to perpetuate dependency only rather than development. Because of a dependency syndrome, maintenance of vernacular languages is necessary. It also will help to erase the notion that wealth of knowledge is to be taken, not made. The temptation to demand from others will be replaced by a sense of duty in creating one' s information by using vernacular languages.

5.5 Rationale for Preserving Vernacular Languages

In the past, African languages have received little recognition, thus forcing the users to attach little or no value to them. African history was misrepresented because limited information has been recorded by Africans in their languages. The African languages must be used to correct the record, to write African history in a positive way, and to interpret accurately the African past. Vernacular languages are the best instruments to disseminate the rich store of information currently existing in the minds of Africans throughout South Africa.

The rationale for the preservation of African languages is to dispute the myth; that is, nothing is documented in these languages that the speakers do not know. For example, Roberts (1956) stated the following regarding the Zulu/English dictionary:

> Those, however, who wish to consult it, need to be guarded against the error into which some Colonists have fallen, of supposing that every Zulu, or what is worse, young Natalian, who, to a certain extent, speaks the vernacular fluently, is thoroughly acquainted with the language. (p. iv)

Such a conclusion is, of course, absurd; it implies that, if people do not document events in their language, then it means they cannot be trusted with what they say, even if they use their vernacular. Therefore, if African languages are to gain respect, they must be valued by the speakers. Documentation of life events through written form of these languages is one way to promote their use. Major contributions to cultural development are documented in various languages.

Through the use of vernacular languages, black South Africans will be able to help future generations to develop inner capacities, that is, their intelligence. Intellectual independence is a necessary condition for achieving economic, social, and, above all, political independence (Cilliers et al. 1994). The use of one's language is a good way to achieve intellectual independence. Creative thought is stimulated through one's language, but it also transfers to other situations.

The use of vernacular will assist in promoting African students' academic growth and develop in them a strong sense of confidence. Historically, African schools in South Africa have reflected the societal power structure by placing African languages at the bottom. School failure among African students, in part, is attributed to being taught in a foreign tongue such as English, and, yet, failure is usually attributed to inherent deficiencies of students (Morris 1986). Therefore, African languages, when used as a medium of instruction, will reverse the African students' educational failure.

The maintenance of vernacular languages in South Africa is essential in avoiding the slow death of African cultures and identity. In a multilingual society such as South Africa, literacy among Africans is likely to be achieved only through the use of all the local vernacular languages. However, African languages in South Africa possess no extensive literature of their own. The task of developing books and/or literature in African languages is the challenge of a postapartheid education.

The study of African languages must be promoted at all levels of education, with teachers exerting positive attitudes on pupils toward their own languages. Encouraging black youth and professionals to write in their languages will help to develop such vernacular. Deeper thinking skills and problem solving are nurtured through the use of a vernacular language. According to Dakin et al. (1968), there is a great need to train African linguistic scholars. The death of any language limits the store of ideas, as well as different ways of looking at the world (Wheeler 1994). In South Africa, the preservation of black languages is crucial in order to prevent extinction in the coming century. Wheeler (1994) described each language as a storehouse of knowledge about craft, culture, and religion. Because there is little written information in black languages, more use of vernacular will reverse that trend. Documenting African languages will ensure the passing of crucial information from generation-to-generation. Emphasis on vernacular languages will help to revive linguistic pride. Children also must take pride in their native stories. More children's books in African languages are yet to be written. Historical events recorded in African languages will play an important role in the intellectual life of Africans. Approaching knowledge in one's language enables students to be critical and creative. Learning to read must be developed from stories written in the vernacular about children's lives.

The only way to encourage young writers in African languages is to instill a love of books, particularly books written in their languages. When children are comfortable about what they read, it makes reading a pleasant, rather than a boring, experience. Reading for pleasure has never been a common practice for black South Africans. A lack of libraries and a shortage of books are attributed to a poor culture of reading. However, with more books written in the vernacular, the situation will improve. Armed with well-developed languages, blacks will be able to transform their environment.

The continued use of vernacular languages among Africans would enhance, rather than retard, the ambitions of black South Africans. Beyond the primary level, students need to choose whether or not they want to learn a foreign language. Currently, black pupils throughout their schooling speak various vernacular languages indigenous to South Africa. Even though English is a popular and preferable language among blacks, there are not sufficient numbers of black teachers to teach it. English is considered a neutral language, but it cannot be used as a national language at the expense of indigenous languages. Moreover, languages are part of human rights. Therefore, all individuals must have the greatest freedom in the use of their own language (Satyo 1988).

Language is a form of identity and national pride, and it needs to be enriched and preserved. Schools and libraries are the best sources of language preservation. Spoken, as well as written, knowledge in a vernacular language serves to promote and preserve cultural heritage. When fully developed, indigenous languages provide access to education, politics, and, possibly, economic development. European languages are associated with economic opportunities. Therefore, language becomes an issue when people are dependent on their colonial rulers for economic reasons. Thus, black South Africans will continue to emulate English or Afrikaans as languages of enlightenment and/or economic emancipation because they are linked to work opportunities. When Africans are able to provide for themselves economically, language will not be an issue. Language is power. Africans who have no economic power have been forced to acquire languages other than African for survival. Consequently, African languages have not been developed for technical, academic, and scientific instruction (Baine and Mwamwenda 1994).

For example, when promoting African languages to equal status with English and Afrikaans, blacks must regard their languages as important as other spoken languages. Historically, there has been a language inferiority complex in South Africa, stemming, perhaps, from a low regard of African languages over the years. In part, some blacks have been ashamed of their languages because they did not lead to economic prosperity.

The future of African languages, whether linked to economic opportunities or not, rests in the hands of those who speak these languages. Language need not be associated with the failure or lack of competitiveness of the speakers; people are responsible. Therefore, language must be regarded as the only tool to use in solving one's economic condition. Advanced knowledge can be imported from other parts of the world using vernacular languages. Imported knowledge is useful only if it is adapted to suit the local needs of the people. Vocabulary is lacking in many African languages. However, an attempt can be made to include scientific knowledge in these languages before textbooks are written.

Language alone cannot provide for the people economically, but it might enable them to cope with the environment and to enhance interactions, thus building knowledge of the world and themselves. Through speaking and writing language, people create and develop world views and are able to pass information from generation-to-generation. Black South Africans, as well as others, cannot learn about achievements, victories, and defeats if they are not documented. Preserving and improving African languages through solid contributions are valuable to the world.

Despite the long history of apartheid, there is accumulating evidence (Twala 1994) that African languages in South Africa have survived extermination and will continue to survive through the determination of its speakers. The storage of knowledge through books written in indigenous languages will significantly preserve these vernaculars. Language carries the culture; therefore, African values and ways of life are strengthened when the language is established (Stairs 1994).

Each spoken and written language is associated with rationality, critical ability, and productivity, as well as the accumulation of knowledge, communication tools, sound judgment, and morality. When Africans deprive themselves of their languages, they limit all that is worth preserving. Language, when properly used, enables its speakers to problem solve. The use of a foreign language contributes to the superficiality of African children' s concepts of themselves and that of the world. In order to participate in the world of knowledge, African children must be fluent in their languages.

Concepts are better understood in one' s own language. Language connects people to their past, present, and future, and it provides continuity to their existence and future generations. On the other hand, the use of colonial languages promotes continued reliance on colonial countries' expertise, methodologies, materials, and teachers (Phillipson 1992). The nations of the world derive the image of themselves through the use of their languages. The importance of written languages was supported by Barbour (1984):

> It is by the writing and publication of books and articles that original thinkers can hope to achieve the crystallization of their ideas and their effective dissemination, even if these require to be translated and re-presented in the various media before they can reach the majority of the population. (p. 95)

5.6 Recommendations

The following criteria must be considered when planning language in South Africa:
1. The selected language ought to be one that has *relevancy* to the needs of the majority in their daily and future lives, that is, minimizing the use of foreign languages in which the utilization of such languages poses additional problems.

2. The language selected must be *functional* for the user in a particular place and at a particular time.
3. The language selected needs to be *practical*, that is, whose interests are served in promoting the language to official status or using it for educational purposes as a medium of instruction. The available resources and the method of distribution also will determine the choice of language.
4. The selected language must be the most *popular* language spoken. The language choice also needs to be supported by all its speakers.

In a multilingual country such as South Africa, selecting a medium of instruction is a complicated task. Yet, all groups have the right to enrich and maintain their language. All South African children need an opportunity to read and write in their mother tongue.

More written materials for preschool children in vernacular languages must be promoted. Writers of vernacular languages are to describe familiar scenes (socially significant) that intellectually motivate children to use their mother tongue to express their thoughts, feelings, knowledge, and opinions (Rubagumya 1990).

Language defines who people are and enables them to create their future. Language, written or oral, is intrinsic to life. Through language, people are able to view the world, understand concepts, formulate ideas, and express themselves. Therefore, adopting a foreign language does not allow Africans to communicate or record their daily experiences effectively. Even though the English language seems to be popular for economic and practical reasons, promoting indigenous languages must be extended at all levels. It is suggested that students be encouraged to write poems, plays, and essays in their own languages. The wealth of textbooks and reference books in vernacular languages, which is lacking in most black schools in South Africa, can be improved by creative and insightful teachers. Because teaching materials in African languages are scarce, regions serving various groups, when assisted by the state to produce reading materials on duplicated paper, will help to minimize the problem (Rubagumya 1991). Teachers at local levels must be involved in writing books and manuals required in schools.

An attempt must be made by each school to establish mini libraries that contain books and reference materials written in a vernacular language. Books also could be translated from other languages when permission is sought. When books of all types and levels are available, reading for pleasure is facilitated. For example, book reports in the primary school are believed to instill the love of books among children.

Clear objectives regarding the language policy in a new South Africa will contribute to the success of this policy. The new government must invest a lot of money and personnel in order to promote previously neglected African languages. Only the African language will convey the authentic cultural heritage of the ethnic groups of South Africa (Phillipson 1992). Thus, African languages ought to be used as the medium of instruction throughout schooling, with English as an exception.

Emphasis must be placed on the importance of each spoken language in South Africa. A language policy is crucial to one's culture, heritage, and identity ("What National Language Should We Speak" 1994). Therefore, suppression of other languages in favor of one national language can prove harmful to students, society, languages themselves, and, consequently, future generations. Establishing a strong foundation in one's language will instill a sense of pride in a student's heritage. Stairs (1994) said:

> The purpose of education is cultural survival. Cultural has to do with our food, our housing, our clothing, and our methods of survival. It has to do with our view of the world, its creation, and the interaction of the plant life, the animal and the bird life, and human life. It has to do with the ways we organize our society, with the government, and with the regulation of our society. It has to do with the games we play, the songs we play, the songs we sing, the dances we dance, and the art we create. But most of all it has to do with our language, our philosophy, our relationship with the Creator, our attitudes, our beliefs, and our values. All human beings have a culture. There are many different ways of being human. We still educate our children for cultural survival. (pp. 73-74)

In addition, for practical and realistic purposes, the language of education ought to be accessible to the majority (Rugemalira, Rubagumya, Kapinga, Lwaitama, and Tetlow 1990). This process also encourages the development of languages spoken by the majority. Accumulation of knowledge in these languages will be enhanced greatly if their status is raised. Furthermore, significant texts and the development of a body of literature in vernacular languages are accomplished when seriously considered by speakers and when additional money is spent on developing them. Textbooks in these languages must be written. Languages struggling for recognition in the postapartheid era will depend on exposure through various publications, the media, and consumer preferences.

A flourishing form of indigenous writing such as children's books, diaries, autobiographies, histories, and essays will add to the body of knowledge. Rationality, critical ability, productivity, and storage of knowledge are important values commonly associated with Western cultures. These values tend to be equated with literate societies and schooling (Stairs 1994); in fact, even indigenous learners can nourish and acquire these values if they have the desire to do so. Documenting historical events, scientific knowledge, ordinary stories, and, in fact, anything in vernacular languages contributes to the wealth of these tongues.

Several factors contribute to the problems of making indigenous languages popular. First is an unjustified sense of shame about the use of these languages, thus creating serious misconceptions about their inherent nature. Second, these languages do not have sufficient written documentation on which to rely (Wheeler 1994). In order to close the gap among languages, specific steps must be taken. The following steps are practical solutions to indigenous language development:

1. The language policy must have government support.
2. Debate on language issues ought to be stimulated at various levels such as in the schools, media, and institutions of higher learning. Workshops must be organized in which professionals, teachers, parents, students, and lay people share their views. It is recommended that the existing language policy be challenged based on needs assessment of the community at large. Linguists, researchers, language teachers, library workers, and ordinary citizens must be invited to share their experiences and how they view language in the context of their daily experiences. Retired professionals, as well as the elderly, will have to express their views on the language issue and how it affected their lives.
3. Policymakers ought to consider the development of appropriate resources aimed at forming language project groups at various levels. School children need to form language groups in which they research small problems by writing poems or stories in their language and by providing a forum to share ideas. Teachers or university instructors could provide guidance in such activities. Permission must be requested to translate

books written in other languages. Simple books must be created to circulate in the school library, as well as in the classroom. Book clubs, when possible, are to be formed specifically for vernacular languages in order to encourage reading for pleasure for adults and children. "Mother-tongue days" are to be scheduled at school in order to revive linguistic pride. Special programs are suggested for aspiring young writers, as well as for those who have special talents in essay writing and poetry.
4. Positive aspects of indigenous languages will be provided at all levels to remove the inferiority associated with these languages such as explaining to students that they are capable of great inventions and great deeds in their own languages, discussing the actual causes why some languages are regarded superior and others inferior, and giving historical perspectives on language policy in order to clarify misconceptions about other languages.
5. Community support needs to be created. For example, students must feel free to use their communities as language resources.
6. In light of the issues addressed above, educators need to consider the development of innovative curriculum. That is, teachers must have more control over what they teach, and flexibility in the classroom must be accommodated rather than rushing to complete the prescribed syllabus.

In short, the language policy in South Africa is to be determined by those whose languages have been ignored. The responsibility of developing these languages is on the speakers themselves. If the majority of South Africans seeks liberation from its unique conditions, then a new language policy aimed at creating a condition in which all citizens must benefit needs to be implemented.

True democracy is based on acceptance of differences and tolerance of cultural diversity. In order to achieve national integration, social adjustment must be present, making possible the preservation of all cultures (Sure 1991-92). In South Africa, a new trend is to be established in order to expand the functions of African languages. The high failure rate in African schools is traced, in part, to the early introduction of instruction in English (Baine and Mwamwenda 1994; Kachelhoffer 1995). African languages, when fully developed, will make learning easier and more pleasurable.

5.7 Conclusion

In order for Africans to rewrite history in their terms, they must use indigenous languages. Africans have a history of their own, but it has never been told by Africans. This challenge is for South Africa if it is to survive what Phillipson (1992) called "linguicism" or "linguistic imperialism." According to Phillipson, linguicism is a colonial language dominated at the expense of indigenous languages.

In a postapartheid South Africa, there must be a consistent policy of promoting each language, particularly those that have been neglected. Expanding the functions of indigenous African languages lies with the speakers. Existing materials in African languages ought to be expanded. Additional books in these languages must be written; in fact, even translation of advanced knowledge available in foreign languages must be conducted. This exercise will increase the richness of African languages.

Black South Africans have always been exposed to learn in languages of the minority culture while failing to contribute to their own languages. If African languages are to develop and benefit from black writers, more focus must be given to literature, art, and scientific research. Viewing foreign languages as a route to employment and prosperity without developing one's knowledge base using one's language is neither essential nor desirable. Preservation of African languages will help to ensure that all voices within a society have an opportunity to be heard.

Chapter 6

Teaching And Learning In Black Universities

6.1 Introduction

This chapter addresses the current status of teaching and learning in black universities of South Africa. An historical background is provided of these institutions of higher learning and their relationship to the wider picture of sociopolitical and economic conditions of South Africa. Such an outline is deemed necessary in order to understand the underlying factors that impact teaching and learning in black South African universities. Finally, suggestions are made for the future of South Africa.

The problem of education facing black South African universities has a long history. Students admitted to these institutions are underprepared because of inequities experienced throughout their education. Therefore, teaching and learning in black universities have suffered the consequences of being at the receiving end of the inequalities of a segregated school system (Gwalla 1988). The challenge is how to provide quality education for all students. Adoption of creative and innovative teaching practices will create new forms of learning behavior and, consequently, new ways of thinking.

Change in teaching and learning is likely to be gradual. Compensatory in-service programs such as international teacher exchange, as well as attendance at national conferences, workshops, and seminars, should be encouraged and conducted regularly. These undertakings will expose instructors to current teaching methodologies. However, improving teaching strategies will be a demanding task; in fact, years will pass before its benefits filter significantly into these institutions (MacKenzie 1993).

In order to comprehend the process of teaching and learning in all black universities in South Africa, it is important to explain how it relates to the overall aims of Bantu education. Teaching and learning in all tertiary institutions of South Africa have been controlled and molded by apartheid ideology. The flow of university graduates, particularly blacks, has been restricted and based on a capitalist market economy. As a result, the amount of inequality has been matched with the size of the economic surplus, concentrating on political power (Nordkvelle 1990). The economic power of the state has dictated what occurs in black institutions of learning.

Teaching and learning strategies in black universities have been strongly influenced by the former central government's ability to produce qualified black intellectuals in order to suit its political and economic interests. University education for black South Africans is based, to a large extent, on the types of opportunities in the society, economy, and belief system (Nordkvelle 1990). Thus, this type of education is more a function of economic stratification and subjugation than of human growth and development (Watkins 1990).

Establishing black universities in South Africa was intended to supply the labor market in which African workers were needed (Dube 1985) such as in agriculture or the liberal arts. Black universities have failed to stimulate the growth of black intellectuals such as researchers, thinkers, philosophers, and scientists (Dube 1985). However, the failure of black universities to produce such intellectuals must be seen in the limitations imposed by the state and the intentions of Bantu education.

6.2 Historical Background

The first university (Fort Hare) to serve all blacks in South Africa was established in 1916. Prior to the establishment of black universities, selected white universities admitted blacks on a limited basis. However, with the passage of the Separate University Education Bill in 1957, white universities were no longer allowed to enroll black students.

As a result, several racially segregated universities were developed: The University of the North for the Tsonga, Sotho, Venda, and Tswana peoples was established in 1960; the University of Durban-Westville for Indian students was established in 1960; the University of the Western Cape for colored or people of mixed race, Griqua, and Malay students was established in 1960; the University of Zululand for Zulu and Swazi students was established in 1960; and the Medical University of Southern Africa (MEDUNSA) for black students was established in 1976 (Nordkvelle 1990).

Black universities are shown in Table 6.1. With the invention of apartheid, other black universities emerged such as the University of Transkei (1977), the University of Bophuthatswana (1979), the University of QwaQwa (1979), and the University of Venda (1979). Several black university branches in major townships also were opened in the 1980s such as the University of Vista in Transvaal and the University of Umlazi in Natal.

Historically, establishing new institutions promoted the development of independent Bantu national units (Nkomo 1984). The hidden intentions in establishing these institutions were to manipulate society' s norms and to perpetuate social segmentation and restratification along tribal lines (Johnson 1994). The hope was that Africans would support the notion that they constitute different nations, justifying the false claim that South Africa is a nation of minorities.

Even though many of the restrictions regarding admission to various universities were removed in the 1990s, the quality of teaching in most historical black universities continues to be difficult or impossible to actualize. A new generation of teachers in these institutions will improve teaching. Most of the instructors currently employed in these institutions are the products of apartheid education. Change in the structure and content of these universities is unavoidable. Therefore, major elements are still intact, including the administration and staff composition, curriculum, teaching methods, and academic freedom.

Table 6.1

Major Black Universities

Name	Medium of Instruction	Group	Enrollment 1989
Fort Hare	English	African	4,134
The North	English	African	9,424
Zululand	English	African	5,555
Durban-Westville	English	Indian	7,402
Western Cape	Afrikaans	Colored	11,934
Transkei	English	African	4,694
Bophuthatswana	English	African	2,330
Medunsa	English	African	1,810

Source: South African Institute of Race Relations, *1990 Race Relations Survey*, Johannesburg, South Africa: South African Institute of Race Relations (1994):872-73.

6.3 Administration and Staff Composition

The administration of black universities rested solely in the hands of government-appointed white officials, that is, Afrikaners (Marcum 1982). These ethnic universities were managed and funded by the state under the direction of the Department of Education and Training (formerly Bantu education) or the Department of Internal Affairs (for coloreds and Indians). It is unlikely that the situation will change drastically, even with the new government of national unity.

Until recently, the faculties remained predominantly white. For example, Marcum (1982) found that, as of 1980, out of 621 lecturers at African universities, 441 were white. Unterhalter et al. (1991) reported that in 1983 only 28 percent of the lecturers at the University of Western Cape, 36 percent at the University of Durban-Westville, and 25 percent at the African universities were black. These black instructors were concentrated at the lower rung of the staff hierarchy. Marcum (1982) concluded that this structure has enabled Afrikaner educators unable to secure jobs at the more competitive white universities, thus perpetuating the ideology of the ruling elite.

Black teachers have always found it difficult to secure positions at white universities, which has enabled white junior university teachers to utilize black universities as springboards for entering white universities (Danaher 1984). Since 1983, a small number of black academicians has succeeded in occupying posts at white universities primarily in the field of African studies or African languages (Nordkvelle 1990). Several studies have found that the difference in funding, as well as other working conditions, at black and white universities are considerable at all levels. File (1986) stated that salaries and expenditures on equipment are much lower in black universities.

Poor funding in black institutions directly or indirectly affects teaching and learning. Thus, talented instructors generally are not attracted to these institutions. Imbalance in the teaching staff has always been associated with social control, that is, economic power of the state. Therefore, black universities of South Africa are staffed by more whites than blacks.

This arrangement has been in sharp contrast with the former South African government's claim that such institutions were intended to supply the developing non-European nations with their own national universities. If true, these institutions would have been staffed by more black professionals than currently is the case. Table 6.2 provides the percentage of lecturers at South African black universities.

6.4 Curriculum

The acquisition of funds from the state illustrates the process of social control and how the state has dictated curricular content. Danaher (1984) observed that black universities were forced to follow an inferior curriculum compared to other universities. Black universities are less well-equipped and have a narrower range of curriculum than their white counterparts. Furthermore, the curricula in all black universities have a narrow focus, offering no opportunities for research.

Table 6.2

Percentage of Lecturers at South African Black Universities

Group	Year		
	1983	1990	1991
Africans	25.0	6.0	15.0
Indians	36.0	3.0	4.0
Coloreds	28.0	2.5	5.0

Sources: M. O. Nkomo, "Democratizing Higher Education: Imperatives of Quality and Equality for Development," in E. Bitzer and A. Beylefeld (Eds.), *Quality and Equality in Higher Education: Proceedings of the 1992 SAARHE Congress*, Bloemfontein, South Africa: University of the Orange Free State (1992):72; E. Unterhalter et al., *Apartheid Education and Popular Struggles*, London, England: Zed Books Ltd. (1991):88.

A legitimate university is defined in terms of its highly trained manpower and a place in which each nation's brain power is concentrated (Peresuh 1994); this is not the case with black South African universities. University staff in other parts of the world are expected to study and research problems currently facing their communities, but this is rarely encouraged in the black universities of South Africa. Peresuh described the role of universities as creators of data and storehouses of information.

In an examination of the portfolio of faculties, Nkomo (1984) stated that there is a strong liberal arts orientation in South African black universities. For example, there seems to be more emphasis in liberal arts than science. Unterhalter et al. (1991) argued that, with exceptions, the dominant curricula orientation in black institutions of higher learning are conservative or, at best, liberal and that radical social theories and writings are largely ignored. Under such an atmosphere, critical investigation and discussion are nonexistent in black tertiary institutions.

The neglect of science is deliberately aimed at preventing blacks from competing with whites economically (Dube 1985). Moreover, the intention of Bantu education has been to produce subservient individuals with skills needed to administer to the needs of the white economy rather than to develop critical thinkers (Nkomo 1981). Training blacks in universities has been designed to maintain a state of intellectual underdevelopment and dependency (Nkomo 1981). Thus, university education for black South Africans is used as a form of social control and defines the position of blacks and whites in the country' s racial hierarchy.

Official emphasis on South African history and culture is on African ethnic differences and the "backwardness" of the latter while glorifying Christian civilization (Nkomo 1984). For example, European wars such as the First and Second World Wars are portrayed in South African history books as symbols of heroism, whereas wars waged by Africans against colonialism and domination are portrayed as acts of savagery and backwardness (Thompson 1990). Furthermore, rote learning is promoted in subjects such as history. Hey (1961) reiterated that black students learn to record events in terms of dates that relate to world history rather than to the local area. Students are never encouraged to engage in critical inquiry regarding what is taught. Thus, black students are never fully taught the reality of their past history.

Religion classes taught at the university level reinforce the idea that Africans are inferior and that their servitude to whites is divinely ordained (Regehr 1979). In this regard, blacks are encouraged not to question their sociopolitical and economic exploitation. Therefore, courses in South African black universities, as one observer noted, are designed to inculcate order, obedience, and industriousness--all qualities that imperial rulers desire to be instilled in their subject race (Nkomo 1984, p. 75).

The geography syllabus, for example, is supportive of the defunct homeland system that limited Africans in their citizenship. Nothing is said about the land issue that allows 15 percent of the population to occupy 87 percent of the land, whereas the black majority that comprises approximately 80 percent of the population is placed on 13 percent of the land (McClellan 1979). African geography, which is more applicable to students' daily lives, is not taught. Thus, the content in most courses does not incorporate important practical issues and case studies of relevance to South Africa.

In short, curricula in black South African universities are excessively theoretical, biased, lacking in positive objectives, fragmented into rigid disciplinary units, and evaluated only occasionally (Bor and Shute 1991). Consequently, most black students never learn to address societal problems as multidisciplinary and multifaceted entities (Bor and Shute 1991). The policy of controlling teaching and course content in black universities was part of the overall aim of Bantu education, that is, to retard the intellectual development of Africans (Dube 1985).

6.5 Teaching Methods

Curriculum, as well as teaching methods used in black universities, were devised by Europeans, thus reflecting their viewpoints. Consequently, creativity and adoption of modern teaching methods have been difficult to implement because of restrictions placed on teachers and students. Black instructors who attempted to teach differently risked their jobs or even detention.

Another factor that prevented improved teaching methods in black universities was the instructors' limited frame of reference. For example, most black instructors were trained under apartheid and were victims of poor training themselves. They tended to apply the outdated teaching methods implemented by their instructors. This entire exercise resulted in a vicious circle. That is, instructors tended to teach the same way as they had been taught, relying heavily on outdated teaching methods such as overemphasis on examination and rote learning. Their white counterparts, on the other hand, were graduates of English and Afrikaans universities, both known for their conservative orientation (Unterhalter et al. 1991). They summarized the teaching methods in black universities: "There are considerable controls on teaching. The use of enlightened methods and course content is met with strong opposition from those who effectively control the campus" (p. 89). Such controls often lead to a restricted flow of knowledge, creativity, and imagination, resulting in reliance on rote learning. Previous state intervention has made it more difficult for black instructors and students to engage in free inquiry of knowledge. In fact, more emphasis has been placed on examinations than intellectual enrichment. Case studies, based on the local environment, group discussions, essays, and research projects, are often ignored. Methods of teaching that are practical and aimed at providing public service, encourage critical thinking, and develop student reading and writing skills are lacking. However, Bantu education was never intended to train blacks for constructive roles in South Africa; thus, African universities were not designed to train and produce productive and critical thinking intellectuals. These institutions of higher learning ought to adopt new roles to meet the demands of a postapartheid South Africa. Peresuh (1994) defined these roles as (a) researching and promoting scholarship, (b) teaching and training, (c) being a storehouse of information, (d) disseminating information and ideas, and (e) producing appropriate manpower and other public service.

In black South African universities, research must be conducted on social, economic, environmental, and political issues. For example, testing instruments could be researched and developed in vernacular languages to assess children with disabilities.

Research on African languages is recommended, as well as producing culturally relevant books, teaching materials to promote critical thinking and problem solving, and creating scientific terms in vernacular languages. Reading for pleasure is enhanced when a body of knowledge and information exists in a particular language. Those who teach African languages should encourage students to write books, diaries, essays, biographies, poetry, and short stories.

In terms of special education, black universities must take the lead to develop adaptive equipment for the handicapped. This equipment can include prosthetic aids, wheelchairs, hearing aids, and canes--all affordable and functional in a South African context. Research must not be seen as a time-consuming exercise. African academicians are obligated to engage in self-initiated research to learn and discover solutions to their community's problems. Research has been reserved for specific groups in South Africa, which has led to the image of an "elitist ivory tower activity" (Swarts 1994). Such beliefs ought to be challenged in order to prevent intellectual laziness among Africans.

Historically, black South Africans have been treated as sources of data rather than invited to contribute to the research venture, including problem identification, interpretation of information, and reporting of findings (Nkomo 1990). This minimal involvement of black people has led to the publication of biased information and distorted views about blacks in general. Non-African researchers typically study areas of interest to themselves rather than to those of Africans. In order for this trend to change, black professionals must lead the way in research to avoid victimization in the literature.

Research conducted by Africans is significant in finding solutions to African problems. Valid projects are measured in terms of their usefulness to the people they are intended to help. Universities are not designed to be government puppets. Their direction is to conduct research aimed at benefiting humanity and to be data banks. When universities are used for government interests, they lose part of their identity as well. This authoritarian rule results in repression and, at times, corruption, while instructors become docile with no commitment to improve their university environment (De Clercq 1991). Thus, black institutions of higher education have been unable to teach freedom of thought and inquiry, as well as concepts of democracy and egalitarianism, and to encourage originality and productivity (Sherman 1990). According to Sherman, depriving black universities of fundamental principles and concepts dooms Africa to marginality and subservience. The world continues to be an ever-changing place that requires productivity.

Even though some black instructors display strong interest in the use of innovative teaching methods, they are challenged to teach within an ideological framework over which they have no control, fostering resentment and suggesting the inferiority of African intelligence. Teaching and learning is even further complicated; that is, the majority of white instructors in black universities is Afrikaner educators who use English as their second language. Their teaching places considerable stress on rote learning because of their inadequate command of the language. Another factor that contributes to poor teaching methods is the instructors' attitudes toward themselves and their educational experiences.

Currently, sufficient creative and inexpensive steps are not being taken to address the deficiencies in instruction and staff development in black universities. First, resources are limited in most black universities such as poorly equipped libraries and laboratories. Second, research is not encouraged in such institutions. Finally, too many restrictions are placed on black instructors that prevent them from conducting research. For example, black faculty members in these institutions are isolated from one another by tradition and geography. As a result, they cannot share research ideas or knowledge sufficient to benefit students and communities.

Furthermore, staff development is hampered because most university-based researchers lack basic equipment, transport facilities, the help of well-trained research assistants, and communication (Bor and Shute 1991). Furthermore, an adequate research environment must have the support of a well-developed research management system, which does not exist in black universities.

6.6 Academic Freedom

Black staff and students are heavily regulated in terms of what they can do, how they can do it, what they can or should say, and when they can say it. Anyone openly criticizing the government can be fined or summarily discharged. Reports indicate that black and white staff have been dismissed when criticizing the government. Many students have been detained, given low grades as a penalty, and expelled for political activism (Nordkvelle 1990).

The claim of academic freedom, as indicated above, is justified only when students and faculty members have the same rights inside the academy as they have as citizens in a free society. In South African black universities, classical academic freedom has been seriously affected by state intervention. Thus, hindrance of this freedom of inquiry among students by instructors makes it more difficult for them to learn and for teachers to teach.

If South African black universities are to participate in the creation and discovery of new truths, they need to exercise freedom of expression and freedom of inquiry. A university that allows diversity of ideas in an effort to raise the quality of learning will equip its student body with an ability to apply knowledge to solve life' s problems. Academic freedom forms the backbone of university teaching and learning. Exploration of popular and unpopular ideas is made possible by academic freedom. Higgs and Higgs (1994) suggested that academic freedom means that

> a university must be free to follow its traditional role of pursuing the truth; a university must be free to weigh up different schools of thought, political, economic, and social; a university must be free to disseminate insights flowing from scholarly activities; a university must be free to appraise trends and tendencies in society based on scientific research; a university must be free to pass on its knowledge to all students who are capable and wish to learn; a university must be free to establish a climate in which its members may contemplate and be creative. (p. 45)

6.7 Recommendations

Teaching and learning in black South African universities reflect, as well as confirm, the surrounding social and racial structure. Therefore, significant changes in teaching and learning in black South African universities will require a change in the political, economic, and social structures of the society. Such changes will occur only with the collapse of apartheid.

Considering the abundant resources, it is recommended that the educational policy be designed by all South Africans in order to suit the needs of all citizens. A central educational authority must assume more of the responsibility of bridging the gap in financing education for the total population. De Lange (1981) reported that attention has to be given to the application of measures in education that will lead to better utilization of scarce resources such as teachers, buildings, and grounds. For example, integration of students and academic staff in higher education will help reduce the scarcity of physical materials and manpower. Educational inequalities at all levels of education are serious problems that must receive urgent attention. Compulsory free education recently introduced from ages five to seventeen is meant to benefit all South African citizens regardless of religious, political, and economic backgrounds.

Cultural dominance, which has been the pattern in South African black universities, is now to give way to more acceptable democratic principles. Instructors must be free to make adaptations in the curriculum and their teaching in order to reach people of all backgrounds. Courses offered in these institutions need to relate to the students' experiences, as well as the use of contemporary teaching methods. Sherman (1990) argued that universities, like other institutions, grow and become dynamic as they provide positive responses to the needs and challenges of their environment. Therefore, South African black universities are no exception. In terms of future administration, greater control of these institutions need to be placed on the private and community bodies comprised of equal representation of all racial groups. Universities governed by such administration will operate under state-established standards of quality, preventing future government from imposing or dictating its ideology. The state, however, will continue to provide financial support to these institutions without having direct control.

In order to improve staff development, all barriers of isolation currently in place among South African black universities are to be removed. Televised instruction or computer networking are possible tools to achieve such an undertaking. Information will have to be shared among professionals, thus reducing duplication. Such cooperation is likely to enhance teaching and learning. The quality of teaching and learning is likely to improve if black professionals interact freely with each other and are willing to share current trends in teaching and learning, even to engage in planning collaborative research projects. In the light of these recommendations, programs for interuniversity cooperation must be planned over a period of time, but trial programs are suggested on a limited scale and must be implemented immediately. Research endeavors ought to be directed at benefiting communities rather than individuals. Activities such as the development of mentor programs for school children, at-risk students, adult schools (night schools), and the eradication of illiteracy, as well as helping the elderly, sick, or handicapped, foster the application of knowledge needed to solve societal problems (Bor and Shute 1991). This process gives students an opportunity to use their communities as subjects for research purposes (Sherman 1990). Engaging students in actual practical problems experienced by the community has a lasting impact in the learning process.

Long-term efforts to upgrade the academic qualifications of staff must be a priority. One way to achieve this process is by organizing workshops and seminars, sharing ideas through the use of computers, providing postdoctoral fellowships, conducting collaborative research, having professional links with foreign universities, and funding centers of excellence for postdoctoral education and research. Such initiatives are to be based on how individuals within the institutions perceive and perform their jobs. In other words, commitment and dedication must be their responsibilities. As long as staff members do not have the technical skills, didactic expertise, motivation, and proper understanding of students' learning needs, solid syllabi for students will not be produced. Improvements in material conditions, combined with proper programs for staff development in subject matter and instructional methodology, are recommended.

Victimization of instructors and students used to suppress unpopular debate has to give way to a more just and tolerant exchange of ideas. Political interference in universities needs to be limited to mutual beneficial terms rather than to manipulation and deprivation of intellectual advancement. Students must have more control over academic materials. In most black universities, the common practice is to maintain the final scripts of students. This practice has resulted in grade victimization of many students. Such procedures are undemocratic and should not be used.

Another factor that contributes to poor teaching and learning in black universities is the unstable political situation that results in school disruptions. Police and even the presence of the military on campuses have been regular events, which render learning impossible. For example, at the University of the North, approximately 50 percent of teaching time was lost in 1986 (Nordkvelle 1990). The situation continues in other black institutions. Free expression, which is a source of creativity and imagination, should be permitted in order to avoid student unrest. Black universities, like white universities, must be able to enjoy autonomy with no government interference.

South African black universities should aim at equipping people with the ability, as well as the willingness, to develop themselves and their communities. This practice involves teaching skills, along with solving practical societal problems. In order to achieve this enormous task, radical revisions in the curriculum, as well as in teaching and learning strategies, must be implemented. Black instructors at primarily black universities should begin the transformation of teaching and learning, laying the foundations of social and political progress. In order to be considered effective, teaching methods are essential relevant to the pressing needs of the black community. Rural poverty, health issues, joblessness, violence, and land concerns must be incorporated in the curriculum. Instructors must encourage the use of more participatory learning methods than the standard lecture method or chalkboard copying. These teaching methods will help black students to develop intellectually by encouraging free inquiry, creativity, and imagination.

This situation will be rectified only by a serious and deliberate effort of the ruling party and by the removal of the apartheid system. Thus, the restructuring of teaching and learning in South African black universities will succeed only when performed by a government and people committed to quality education for all citizens. University learning needs to make people aware of their past and present, striving for a better future (Nyerere 1985). Without sufficient teaching materials such as books, laboratory materials, overhead projectors, televisions, tape recorders, photocopying machines, and other teaching aids, it is difficult to implement innovative teaching methods or to conduct promising research. The shortage of physical facilities still need to be addressed by fair use of what is available throughout the education system. This process will be accomplished by eliminating segregated educational facilities that are expensive in terms of physical and human resources. African universities in other parts of the continent also are in the position to provide South African black universities with usable information, ensuring that mistakes are not repeated.

Efforts to transform the content and teaching in black universities are to be based on providing new textbooks written by Africans, thus reflecting the African environment and experience, and adopting teaching methods aimed at intellectual growth. Science teaching in the university curriculum must be encouraged because of increased demand for high-level scientific jobs. This endeavor cannot succeed without training more teachers in the field of science.

The current situation in black universities is the result of poor preparation of black students at each level of education. Therefore, attention is to be given to the provision of quality education at each level, particularly ensuring a solid foundation at the primary level. University students should be prepared for critical and creative approaches to knowledge. This process requires instructors with confidence and expertise, motivated by a teaching culture geared towards experimentation and innovation.

A great deal of training and time will be required for the majority of instructors in these institutions of higher learning in order to change their attitudes regarding teaching and learning. In the end, a key ingredient of the quality of learning is the quality of teaching that occurs in an institution of higher learning. Quality learning at any level of education is heavily influenced by the quality of staff, as well as their enthusiasm, motivation, and expertise. In order to improve teaching and learning in black universities, teachers' morale must be improved with adequate professional support. All instructors must be aware of available educational possibilities through informative pre-service and in-service training. Universities must encourage information dissemination of research conducted by instructors through grants. Joint research by instructors and students is essential in building healthy relationships among professionals.

A further issue relates to providing a wide range of courses to students without imposing restrictions on course selection. For example, black universities in South Africa must focus their curricula on the areas of modern technology, mathematics, and natural sciences. These areas are essential in building a nation, particularly in economic growth and development. Therefore, university teaching and learning ought to be organized to provide the maximum degree of flexibility for learners in order to meet societal needs and their changing conditions.

Researchers have reported that without solid college preparation most students will not be able to enhance their knowledge base and, thus, will not be able to make valid contributions to society (Bor and Shute 1991; Nkomo 1992; Sherman 1990). Therefore, black universities in South Africa must not restrict individual growth if their pupils are to contribute to the world's intellectual and cultural stream. The challenge of universities is to create a new society capable of understanding its needs and actions and to provide opportunities to further knowledge through research (Nyerere 1985). Functions such as student-initiated study skills programs, tutorials, seminars, field trips, off-campus projects, internships, and summer workshops are vital elements in the university's commitment to quality teaching and learning approach (Watkins 1990). Consequently, curricula must be reconceptualized and revised if significant improvements in university teaching and learning are to be realized.

In order for black institutions of higher learning to succeed in their mission to prepare students for a positive future, substantial financial assistance must be available from the government and private sector. However, financial assistance to these institutions does not imply that they have the right to exercise political intrusion on academic freedom. Unless the university is free from political pressure and manipulation, it will not be able to perform significant inquiry. Training in conducting research in various fields of study, as well as the use of specific research techniques, must be a high priority in order to improve teaching and learning.

The quality of university teaching and learning is improved through professional development, teacher exchange networks, dissemination of appropriate instructional materials, and interuniversity coordination services (Bor and Shute 1991). However, implementation of the proposed measures is more likely curtailed by the difficult financial situation currently facing black universities in South Africa (Vergnani 1993b). The discrepancies in the distribution of educational resources has greatly affected teaching and learning in black South African universities. Historically, the racial basis of education tended to favor whites in the allocation of resources. On the other hand, blacks suffered the restrictions of opportunities in education, as well as in other life necessities.

Black universities, given the opportunity and resources, are capable of changing their roles in teaching and learning. They also can increase the production of black intellectuals, deepen understanding of the educative process, and uniquely serve the most troubled communities (Watkins 1990). The following reasons must be considered as the objectives for having a university: (a) to create, save, and share valuable information with students and the public; (b) to nurture and promote intellectual talent intended to benefit the whole society; (c) to encourage research projects aimed at easing societal problems such as reduction of violence, street children, poverty, joblessness, and diseases; (d) to cooperate with other agencies in conducting research aimed at benefiting all South Africans; (e) to stress the importance of community service rather than the overemphasis of certificates and diplomas; and (f) to encourage the value of scholarship and continuous publication among faculty members and students in order to contribute in the pool of knowledge.

6.8 Conclusion

In an ongoing demand to address the educational crisis in South Africa, black universities seem to focus, in part, because such institutions of learning are generally regarded as centers imbued with the task of generating and applying knowledge beneficial to the needs of society (Sherman 1990). In order to reform education, black universities and colleges are expected to take the initiative in preparing students who will transform schools.

Therefore, a university must not be a place of distributing meaningless diplomas or degrees, but it is a place in which building an individual's intellectual foundation is stressed. Students need to be encouraged to register for disciplines that will benefit the community. Reduction in enrollment in some fields has to go hand-in-hand, with selective increases in others such as teacher training and postgraduate programs in the physical sciences, engineering, and social sciences (Sherman 1990).

Chapter 7

Gender Issues In Education

7.1 Introduction

This chapter focuses on the conditions of black women in South Africa. In addition, it explores areas such as laws that affect black women, in particular, and educational opportunities available to them. The past and present status of black South African women, movement for change, and critical needs also are addressed. The important roles played by black women such as holding families together and being the providers, disciplinarians, and head of households are briefly discussed.

The argument in this chapter highlights the importance of education for women in order to free themselves from oppression, but it is not sufficient in itself (Unterhalter et al. 1991). The underlying factors responsible for class, race, and gender inequalities in South Africa exist outside the educational terrain and within it. The extent to which positive impacts can be experienced in the education of women depends, in part, on the political, economic, and social conditions in South Africa, as well as the manner in which black women struggle and fight against gender oppression.

Education alone is less likely to decrease women's subordination because it is an attitudinal problem experienced by women worldwide. The extent of women's subordination varies from country-to-country, with women in industrialized countries being better off. In South Africa, the greatest challenge in empowering women is attitudes and expectations about black women.

7.2 Historical Background

In South Africa, as in any other African country, black women have been poorly represented at almost every level of education, with females experiencing greater repetition and dropout rates than males (Davidson and Kanyuka 1992). Apartheid laws and the cultural myth that black women are inferior to men and to women of other racial groups have placed them at the bottom. Educational inequality that affects blacks, in general, tends to affect women even more. For too long, black parents have preferred to educate their sons and openly denied their daughters the same opportunity. In some instances, girls were forced to marry early or kept at home.

In the primary school, the number of black girls enrolled is almost equal to the number of boys. However, the trend changes at higher levels in which girls drop out of school or disappear into "female sectors." These sectors include domestic science, teaching, and nursing. Very few women have succeeded academically and/or economically. According to Kuzwayo (1985), several generations of women have been condemned as unproductive, unintelligent, and/or incapable; that is, they are viewed as male property, whether single or married, and, by law, categorized as minors.

Unterhalter et al. (1991) observed that only a small number of black women reaches the university level. Even though their numbers have increased absolutely and proportionately, they have not attained a position of equal access (p. 68). While few black women attend universities, many attend teachers' training colleges.

For approximately every ten males, only six females are enrolled in secondary school (OAU 1992), which is a clear indication that black women lag behind men in education. Therefore, as a result of the gender-biased education system, approximately 65 percent of African women over the age of fifteen are illiterate compared to 40 percent of men (OAU 1992). High levels of illiteracy among women, coupled with being denied access to education, are closely associated with the lower status of women in the society, as well as the traditional heritage of inferiority.

The status of women will undergo a fundamental change in South Africa only when laws that control and disrupt the lives of black women are abolished. Black women are to be included in decision making at both the national and local levels. Women must receive adequate protection under existing civil and customary laws. The protection of women cannot occur without their participation. Therefore, black women must not be left out as the country progresses.

Even though opportunities in education are beginning to open, they remain limited to black women. Gender equity is still a debatable issue, even in developed countries. Women throughout the world are still underrepresented in higher levels of education and in male-dominated professions. However, the situation for black women is even worse in South Africa. For example, race, gender, and class are all determining factors that limit access to education.

Even as South Africa adopts a more acceptable form of democracy, equality of the sexes is still unattainable, in part, due to mental attitudes imposed on women by social customs, as well as apartheid that reinforced subordination. In South Africa, people working for change in the treatment of African women are likely to encounter difficulties in changing old attitudes. Patriarchal views, based upon the notion that men are superior to women, are evident in African tradition, as well as the civil law of the country.

Historically, black women have not been protected under the law and, thus, have found themselves caught between apartheid laws and their African social traditions. Apartheid laws did not legally recognize African women as adults with rights to the land and/or property, thus undermining their self-worth (Redding 1993). In South Africa, the state relegated African women to a level below that of their sons. As a result, African women are regarded as human only in association with their male counterparts. This status exposed African women to all forms of exploitation, making them more dependent on men (Redding 1993).

Apartheid laws exaggerated the African woman's role in society, but the African society also contributed to this belief. Taylor (1994) asserted that most African men want women to be versed in sewing, cooking, and child care at the expense of economic and educational advancement. The position of African women in society is reproduced and manifested by educational institutions (Taylor 1994). African women learn at school only what is considered good for a wife or a mother, thus perpetuating gender division at all levels.

7.3 Problems Faced By Black Women of South Africa

A combination of many factors accounts for black women's failure to achieve academically. Limited opportunities, gender discrimination, lack of appropriate role models, and sexual harassment are only a few factors that prevent black women from reaching their highest potential. The majority of women who reach higher levels of education is concentrated in the caring professions such as teaching, social work, and/or nursing. Black women are few in scientific fields, as well as other well-paying professions such as medicine and law, but this is also true of South African black men.

The answer to many problems currently facing black South African women is embedded in a complex mix of historical forces related to colonialism, apartheid laws, gender perception within the community, and cultural/traditional dynamics. Black women in South Africa are seen as experiencing a triple burden, that is, the burden of being working class, black, and governed by civil and customary laws (Gardner 1994). The subordination of living in South Africa is obvious and can be seen in various ways; for instance, black women are underrepresented politically and educationally.

Sachs (1990) stated that colonialism and apartheid have whittled away at the democratic aspects of traditional African society and law, emphasizing vertical power and patriarchy. He asserted that African women have been left in limbo, stripped of a secure (if junior) position in a traditional society and denied individual rights by state law. Even though changing rapidly, gender equity is essentially nonexistent in South Africa.

Black women are forced, through circumstances, into multiple roles. Women and girls are primarily responsible for domestic tasks such as cooking, child care, cleaning, fetching water and wood, and contributing to home maintenance and repair. If money for school is in short supply, a girl is more likely to be withdrawn from school than a boy. For additional babies born into the family, older girls are required to help with child care. In extreme cases, an older girl is forced to leave school early in order to care for her siblings. Such practices always place a girl at a disadvantage, sometimes robbing her of an education. In short, girls in South Africa continue to bear the brunt of their families' poverty.

Most black women are forced to work in order to support their families. Many women become victims of gender discrimination, that is, the last ones hired and the first ones fired. Women of childbearing age also suffer in employment settings in which maternity leave is not available. Because there are few child care facilities, working black women experience extreme hardships in ensuring the security and happiness of their children. In a profession such as teaching, unmarried pregnant women are expelled but male teachers who impregnate them are not. Gender discrimination retards the progress of many black women academically and socially.

The migratory labor system robs many black women of their family lives, companionship, and economic tranquility. The system is based on the assertion that Africans are "temporal sojourners" in the "white" areas of South Africa (Regehr 1979). Consequently, the government has pursued a policy of making homelands the permanent homes for Africans; dismantling established African communities in rural and urban areas; taking husbands, brothers, and sons away from their families; and replacing family residences with vast single-sex hostels.

In many instances, women are forced to assume the roles of their absent husbands. These roles include being head of households, working on farms, and making life more difficult than it would be in the presence of their husbands. The migrant labor system is purported to be the cause of much of the mental illness experienced by Africans, in general, and women, in particular. This assertion is supported by Whittaker (1991). He contended that various mental illnesses, economic insecurity, marital disharmony, and material and emotional misery among blacks were a result of the migrant labor system. Psychological disorders such as depression and hysterical behavior (associated with the insecure position of African women) also are attributed to the negative side effects of the migratory labor system.

The policy of forced removals, coupled with family and community disruptions, is devastating for blacks and, in particular, for women. Enforced separation of families deprives Africans of the fundamental human right of working and living within the security and comfort of their families. For example, women in rural areas involved in large-scale farming, when forcibly removed, are deprived of access to the land, as well as domestic employment.

Black women who choose to follow their husbands are forced to work in unskilled or semiskilled jobs. Education may be a factor in finding a good job, but for most black women racial classification that favors other racial groups cannot be overcome. The education of women needs to be linked with laws that aim to eliminate race, gender, and class discrimination. Gender discrimination is still evident in most developed countries of the world, suggesting that even with education such oppression will continue to exist.

7.4 Rationale for Educating Women

Numerous studies have indicated that there are many economic and social benefits derived from women's education (Davidson and Kanyuka 1992; Stromquist 1990; Taylor 1994). A strong relationship between the education of women in developing countries and their active participation in socioeconomic development has been established in many studies. Education for women is believed to bring an improved sense of self-worth and well-being, as well as liberating them from being economically dependent on men.

If African women are to play major roles in the economic, political, and social transformation of their country, they must be educated. Education will encourage African women to question or alter their present condition of subordination (Taylor 1994). Access to education and the acquisition of knowledge are important components for women to reflect critically on their position in society.

When women become vocal on issues that affect them, it will help change the attitudes and behaviors of men, as well as society at large. The meaningful education of women must be more holistic; that is, women should be encouraged to look beyond their present needs (Taylor 1994). Women must understand sociocultural attitudes that begin with their families and then transfer to all aspects of their lives, thus reinforcing their oppression. Therefore, changing attitudes must be taught at home in order to transfer to other aspects of life.

Research studies have confirmed the notion that as long as oppressive social values such as sanction and acceptance of male dominance continue and women's exploitation is tolerated the education of women cannot bring empowerment (Ramphele 1990; Stromquist 1990). Nevertheless, African women armed with education have more control over their lives. Education is a freeing agent to those women who are gripped by a sense of powerlessness and helplessness. A self-sufficient woman does not fold her arms and wait for her male counterpart to rescue her. If a woman is capable of earning a living, it eases the burden on her, as well as on her family. Education gives women a sense of purpose and enables them to utilize their potential. Chatterjee (1995) stated that the more informed women become about their opportunities that the more they will reject the life of continually bearing children, which is forced upon them in developing countries. Therefore, the education of women can be seen in providing more choices.

Researchers (Chatterjee 1995; Ramphele 1990; Stromquist 1990) have reported that more education for women results in fewer children per family, less infant mortality, marriage at a later age, more healthy children, and better-reared and better-educated children. Economic and social benefits are derived from women' s education.

According to Stromquist (1990), educating women makes them better mothers and wives, and it enhances their ability to think more analytically. Women with positive self-esteem cannot be taken advantage of economically and personally. Education cannot eliminate women' s subordination, but it can help them to become productive members of the community.

7.5 Empowering Black Women: A New Vision

In the past, inculcation of African values and mores was concentrated in the education of African women. Stories were told by elderly women passing important cultural values from one generation to the next. Black women in South Africa, like women throughout the world, are teachers first. Well-informed parents, particularly women, raise well-informed children. Empowering black women in South Africa is key to implementing cost-effective program strategies for African children, particularly the millions in especially difficult circumstances (OAU 1992).

Education will not solve all the social and economic ills of South Africa, but access to economic and political power is possible through education. Self-sufficiency also is possible through knowledge and exposure to education. Therefore, a new South Africa must invest in human development that will provide opportunities for black women to become economically independent. Furthermore, improving the health care, access to social services, and education of women will pay large dividends in child survival, growth, and future productivity (OAU 1992). Researchers have indicated that nations demonstrating the capacity to sustain social and economic development also have emphasized education and training in order to increase their people's capacity to accumulate knowledge, communicate information, and coordinate and organize themselves productively (Nkomo 1990; OAU 1992).

Black South African women are important figures in local development such as head of households, household providers, disciplinarians, workers of the land, and community leaders. Despite their roles and potential, South African black women remain excluded from various sectors of society, including decision making in the education of their children, health issues, and political matters. Stromquist (1990) reported that male resistance to women's literacy also has been found in several African settings. Education for African women is seen as a potential challenge to patriarchy by their male counterparts.

Basic education, particularly for women, is strongly associated with lowered child mortality rates, fertility rates, and family welfare (including health and nutrition). Therefore, empowering women is important for the well-being of the family and is crucial for the well-being of the nation. Informed and well-educated women give rise to informed leadership.

Special attention should be focused on the learning needs of girls and women because they constitute the largest group still untouched by formal education. This effort requires immediate attention, but its urgency requires it to occupy an integral part in the educational reform initiatives. African women at all levels must work together in order to bring social change.

7.6 Steps To Be Taken in Empowering Black Women

Implementing well-focused policies to reduce gender disparities is one of the best methods of improving access and restoring growth to the basic education system of South Africa. Special policies must be implemented to attract girls to school and, once there, to retain them until they complete basic education. Parents must be encouraged to educate all their children, regardless of gender. More female teachers should be recruited and trained to attract and retain girls. Female role models must be evident at all levels of education to encourage girls to remain in school. Educating women will help to decrease the level of illiteracy among blacks; that is, more measures must be taken to improve black women's literacy and to expand educational provision, particularly for adult women. Women must demand that legislation guaranteeing them the right to job security and adequate maternity leave will be implemented (Nkomo 1990).

Providing financial incentives or scholarships will encourage poor parents to send girls to school. Emphasis on sex education will help prevent early pregnancies, which is another factor that causes girls to leave school early. Providing school meals also will help to reduce the school dropout rate, which affects girls in greater numbers.

Empowering black women through education will give them a voice in a country that has silenced them. Education will help many black women find themselves and realize their full potential. Education also will give black women an opportunity to be independent. African women must be given the option to choose their profession. Stromquist (1990) found that in many developing countries the qualities prescribed for women are traditional such as sacrifice, abnegation, living for others, docility, love, and softness.

Empowering black women will utilize all their talents for economic growth, giving them the confidence to approve self-worth, exercise their rights, and make decisions. Most women are not able to exercise their rights such as making the decision on how many children they wish to have based on income. Rather, they are forced to make motherhood their career without consideration of self-improvement. In many instances, black women are in perpetual dependence and poverty because their lives are planned by others.

African women must be exposed to knowledge in order to understand better their subordination. Knowledge is needed about the existence of patriarchal ideology and cultural forms of subordination among African women. Such knowledge will make them better negotiators with their male counterparts. Moreover, it will help them to reject any imposition of unfair treatment. Exploitation of women's labor and all forms of discrimination experienced by them will be minimized by their voices.

7.7 Conclusion

In South Africa, black women do not publicly voice their opinions, but the trend is changing. The change will be remarkable when black women fight for their rights; that is, the war is not won unless it is fought (Sachs 1990). The only way to address gender issues is to understand the deep sources of women's subordination, including the role of patriarchal ideology, as well as the African tradition. Progress in gender issues is not possible without attacking patriarchal ideology and African tradition (Stromquist 1990).

Stromquist (1990) suggested that the political nature of women's subordination must be identified and education must be seen as an additional expression of uneven power relations. Gaining support from men will play a major role in changing the image of black women. The positive portrayal of women by men in the media, in general, will benefit women. The existence of black women in major leadership roles will help to change South African society.

With education and empowerment comes self-expression. Therefore, black women in South Africa, if given an opportunity to learn, will be able to create conditions that make it possible to establish their demands and priorities. Education will help African women control their lives, as well as their immediate environments. Control will be accomplished by participating in all aspects that deal with laws regulating their lives.

The change of attitude regarding the education of women will be a long process. Any challenge to patriarchal ideology and traditional gender beliefs will require men to acknowledge their roles in perpetuating women's subordination. Once achieved, education through all available mediums must be attempted. The process of changing attitudes about gender should begin at home, then transferred to schools, and finally given to society. Davidson and Kanyuka (1992) found that parental and societal attitudes must be challenged, as well as those of school staff, toward female learners. Teachers have the responsibility to implement changes in their classrooms, as well as within the school community, that facilitate gender equity in education at all levels (Davidson and Kanyuka 1992).

The gender issue is still crucial in developed countries, but in developing countries it is just beginning to acknowledge the contributions of women. Black women must be aware that they should be neither passive nor act as victims in their struggle for equality. If black women in South Africa are to envision a better future, it will not come by itself but will be created by dedicated women. The new government must provide the financial support that women need to further their education.

Chapter 8

Aims Of Education

8.1 Aims of Education in a Future South Africa

In South Africa, if credible alternatives to Bantu education are achieved, educational changes should be guided by goals that offer a blueprint for the process of change. These educational aims must help black schools to structure their curricula, syllabi, and teaching methods. Future goals of education ought to differ from those of Bantu education. Postapartheid education need to focus on the development of its most valuable resources: human resources.

What are the goals of education? Goals provide directions in which educational programs must be conducted. Educational goals, according to Dillman and Rahmlow (1972), tend to be broad and less explicit. Thus, the goals of education are defined as broad, general statements that describe educational intent in terms of the desired learning outcomes. Aims of education are specific enough to provide direction for learning, including the content, teaching methods, and evaluation of the educational outcomes.

Because educational aims are prerequisite in planning and implementing educational endeavors, they are theoretical and practical. The use of educational goals as a guide markedly assists educational planners and teachers to enhance the quality of their work through tangible means. A further significant advantage of educational aims is that they give direction to educators. Therefore, educational goals are the guidelines that educators seek to follow to impact learners.

White (1982) asserted that education is a preparation for life within society, forming its future workers and citizens. This definition implies that meaningful and valuable aims of education are directed at producing good citizens, competent workers, and sensible thinkers. Thus, education is seen as a preparation for all aspects of life. Education, as described by White, is similar to raising children. The aims of education also are explained in terms of what one wants to instill in children, translating to achievements, character, intellect, or other attributes. A school is seen as a place in which children have an opportunity to experience reality while being prepared for later, more complex social realities.

Unless those who work in education, particularly black professionals, are clear on what they want children to learn, the quality provided will suffer. Participation of all parties is crucial in formulating educational goals, including teachers, parents, and professional educators.

The demand to end Bantu education and the provision of quality education in postapartheid South Africa require the full participation of blacks. Postapartheid education ought to teach blacks how to think critically, make sound judgments, control their destiny, and participate actively in shaping their lives. Future education will have to prevent blacks from being passive receivers of information designed to control rather than to liberate them. Unless blacks make major contributions in their education, the aims of Bantu education will linger for years.

The objective of postapartheid education needs to ensure that black students have systematic access to programs that will equip them with economic opportunities or ways to become self-sufficient. Education is essentially concerned with the elimination of ignorance and the provision of opportunities to improve one' s circumstances. The aim of education is to nurture rather than stifle the aspirations of black students. Value of work and a desire to achieve must be instilled in all black children, mastery of which is necessary for survival.

Character molding and/or acceptable behavior are to be taught. South Africa has experienced hatred, violence, and disrespect for property; thus, children need to learn positive behavior and respect for human life. Schools need to take every opportunity to work hand in hand with parents in their children' s education. Black parents have not been fully utilized in the educational process of their children. No defined role for parents regarding the education of their children has been determined. The school and the home have worked as separate entities in the education of black children. This trend must change. A strong partnership between the school and the home is central to a commitment to quality education. Youth in South Africa must be taught skills that will ensure responsibility of their actions. Values that cut across cultural, political, economic, racial, and religious lines are beneficial such as those cited by Minnery (1994):

> 1. Trustworthiness. Honesty, integrity, fidelity, moral courage, and keeping your word.
> 2. Respect. Courtesy, decency, and recognizing and valuing all people.
> 3. Responsibility. Diligence, hard work, self-improvement, self-restraint, accepting blame, and not claiming credit for others' work.
> 4. Justice and fairness. Equity, due process, openness, consistency, impartiality, and refusing to take unfair advantage of the mistakes or ignorance of others.
> 5. Caring. The Golden Rule: Do unto others as you would have them do unto you. Seek to maximize benefits and minimize harm to others.
> 6. Civic virtue and citizenship. Duty that lies beyond one's self-interest. Voting, reporting crimes, public service, obeying laws, and opposing unjust laws, social consciousness. (p. 139)

Morality and responsibility are universal principles; these principles benefit all humanity; they cannot be limited to a race or country.

Education is an ever-changing process that keeps pace with the rate of change in the outside world, and it is a connecting force to the common stream of society. Black students must be taught not to be passive receivers of knowledge but that they are capable of becoming critical procreators of wisdom and insight. The goal of education is to enable blacks to look beyond their immediate needs. Formal education goes beyond learning how to read and write. Meaningful education prepares its students to be critical thinkers and to have the ability and means to change their environment. This approach enables students in the process of conscientiousness in which they learn to perceive social, political, and economic contradictions, as well as to take action against the oppressive elements of reality (Taylor 1994).

In a South African context, students must perceive the underlying causes of unemployment, poverty, and ignorance, as well as other elements that make people vulnerable to exploitation. Their awareness of these social ills will enable them to take action. Raising people's consciousness regarding their circumstances will change the way they look at the world, and it will change their negative views on reality. Self-reliance is a crucial tool that must be taught to all students.

A more democratic, open South Africa will value the contributions of all its citizens. Postapartheid South Africa must welcome the contributions of all its citizens, including blacks, if quality education is to be a prerequisite. Quality education for blacks will be realized with improvement in curriculum issues, teaching methods, and scope.

8.2 Curriculum Issues

The Bantu education legacy also influences current curriculum issues. The Bantu education system was designed to suit the needs of the economy and to ensure African subordination. Bantu education was never intended to provide blacks with sufficient education in order to allow them to participate intelligently in conducting their lives. Bantu education, like any other colonial education system, is dominated by the Western model of education.

Western education, currently dominating black schools, exposes Africa's young to study England and Europe but are taught almost nothing about their surroundings or those of their African neighbors (Van Hook 1994). Thus, the status quo continues because people whose culture, language, and contributions are not stored in history books are vulnerable to exploitation. Moreover, history is recorded only by those whose contribution is documented in their languages and shared by others. Therefore, the world learns from those whose information is available.

Black South Africans must be contributors to educating their children. Curriculum in black schools that is based on the experiences of black people will lessen a gap between what is taught at schools and what actually takes place in real life. When blacks fail to create knowledge based on their circumstances, it encourages them to compete for limited occupational choices made available by others. Decisions about black education ought to be made by the people it most affects. Defining the role that postapartheid plays in the lives

of blacks must become an integral part of those most likely to benefit.
Curriculum in black schools was designed to restrict the mobility of blacks, and it placed a ceiling on the opportunity for academic improvement (Evans 1992). This curriculum restriction has resulted in a few young people of African descent to receive an academic education. Van Hook (1994) asserted that vocational education training is considered more useful and politically safer for the majority of African students.
Currently, many schools in black communities are being converted into vocational or commercial schools (Collins and Gillespie 1984). This tracking of black students to more vocational training is deliberate and has a hidden intention. Collins and Gillespie suggested:

> Pupils from privileged middle-class backgrounds will be channelled into academic schools, universities and, in time, into professional and managerial jobs. Black working-class children will be forced to make do with technical education or will be pushed out of school on to the job market after an initial period of literacy and numeracy training. (p. 629)

Thus, postapartheid curriculum must promote academic education with strong emphasis on mathematics and science.

The narrow curriculum provision of Bantu education limited the horizons of African young people. In black schools of South Africa, for instance, science is considered appropriate for other racial groups but not suitable for Africans. This view has been a self-fulfilling prophecy to many blacks intimidated by mathematics and science. In order to compete in a technological world, Africans must be competent in science. Attempts to encourage blacks to view science as a necessity will be difficult to accomplish.

Postapartheid curriculum must be viewed in the light of changing circumstances. A modified system of education needs to recognize the importance of African languages and view them in a positive light as English and Afrikaans. The promotion of African languages is likely to encounter several obstacles. As a result of the apartheid legacy, many black people view their languages as inferior and suspect; that is, their languages are denying them access to economic and social opportunities. They also lack an appreciation of the importance of African languages to economic development in the fields of technology, science, and trade, as well as a lack of appreciation of the development of African languages and culture.

The language issue needs to be addressed by encouraging universities to develop vigorous faculties and departments for the study of African languages. Black professionals at all levels must be encouraged to develop materials in vernacular languages. When African languages are fully developed, they will enable blacks to create information and/or knowledge necessary to improve their circumstances. Future curriculum will have to stress the importance of indigenous languages; that is, languages carry the history of the people. Neglecting one's language is akin to neglecting the history of an entire people (Ngugi 1993).

Postapartheid curriculum must instill a high regard for all languages spoken in South Africa but particularly those of blacks. Encouraging blacks to record events that relate to their history is a good start. Blacks are more likely to learn about world history than their local history (Hey 1961; Van Hook 1994). This trend must change if blacks are to gain a full understanding of their history. Blacks must record their history, using their languages, thus reflecting an African point of view. Allowing others to write their history and to record their views will limit their contributions.

Africans will continue to be subjects of data rather than contributors to research of their circumstances if they do not use their languages to record their findings. Dependency on others for information will not cease unless blacks begin to create information based on their languages. If an attempt is not made to provide more education materials in African languages, alienation of these languages will continue.

Baine and Mwamwenda (1994) recommended the following curricula design for the future South Africa:

> -Curricula should be ecologically valid. That is, curricula should teach the knowledge and skills required to function effectively in the political, cultural, economic, and geographical contexts in which students live and in which they are likely to participate in the future.
> -The knowledge and skills taught in curricula should be based on an analysis of local, regional, national, continental, and international trends in technology, industry, and population migration, in addition to other types of changes that may influence future conditions.
> -Given the high dropout rates in schools, especially in the early years, primary level training should not prepare students merely for successive levels of academic training, but for fulfillment of common, daily tasks which students are or will be required to perform in the environments in which

they live, now and in the future. Basic education should involve a careful blending of academic and practical skill training aimed at making students more productive after school.
-Academic subjects such as history, social studies, and geography should initially be related to the context within which students live so as to make the teaching more relevant to them. However, to avoid a narrow perspective, as early as possible, and to the extent possible, the curriculum should expand to a broader, comparative perspective, recognizing regional, national, continental, and international contexts.
-The curricula should promote reflective education that goes beyond rote learning, while teaching students to critically evaluate the acquisition and use of knowledge and skills. A reflective education should be related to personal and cultural development. Students should be taught methods of problem solving, application, analysis, synthesis, and evaluation of knowledge. (pp. 128-130)

Curriculum development for the future of South Africa must reflect current changes in the world in order to be practical and up-to-date. Social change must be accompanied by change in attitudes, as well as change in education.

8.3 Teaching Methods

Teaching methods in black schools need transformation in order to meet new demands in a changing environment. For black students to function in a global society, they must be competitive. Analytical thinking and major scientific contribution will help black students cope with profound change currently occurring in South Africa, as well as in other parts of the world. Updated and creative teaching methods adopted in black schools will help to enhance competitiveness among black learners. Meaningful teaching methods to be adopted in black schools are those that foster the involvement of the total person (physically, emotionally, and cognitively) in an atmosphere that is pleasant, supportive, and warm (Cilliers et al. 1994).

Teachers in black schools must change their method of teaching from one of "stand and deliver" to interactive teaching and learning. They must realize that allowing students to participate in their own learning gives them the opportunity to be creative and imaginative, and it creates the conditions in which the latent potential of the learners is released (Cilliers et al. 1994). By adopting a variety of teaching methods in their classrooms, black teachers will be able to identify what works best for them. Black teachers must be flexible in order to be effective in their teaching methods. Projects based on real-life situations are to be encouraged at all levels in order to enhance children' s imagination and creativity. Developing a habit of reading for pleasure is crucial for black teachers, and it will make them more aware of new teaching strategies. Teachers who are widely read are likely to instill the same values in their students. Moreover, having more tools to experiment with is another positive way of teaching. According to a report by Effective classroom presentations employ a variety of techniques, including demonstrations, small group activity, peer tutoring, and individual work ("Keys To A Quality Multicultural Curriculum" 1992).

Teachers in African schools ought to learn how to use their local environment and to expand from it into the larger world. That is, they must teach children what is familiar or is of interest to them before teaching about remote subjects. Such experiences will help students build a solid knowledge base. Supplementing teaching materials, whenever possible, will make learning experiences more challenging, including the use of the radio, videotapes, slides, television, and press cuttings.

Teachers in African schools need to realize that they cannot prepare students for the rapidly changing world by using outdated teaching methods. The skills that most black students will need are varied, thus requiring several methods of teaching. If teaching methods are not improved in black schools, they will continue to lag behind.

The following characteristics were reported of flexible teaching styles that respond effectively to a wide range of student needs:

-Genuine interaction between students and teachers.
-Support for student-directed learning.
-Encouragement of collaboration among students.
-Integration of language skills with the entire curriculum.
-A focus on reasoning and problem solving rather than simple recall of facts.
-Stimulation of internal, rather than external, motivation. ("Keys To A Quality Multicultural Curriculum" 1992, p. 5)

Even though overcrowdedness and lack of teaching materials are issues of great concern in most black schools, creative and innovative methods are still to be adopted. Teachers are to be encouraged to use what is available in order to help students. Good teaching methods can help students to develop lifelong skills.

8.4 Community Involvement

If black schools in South Africa are to be fundamentally transformed to allow black children access to quality education, then all members of the school community must participate. These members include parents, educators, advocates, community leaders, and policymakers. Education reflects the essence of all communities; therefore, community involvement forms part of black education in a postapartheid South Africa. In order to begin this difficult task, a massive campaign will have to be attempted in order to eradicate illiteracy among blacks. Given the fact that there is a 46 percent illiteracy rate among Africans ("Black Power in South Africa" 1994), it will not be an easy task. The habit of learning, which is lacking among Africans, must be nurtured if illiteracy is to be reduced. Adult education and informal education have to be supported and encouraged. Increasing the opportunity to travel also will help to expand one' s frame of reference.

Black parents need to become actively involved in the education of their children; one way to accomplish that goal is by attending all school meetings dealing with educational issues. Open avenues ought to exist between the home and the school for reporting problems such as truancy, vandalism of school property, theft, and violence. Positive aspects also must be shared with parents, and, where possible, with community members who wish to be involved. Students bring community problems to school; when the school works hand-in-hand with communities, some of the previously discussed problems are reduced.

The assistance of parents in schools is not to be overlooked. For example, those who have certain expertise, such as teachers' aides who can help with discipline and offer student support, must be sought. Other avenues within the community might help to eliminate school dropout. For instance, girls required to assume more responsibilities at home must be offered help to prevent them from leaving school early. Formation of community agencies is one way to provide support groups, as well as school enrichment programs, that will help in the improvement of black education. Because new programs require extensive funding, community members who have the finances to fund black education must be encouraged to do so.

Parents are to be encouraged to help with school field trips. When parents are included as part of the educational endeavor, it changes how students view their education. Moreover, education begins at home; this commitment must be stressed to all black parents. The type of curriculum taught and the methods of teaching used are important for black students (Ogbu 1992); however, more is involved. What the children bring to school, their communities' cultural models or understandings of social realities, and the educational strategies used are as important as within-school factors (Ogbu 1992).

Sebidi (1992) cited the following reasons for allowing parents to participate in the education of their children:

-It will have the good effect of anchoring education where it traditionally belongs: in the community.
-It will destroy the myth that black parents are disinterested in their children's education and have abdicated in favor of total governmental control.
-It will temper the natural impetuosity of young students and help channel their great energy and enthusiasm in positive directions.
-It will lessen the traditional fear parents have in communicating with the youth about "serious" community matters and minimize the ill effects of the so-called age gap.
-It will make teachers realize, in a way they have never realized before, that, in their role as our children's mentors, they are always acting in loco parentis and in no other capacity.
-And, finally, these parent, teacher, and student coalitions will be the initial anvils upon which much of our educational curricular planning and development will begin to take shape. (pp. 38-39)

Research studies have suggested that the role of the community is important in promoting the learning culture. Students must see the connection between the school and their communities. This relationship provides continuity, as well as the practical implications of education. Community involvement in the education of youth has a significant influence on students' educational orientations and behaviors (Ogbu 1992).

8.4.1 How Communities Can Contribute To the Education of Their Children

An informed community is in a better position to encourage its children toward academic and social success. Libraries need to be established in the communities in order to encourage reading for pleasure. After-school programs, when established and supported by the community, add to the social benefits of society. Successful members of the community should give their expertise without being asked. For example, retired physicians can give lectures on health issues and healthy lifestyles; and, during their free time, teachers can give additional help to students.

Children must be informed that their successes do not depend on books alone but on their behavior and attitudes as well. Black communities who provide their children with evidence that its members appreciate and value academic success contribute to the success of their children. The use of the newspaper, radio, television, and computer has a significant impact on a community's educational, economic, and political benefits. In these media, successful, educated, and professional individuals such as doctors, engineers, nurses, teachers, business people, university professors, and lawyers share their success stories or advice.

Positive contributions by members of the community tend to have a great impact on students by teaching them that education is not aimed at benefiting only an individual but is recognized when it benefits the entire community. People who have achieved academically ought to be acknowledged as a way to promote education as an important investment.

8.5 Teaching Diversity Issues in South Africa

> The beauties of nature come in all colors. The strengths of humankind come in many different forms. Each human being is wonderfully unique. All of us contribute in different ways. When we learn to honor the difference and appreciate the mix, we find harmony. (Author unknown)

South Africa is undergoing social and political changes. These changes require that diversity must be addressed. The long history of racial tension in South Africa, as well as growing concerns about minority rights, are reasons to promote teaching issues of diversity.

The primary reason to teach diversity is to provide information aimed at erasing misconceptions about other racial groups, as well as educating the public about differences, to change attitudes or behaviors. Such an appreciation will lessen feelings of distrust, hostility, and even hatred (Terry 1995).

Teaching positive aspects of diversity helps change attitudes regarding how lower classes are viewed. Moreover, youngsters who learn racial tolerance early are likely to be less prejudiced as adults. Leming (1994) stated that it is important for youth to develop an understanding of people of other cultures that, in turn, will help in developing positive attitudes of other cultures. South Africa has suppressed knowledge about the culture of the majority of its citizens. The trend must change, with all cultures given a platform.

There is no need for one culture to be imposed on the majority. A more inclusive presentation of various cultures is more acceptable. Positive portrayal of those affected by discrimination and oppression is a move in the right direction. Sandoval (1995) cited the following components to be considered for effective multicultural education:

1. Redefining of language diversity as an asset rather than a deficit;
2. Using student's language and culture as foundations to build upon rather than tearing those down as ingredients;
3. Seeking, encouraging, and involving parents and communities in the education of their children;
4. Understanding and accepting bilingual education and other language approaches and services as necessary components of equity educators;
5. Developing and promoting an awareness that all students can benefit from diverse languages and cultures. (p. 3)

8.6 Rationale for Teaching Diversity in Schools

South Africa has experienced an intolerance problem, a lawlessness problem, and a violence problem. None of these problems will vanish until schools teach youth responsibility and appropriate behavior. Discipline and character building are supposed to be taught at home, but schools, too, have a responsibility to teach them. Education in multiculturalism provides communication channels; it is a powerful tool to raise awareness about racial tolerance while embracing diversity. Such an undertaking, when adopted, will change the attitudes of many South Africans.

Even though making students of all races aware of diversity, it also is important for black South Africans to realize that the ethnic emphasis that has divided blacks was created for, and served the interests of, privileged groups within the society and has perpetuated racism, sexism, and inequity. Rather than focusing on this type of diversity, students must be taught to challenge it and to be critical of it. Teaching diversity as a positive commodity is fundamental for South Africa to be productive. Being aware of and understanding cultural differences as assets are talents demanded of a postapartheid South Africa (Strenski 1994). With open communication, people are able to address their fears and mistrust, realizing that each person' s contribution counts regardless of magnitude. Raising awareness among people of different racial backgrounds is crucial in changing attitudes. South Africa must find new channels and forums to reach its diverse population.

Diversity values each member of society, maintaining one' s identity for the common good. Diversity, according to Strenski (1994), presumes difference, that is, "value added." Strenski also stated that if differences are harnessed, then a competitive advantage is established. When each member of society is valued, all will strive to be the best possible. Thus, South Africa will benefit from obtaining the talents of all races.

8.7 Making Diversity a Learning Experience

During apartheid domination, certain cultures and races have been devalued. For example, the contributions of blacks were regarded as insignificant and useless. For many black South Africans, apartheid meant harassment and culturally insensitive treatment. Books used in black schools promoted Western civilization, while lowering the role of Africans (Nkabinde 1993b). This exercise has resulted in low self-esteem among black students. Sweeping political changes in South Africa also are resulting in increasing numbers of students of various racial and cultural backgrounds to attend the same schools. Thus, multicultural education is desirable in South African schools in order to promote an understanding and respect for other racial groups.

Diversity has been used negatively to promote tribalism among black South Africans. For example, enforcement of ethnic differences has never been an issue for other racial minorities, but it has been a crucial issue for blacks. As a result, diversity in a South African context has meant division rather than national unity. Diversity, as discussed in this section, is not intended as division; it is aimed at acknowledging all contributions without lowering those made by others. Diversity is regarded as a learning experience, not a source of conflict.

Diversity is not an imposition of one culture over another but respect for all cultures. The following points were cited as keys to a multicultural curriculum:

-Describe histories, cultures, and languages as dynamic wholes.
-Present events, issues, and concepts from the perspectives of diverse racial and ethnic groups.
-Examine the impact and contributions of various cultures.
-Describe differences among cultures without judging them.
-Focus on concepts of racism, class stratification, and victimization.
-Emphasize the value of decision making and citizen action. ("Keys To A Quality Multicultural Curriculum 1992, p. 5)

Education reflects the culture of people, whereas multicultural education affirms the value of diversity without overemphasizing cultural differences negatively. Educational content must relate to one's life, but it must not limit one's imagination. Education for the sake of culture alone, without the realization of human potential, is meaningless. Historically, black education in South Africa has been dominated by European perspective. Textbooks are written by Europeans, which overplay the achievement of Europeans and underplay the African culture (Hey 1961). Black children usually learn about the history of Europe before knowing their own history, rarely learning about themselves and their environment. Consequently, black children see themselves through the eyes of others.

Multicultural education in South Africa ought to be a strategy to combat negative racial stereotypes and discrimination. This type of education will have to allow all citizens to be valued for what they have to offer. People in South Africa come from many backgrounds; therefore, diversity must be viewed as an asset rather than a disadvantage. Focusing on the strengths of all individuals connects humanity and helps them to work together (Riley 1995). All South African citizens are to be given an opportunity to experience educational content that is personally meaningful. Children from all backgrounds have a right to be taught their history. All South Africans deserve an opportunity to determine their future by making positive contributions socially, educationally, and economically. Multicultural education in South Africa must erase unfounded fears associated with racial differences and prejudice. Tolerance is a positive aspect vital to racial integration. Racial hatred is a learned behavior, but it can be unlearned. South African schools have perpetuated racial hatred, but the trend needs to be changed through multicultural education. Respect for diversity will be achieved by adopting the following strategies:

◄Schools are to become centers in which respect for life or racial tolerance is promoted. Textbooks, the dominant source of information in schools, must reflect the cultural diversity in a more positive light. Books that are offensive to other groups ought to be removed from schools. Much work must be done regarding multicultural curriculum materials. The demand for multicultural education, coupled with changes occurring in South Africa, must be recognized. Teachers' contributions and those of experts in the field will make a difference.

◄The devaluation of African culture and racial features in South Africa need to be discouraged. All societies devalue the culture and characteristics of workers regardless of race (Powell 1994). Devaluing implies that the worth of individuals is to be based on their achievements, not race. Multiculturalism in South Africa does not mean favoritism or reversed apartheid, but it does mean allowing all citizens the opportunity to unlock their inner abilities. Discrimination must not rob people of their opportunity to succeed.

◄Because the media in South Africa is the influential tool that shapes the public' s perception of reality, adopting it to influence positively attitudes on diversity is recommended. For example, the media (television, radio, newspaper, and computer) have not been fully utilized to portray positively those cultures that suffered under apartheid.

◄Local experts invited to institutions of learning to share their views generate mutual gains for all members of the learning community.

◄Learning respect begins at home. This respect will spill over to society, the workplace, and, consequently, everywhere. This attempt is difficult to accomplish, but nothing is impossible.

◄ Diversity among blacks must be challenged, where applied, to divide and rule. Students are to be made aware that even minority groups in South Africa are from different cultural backgrounds, but they live in harmony with each other. If Africans are to avoid conflicts, they must recognize that in unity is strength.

◄ Black students must be made aware that unless they respect themselves and show compassion, cooperation, courage, and self-discipline that they cannot extend those values toward people who are different from them. Schools must nurture values in order to make the youth productive members of society. Reference to black students, in particular, is used because, as a class of people, they have suffered devaluation and discrimination.

◄ Because of apartheid domination, minority groups seem to know more about the majority culture than they know about themselves. Teaching the majority culture through their eyes will strengthen their position.

◄ Even though relevant positive materials on black cultures are insufficient, long strides in that area will be made by Africans. Multicultural education in South Africa will be necessary in order to unite a diverse population while educating the public about positive aspects of each culture.

8.8 Conclusion

Throughout the educational history of South Africa, instruction at all levels has been tied to Western beliefs and ways of life. The views of the majority were systematically silenced. Thus, whatever was presented about the culture of the majority was sometimes distorted. Therefore, black South Africans must be challenged to ensure that their contributions of textbooks, as well as other curriculum components, will determine their educational direction.

The changing faces of South Africa cannot afford to waste the talents of any individual. Embracing diversity is a prerequisite for a future South Africa. Multicultural education is seen as a way to teach tolerance, acceptance, and a commitment to the unique worth of all people as teachable and learnable attitudes (Terry 1995). Teaching students acceptable behavior is neither new nor special. Some students will always ignore what is acceptable and opt for the unacceptable. Some teachers, rather than teaching what is ethically correct, will inject prejudice and hatred. In the final analysis, parents must play the primary role in teaching responsible behavior.

Parents, along with the school, must teach responsibility, showing children the path to academic and social success. The best students are those who can differentiate between right and wrong while performing to the best of their ability.

Chapter 9

Beyond Bantu Education: Changes, Challenges, And Harsh Realities

9.1 Introduction

The integration of education departments was announced in 1995. Under a new regulation, all of South Africa's students will be taught under a single educational system regardless of race. Will a unitary system of education have a meaningful role to play in ensuring quality of education throughout South Africa? Obviously, the answer is "no!" Legislation alone does not mean radical changes. Moreover, the situation in South Africa is unique because it involves a process of integrating a majority group into a privileged minority group (Penny et al. 1993).

Planners of education in South Africa must devise ways of improving black education that benefit all people, including those in remote rural areas. Many rural communities lack access to information, they experience poverty, and they are illiterate. These people require educational structures that address their immediate circumstances. Such an educational system must be more practical and realistic in order to address the lived experiences and aspirations of Africans. The culture of learning and teaching must receive more attention at all levels. A home that values education and has educational materials to stimulate learning will help children form a solid foundation for later achievements.

◄Educational changes do not mean name changes, but rather address ways in which quality education is enhanced in black schools. Change agents such as teachers, parents, students, educational planners, and the community must be utilized effectively for better results. These change agents must be well-informed to be effective.

◄Laws alone cannot guarantee the implementation of quality education. People's attitudes and dedication are responsible to ensure that what is implemented will benefit society. Laws are safeguards against human abuses, and they are crucial in designing educational programs acceptable to all citizens.

◄The government's willingness to encourage local participation in the design of suitable educational programs is encouraging. Teachers who have firsthand experience with what transpires in the classroom are excellent resources. Students, too, when consulted to obtain their views on educational issues are a vital source of information. Financial support will help professionals who have talent but lack the resources to perform their talents.

◄Parents, students, and the community must all make contributions to black education. Education is a collaborative effort. Popular debate about black education includes, but is not limited to, improved quality of education.

◄One challenge facing postapartheid education is the need to make educational provisions that will cater to the hundreds of thousands of black youth frozen out of the troubled school system by political disruption. Violence in black townships, as well as other parts of the country, prior to the 1994 elections, contributed greatly to the breakdown of authority within the school system. This period also was characterized by long periods of absenteeism in many schools. Adult education and/or night schools must be introduced in order to rehabilitate those currently excluded from the educational system.

◄Technical- and vocational-oriented schools in South Africa are options to be used in order to embark on an intensive effort to provide useful skills to blacks in an effort to reduce unemployment. Vocational training will meet the challenge of providing the majority of black people with skills and expertise, enabling them to become contributing and productive members of postapartheid South Africa. People who possess skills that are in demand are more likely to find jobs. Vocational training is an alternative to academic training. The option is to be made available to those who cannot benefit from academic training. Moreover, academic training for all citizens is a myth. The popularity of technical and vocational training, thus, becomes necessary for other sections of society, particularly for pupils who show interest and can benefit from it.

◄ Existing training facilities to teach African languages in all tertiary institutions in South Africa ought to be expanded. Language is seen as a liberating tool in terms of writing and expressing one's views, and it is an instrument of improving one's condition. All languages are capable of achieving those goals, as long as the users make an effort.

The future education for black South Africans must address the following challenges:

◄ Clearly defining aims and goals of education, especially education that will be meaningful and will appeal to all South Africans

◄ Addressing inequities in black schools without compromising the quality of education

◄ Addressing the issue of curriculum modification, writing appropriate books, and providing teaching materials in black schools

◄ Improving black teachers' qualifications and preparing them for new roles in postapartheid South Africa

◄ Rehabilitating the millions of youth who dropped out of school because of political disruptions and making provisions for the unemployed, as well as the unemployable

◄ Empowering communities to take part in the education of their children

◄ Empowering all black people to be agents of change rather than expecting change

◄ Effecting educational changes to address the quality of education rather than the quantity

◄ Educating women to form part of the educational transformation. (Black women in South Africa suffer the dual strict code of compliance imposed by tradition, as well as the law of the country, and they lack the knowledge of their rights, which all add to exploitation.)

9.2 Will a Unitary Education System Achieve Anything?

A centralized education system is necessary for equal distribution of resources, as well as establishing educational standards acceptable to all South Africans. The primary purpose of a unitary education system is threefold: (a) to equalize educational opportunities by allowing the center to distribute finances, resources, and manpower to various regions; (b) to permit and ensure nationally accepted educational standards; and (c) to encourage and support regional educational initiatives. Unquestionably, a unitary education system will not automatically guarantee equality and quality in black schools, which still suffer from the legacy of a poor educational base.

On the other hand, a unitary education system will guarantee basic educational services to all children in South Africa. A unitary education system also is believed to be easier to monitor and control than a decentralized system. Compulsory free education will help when parents cannot contribute sufficient monies for basic educational services or cannot contribute at all. The quality of education for the majority of blacks is likely to remain the same unless radical changes are implemented in teaching methods, curricula, and the organization of black education as a whole.

Comprehensive changes in the content of black education will require a lot of money and highly skilled people to implement. Small businesses and the private sector, when encouraged to provide financial help for the improvement of black education, will help ease the situation. The introduction of a unitary education system is meant to benefit all, particularly disadvantaged groups, but it also is necessary to promote regional initiatives to improve education. A unitary education system has been criticized for making it possible for an elite group to control the distribution of resources to reward or punish regions, communities, and individuals (Kabzems and Chimedza 1995).

For instance, the process of provincialization of the Department of Education, emphasizing regional and local powers, is meant to give freedom to the provinces in order to determine how they want to manage and/or improve their local schools. The provinces also determine how to spend finances in order to address local- and state-identified problems and purposes. Local control of education, while necessary, can cause wide variations in providing education.

A fundamental objective of a unitary system of education is to raise the standard of education through improved schooling for all citizens, as well as the equalization of opportunities. Equal access to information and knowledge, improvement of teaching and learning, and making available numerous courses in order to enhance a variety of career paths will involve the complete transformation of the entire educational system for blacks. Therefore, a unitary education system is aimed at promoting greater effectiveness and affordability of educational services, as well as providing attainable and acceptable educational opportunities to South African communities and, in particular, to the victims of past discrimination and the poor. In order to be effective, a unitary education system must address the following:

◄Development of a well-articulated educational policy that reflects the needs of all South African, thus ensuring accessibility.

◄Promotion of democratic ideals such as recognizing and respecting individual rights, social responsibility, and the freedom of expression, thought, and movement are to be guaranteed for all South Africans.

◄Accountability at all levels of government in the control and management of education is needed.

◄Special services for people with disabilities must be made available to all South Africans.

◄Exclusion of persons in education because of race, religion, political affiliation, and/or handicap is regarded as unconstitutional and ought to be discouraged.

◄Access to information and the contribution of all individuals to knowledge are valued assets to be embraced by all humanity.

◄Cultural domination, which has persisted over the years, is to be replaced by more democratic values in which all cultures share the right to exist and to be developed.

◄All South Africans have the right to develop their potential to the fullest without being discouraged or harassed.

◄A strong foundation in education will enrich the child' s physical, mental, moral, and social development, which will last a lifetime.

◄Teachers must have more input about what they teach, as well as the assessment of their students. In-service and better training of teachers will add to the provision of human resources needed to provide quality education.

◄Promotion of indigenous languages is important and must be supported by the government at all levels. Approximately 50 percent of South Africans do not have the necessary language and life skills to participate in political proceedings and to promote their own development and that of their communities ("Affirmative Education" 1994). Language is a prerequisite for effective communication; therefore, vernacular languages must occupy an important position as well.

◄ Adult education needs to be promoted in order to reduce illiteracy and to cater to the needs of students who are too old to benefit from formal education.

9.3 Conclusion

In the past, Africans who have experienced severe containment in their access to education and knowledge must find innovative ways to replace Bantu education. Unless there is substantial funding for black schools, retraining opportunities for black teachers, and a curricular change, the legacy of Bantu education cannot be expected to change much (even with the repeal of the education segregation policy). Few African children will be able to attend costly white schools. Even if there are more nonwhite children from middle-class families, flocking to white schools is likely to be selective and, in some instances, resisted.

Communities in conservative towns and neighborhoods will maintain racial segregation in their schools, whatever the law may be. Strong regional autonomy also will assist in keeping schools racially segregated. The superior levels of services available in white schools make them more attractive to the nonwhite groups of South Africa. Therefore, the prospect of white children moving into black schools is unthinkable. Consequently, not all black children can be accommodated in the few privileged schools of South Africa. It is recommended that the focus on educational issues in South Africa need to be more on quality and the expansion of opportunities for all children than on desegregation.

Substantial variations in black education need to focus on curricular changes, improved teaching methods, and overall improvement. These changes will not occur quickly because of financial restraints; a gradual process is required. The vision of postapartheid education is, therefore, to improve the standards and quality in black schools. Postapartheid education will help empower blacks to make the most of their lives. The government of national unity must help communities do more for themselves. Education requires communities to take charge of their lives.

Africans in South Africa must be made aware that change is experienced only when participating in the process. Another important component of change is that with new opportunities come responsibilities. In this connection, educational planners, teachers, students, and parents must have a plan of action and a strong commitment to education in order to address current problems facing black schools. Education is about contribution to human enlightenment. The application of knowledge has resulted in creative endeavors aimed at making the world a better place to live. Thus, respect that goes with being educated is attributed to human achievement. Africans in a postapartheid South Africa must demonstrate their commitment to improve learning if they wish to be respected and counted among the world' s creators of knowledge.

Chapter 10

The Financing Of Education

10.1 Introduction

Funding constitutes an important aspect that influences the quality and type of education a country can afford for its citizens. In the new South Africa, financing education has emerged as a major topic of discussion among decision makers. A quality education system requires immense educational resources and finances, which South Africa currently cannot afford. Many black schools are faced with numerous problems such as poorly constructed buildings staffed with poorly paid and poorly trained teachers.

A basic three-year university or technical degree currently costs approximately R35,000 for fees, books, and accommodations, which few can afford ("Investing Cents Will Make Sense for Your Child" 1995). According to the report, in fifteen years, these costs will soar from R110,000 to R250,000. Clearly, the new government has numerous challenges in financing education. Higher expectations among those who have suffered educational deprivation also demand immediate attention.

However, because the level of poverty among Africans is so great, serious inequalities will continue to exist between urban and rural areas and between the rich and poor (Pillay 1992); consequently, the state must use its financial educational resources to reduce these inequities. The previous government used different strategies to amass finances for African education. One method of financing

Bantu education was through taxation. In the historical background of this method, financing postapartheid education needs to be understood.

10.2 Historical Background

Africans have paid directly or indirectly for the education of their children. The methods used to generate educational funds for Bantu education have varied (Hurwitz 1964). Missions and churches prior to 1904 relied primarily on their own resources and the taxation of Africans. In 1904, the mission schools were subsidized by the government, which later took control of all African schools (Geber and Newman 1980). After the union in 1910, different systems of taxation, adopted by various provinces, resulted in the uneven development of African education.

When Bantu education was implemented, the same type of funding of African education continued. The trend was the maintenance of a special account for Bantu education, which, according to Geber and Newman (1980), was R13 million in addition to approximately 100 percent of the taxes paid by Africans in 1963. According to Hyslop (1993), this type of funding negatively affected the educational standards in black schools. A tremendous reduction was realized in per-capita expenditure for each child (in 1953 = R17,08 and in 1960 = R12,46), thus deteriorating student-teacher ratios (in 1946 = 42,31:1 and in 1960 = 54,7:1) (Hyslop 1993, p. 401). The state also abolished feeding schemes in black schools.

The state used two additional methods to recover monies for African education. For example, it had been a common government practice to increase African taxation in order to pay for education. Additional school fees had always been collected from African parents. Geber and Newman (1980) cited the following measures implemented by the government as an attempt to keep the cost of African education relatively low:

(a) The provision that part of the cost of erecting new primary schools in urban areas would be recovered by levying a special tax on Africans living in government homes in the area.
(b) All new postprimary schools erected were to be half funded by the African school boards.
(c) The daily work of cleaning schools was to be the responsibility of pupils under the supervision of teachers.

(d) To bolster the numbers at school, the "hot-seat" or "platoon" system was introduced for preprimary standards, where the number of hours teaching per day was reduced to three, and two groups of pupils were taught successively in the same classrooms. (p. 63)

Occasionally, various volunteer bodies, as well as commercial and religious organizations, contributed toward funding African education. The cost of African education varies, with private schooling the most expensive. Additional expenses in African education include school uniforms, textbooks, writing materials, and other school-related materials, which African parents are required to provide.

Black South Africans have been directly responsible for financing their own education through school fees or taxation. Even though central control has been maintained through the creation of "A Native Development Account," black people have remained responsible for their educational services (Hurwitz 1964). African taxation has continued to increase, as has the population.

The rapid population growth has resulted in limited funds, as well as the increasing demands for education facilities. Consequently, the African community has been faced with increasing demands to finance its own education. This demand has been made more difficult by the limited economic prospects of blacks in general. Job reservation, influx control, and overcrowded Bantu areas have continued to add to economic difficulties (Hurwitz 1964).

10.3 Current Educational Funding

The cost of education for Africans varies according to geographic area; for example, estimates for the Soweto range from R12.50 for the primary schools to R34 for the secondary schools (Geber and Newman 1980). The cost does not include additional expenses such as school uniforms, transportation, field trips, and textbooks. At the same time, the average income for a Soweto blue-collar worker is approximately R160 per month, which is a fraction spent on food ("Black Power in South Africa" 1994).

In 1995, the educational dispensation declared that education was to be free and compulsory for all six-year-old children in South Africa (Malherbe, Naidoo, Meintjies, Nagoor, and Brown 1995). According to the report, this declaration would place between 150,000 and 300,000 children in schools who otherwise would not be attending school. The state's ability to fund free, compulsory education is likely to be severely constrained by the economic realities and growing demands for social needs such as housing and health. South Africa recently experienced a sharp increase in the enrollment of students in the primary school. This increase has led to overcrowding and declining quality in some black schools. In the long run, the South African government will be forced to look for creative ways to fund black education, including merit scholarships, student loans, taxation, school fund-raising, and community financing. Donor support ought to be used as the last resort because it tends to encourage dependency, as well as other problems.

10.3.1 Merit Scholarships

In South Africa, bursaries and merit scholarships have been given to students on the basis of merit and individual need. Many African students in various educational institutions have benefited; however, such schemes have been more popular in higher education. Scholarships have allowed students with greater intellectual capacity and limited financial means to obtain a better education.

Enrollment in higher education among Africans, in general, is low. Most students tend to come from relatively wealthy families, with bursaries usually benefiting a small underprivileged social group. Bursaries and merit scholarships within higher education encourage enrollment among students from poor families. Therefore, the government and the private sector need to continue to offer financial support in the form of bursaries and scholarships.

Even though the state will remain directly responsible for a larger part of educational funding and development, additional funding from donors is a necessity. This arrangement is favored because it does not limit the selection of students from wealthy families at the exclusion of otherwise intellectually capable, but poor, students. Because qualified students from disadvantaged backgrounds cannot be denied access to education, it is desirable and recommended.

10.3.2 Loans

Loans are another method of allowing students to borrow money in order to finance their education. The advantage for loans is that any student, regardless of academic standing, is free to apply for assistance. Pillay (1992) argued that loans improve student motivation, encouraging learners to become more cost conscious and thoughtful about future career prospects. Several disadvantages are associated with loans. For example, many students might avoid using loans because of the fear of accumulating debts. Interest rates also might discourage students from poor families in using the loan scheme. The overall success of a loan depends on the rate of cost recovery.

10.3.3 Education Taxes

Historically, African parents contributed to the education taxes during the apartheid era. Such taxes, no matter how humble, accumulated the needed educational expenditure. This method is to continue, with adjustments where needed. Charging a percentage of one' s income might not be favored by the rich, who will be required to pay more taxes in support of the poor. Equalizing expenditures for all children by raising subsidies to the level enjoyed by privileged groups would consume one third of the national budget and would have crippling side effects on the economy ("School Lessons Remain Unlearned" 1995). Consequently, the government has few choices.

Obligatory education taxes on a sliding scale, according to income, is another option that policymakers ought to consider. Affluent parents, of course, will be able to select schools for their children. Private schools or schooling abroad also are options that might prevent many from paying education taxes.

10.3.4 Donor Support

Foreign donor support is not the answer to the educational problems of South Africa. Donor support is to be accepted temporarily in order to address the pressing needs of the country, but not as a way of life. Many problems are associated with external financial support. For example, this type of support could be withdrawn at any time such as during a recession. Moreover, wealthy countries might become weary of being financial supporters of poor nations indefinitely. Possible pitfalls are associated with dependency on donor support, which South Africans must avoid.

For example, some ex-colonial countries in Africa have experienced their education systems being "colonized" by donor countries. That is, donations were used to influence the education policy and delivery systems to such an extent that indigenous needs and resources were ignored (Van Zyl 1995). External funding sometimes comes with restrictions and/or conditions that might not be favorable to African countries. These restrictions continue to place countries in conditions susceptible to external manipulation and pressure.

Mwamwenda (1994) explained that Africans must solve their problems at the primary school level, as well as at the secondary and tertiary levels. Educational institutions that were nonexistent during the colonial period currently are in abundance, producing employable individuals aimed at benefiting the labor market.

10.3.5 Community Financing

In many developing countries, the idea of education through self-help financing is not uncommon. Kenya, for example, adopted community financing (known as "Harambee") after independence, which has been a popular method of financing education. Since independence, Kenya provides a larger percentage (60 percent) of local financing for its secondary schools than other countries in which community financing is popular (Mwiria 1990). Other countries in which community financing is a common practice are Nigeria, Zambia, Botswana, and Tanzania (Mwiria 1990).

Community financing of schools has become a necessity in many developing countries because of rapidly expanding educational systems, as well as the economic realities faced by many African countries. Community financing schemes vary from country-to-country. Some communities have built schools, whereas others have paid teachers' salaries and/or provided teaching materials. Community financing is not new in South Africa. The pitiful contribution of the state to black education, in some instances, has forced these communities to finance their own schools, ranging from paying teachers' salaries to erecting school buildings. Teaching aids and office equipment also have been provided by community members ("Bright Ideas To Get Our Schools Buzzing" 1995).

However, community financing has been limited. Efforts encouraging communities to finance their local schools could be performed in many ways. For example, local craftsmen and artists could be encouraged to sell their work in order to benefit community schools. For African children to benefit from schooling, they must be healthy; that is, good eating habits make them stronger and more capable of facing challenges associated with learning. Local farmers can support the schools by selling produce. Donations of food by farmers and private businesses are recommended programs to be used in the schools' nutritional scheme. Maintenance of such schemes benefit children from poor communities. Feeding schemes also ensure that no child starves while at school.

Currently, there is a shortage of suitable accommodations for teachers in rural areas. Such a need discourages many qualified teachers from seeking employment in these locations. This situation affects children' s learning; that is, teachers attracted to rural schools are poorly qualified. Community efforts, combined with government support, will help to improve the situation.

Community efforts in financing education are good, but they also can be problematic. These efforts have been criticized for reinforcing, rather than reducing, existing disparities in education (Mwiria 1990). For example, poor neighborhoods do not have the same amount of money or community support as rich neighborhoods, which has a significant impact on the quality of education.

On the positive side, community efforts usually help in fostering links between educational institutions and their communities. This relationship encourages students to become involved in community programs that enrich their communities. Such schemes also promote a sense of ownership in which community efforts are valued by all stakeholders. That is, people support what they create!

10.3.6 Company's Financing

Many companies have sponsored students in various disciplines, particularly at the university level. Employees' children have been targeted for financial support by private companies. In other instances, companies have supported former employees who later contributed to the company' s growth. Encouraging the private sector to fund education is not a new phenomenon in South Africa. Involving the private sector in funding education is valuable.

The private sector' s support of education must be encouraged in order to boost underfunded schools. This support can be manifested in various ways such as providing textbooks, desks, cupboards, and computers, as well as upgrading facilities. Involving the private sector in education will have a positive impact on many African schools that suffer from a lack of resources. Several companies have supported African schools. However, this support has been sporadic and limited, but it must be encouraged.

10.4 Summary

The quality of black education in South Africa is dependent on state funding. Funding levels, whether state or private, determine the availability of school buildings, textbooks, teaching materials, laboratories, equipment, excursions, and virtually all that the school offers (September 1990). The quality of what is being taught and how it is being taught depends on funding.

Therefore, increased economic opportunities for Africans equate to a higher quality of education. In short, African education is not an individual matter but a national responsibility. The new government must help those communities committed to improving the quality of education by donating funds. On the other hand, the government must limit dependency on foreign aid. Dependency is difficult to terminate; that is, Africans recently received political independence, but the economy is still dominated by the minority.

A partial solution in financing African education is to reduce the population. Reducing population growth is necessary in order to realize step-by-step improvements in the economy and education. A large segment of the population in South Africa lives in poverty, with little chance of breaking the chain (Chandler 1995).

More educational funding, accompanied by the efficient distribution of resources, are keys to the improvement of quality education. The state must distribute its financial resources by investing more money in primary education, which will give a higher rate of return (Goldemberg 1988). The concept of free education must disappear from the vocabulary of South Africans. Education has never been free, and it will never be free. Society must continue to fund education directly or indirectly.

Population control among Africans is a necessary condition for the state in order to afford the expansion of educational facilities. The quality of life will be enhanced by educating men and women to see the value of children, not in numbers, but in their overall well-being (Norward 1994). The African population is the fastest growing of all racial groups in South Africa. For example, the fertility rates in 1990, according to Eckstein (1994), were as follows: blacks = 4.7, Asians = 2.3, coloreds = 2.8, and whites = 1.7 (p. 49). The new government will have difficulty meeting the expectations of a rapidly growing black population. The people must be encouraged to be self-sufficient and independent. Incentives for families to have fewer children are recommended. The maintenance and encouragement of local initiatives in funding education remain important.

Chapter 11

Africa's Lessons For South Africa

11.1 Introduction

Africa's educational systems have continued to advance since independence, which began in the late fifties to beyond the sixties. Their successes and failures are lessons for the South African educational system as it attempts to bury Bantu education. South Africa has an advantage to learn lessons from other African countries. That is, people must understand the forces responsible for enhancing educational successes, as well as forces that hinder social and economic developments in these countries. In understanding Africa, many African countries, after independence, had taken over the political infrastructure of their state from former colonizers only (Cowder 1987). Consequently, for many African countries, their economic infrastructures remained largely controlled by colonial powers. These forces include economic, social, and political instability, which is sometimes experienced by African countries.

Many African countries, for practical economic reasons, have found it difficult to rid themselves of their colonial past. Thus, the trend for many has been the adoption of colonial education with little or no adaptations. Such practices have led to continuous dependency in terms of educational materials, personnel, and educational funding. The more issues of colonial education and its aims are discussed, investigated, and analyzed, the better the chances are for the public to comprehend Africa's dilemma.

Colonial education for Africans did not lead to true knowledge and understanding. Such education prepared Africans to be of service to their colonial masters. Clarke (1991) explained that the scramble for Africa and colonialism, led by European powers, threw African societies out of balance. These societies quickly learned new ways of living and educating their citizens. Traditional ways of learning and surviving in the African environment, useful before colonialism and domination, were no longer essential (Clarke 1991). Colonial education proved ineffective for many Africans who seemed to have forgotten much of their own methods of adapting to their own environments; in fact, they had not completely mastered the ways of their colonial masters (Clarke 1991).

Colonial education was never intended to help Africans liberate themselves; on the contrary, it was meant to train Africans to serve alien powers, in particular, those who colonized them. Therefore, Africans became consumers of foreign education in which their educational input was never encouraged and/or desired. Textbooks and teaching materials used in African schools were imported and similar to their colonial masters. This exercise became a good way of allowing Africans to view their world through the eyes of those who controlled them. Moreover, it perpetuated dependence of African people on other people, in particular, their former masters.

In almost all independent African states after independence, the trend did not change. Generally, after independence, African states shared (a) a colonial heritage, (b) an education system inferior in quality and quantity, and (c) economic and financial problems typical of Third World countries (Agar 1983).

After gaining independence, many African states experienced an increased dependence on the advanced capitalist countries, as well as the domination of local economies by a small elite group of the powerful and wealthy (Maliyamkono 1980). The role of education in many African countries has followed a similar trend. For example, foreign funding, imported experts, and foreign educational models have dominated many educational domains in Africa, which has been Africa's dilemma. Dependency, in any form, has never freed a people from bondage.

Given the colonial past of many African countries, it is logical to conclude that educational expansion, far from rendering social upliftment and/or economic development, served to render education little more than a sophisticated mechanism for the recruitment of elites (Maliyamkono 1980; Weiss 1994). Therefore, black Africa needs to define and implement its own educational aims and/or policies before it can rid itself of colonial education.

11.2 The Case of Nigeria

When Nigeria obtained its independence in 1960, the country placed highest priority on education. The end of British rule in Nigeria also left the country divided into three main regions, namely, North, East, and West. This regionalization of the country also meant regionalization of education (Fafunwa 1974). Each of the three regions began competing, trying to outdo the other in providing educational amenities for its own area (Fafunwa 1974).

Universal primary education was introduced throughout the country. When the British colonial administration transferred the responsibility of education to the Nigerians, it meant that the structure of education would remain unchanged (Obiakor 1992). For example, the education structure remained the same as it had during colonial times, i.e., six years of primary education, five years of secondary education, and four years of university education (Obiakor 1992).

11.2.1 Primary Education

The aims of primary education in Nigeria are threefold: (a) to help students master the three "Rs" (reading, writing, and arithmetic), developing permanent literacy; (b) to develop solid standards of individual conduct and behavior; and (c) to acquire some skill and appreciation of the value of manual work (Fafunwa 1974).

The major changes that occurred soon after independence, such as the free universal primary education scheme, were marked with many challenges. Qualified teachers were not available to teach in newly erected schools. Insufficient time for planning resulted in the shortage of buildings and equipment, as well as the mismanagement of education (Fafunwa 1974). Local authorities, expected to meet the financial requirements in providing buildings, did not have the funds.

11.2.2 Secondary Education

Secondary education in Nigeria remained basically the same as it had during colonial times. For example, secondary grammar schools, patterned on the English grammar schools, are still in existence (Fafunwa 1974). At the secondary level, trade schools, technical schools, and trade centers also are available for students unable to continue with general schooling.

In Nigeria, all schools are partially funded by the government whether operated by private individuals, missions, or local authorities (Fafunwa 1974). Examinations are still common evaluation measures of students' performance.

11.2.3 Language of Instruction

In Nigeria, children are taught through their mother tongue during the first three or four years of primary school. The switch to English as the medium of instruction normally occurs after four years of schooling (Fafunwa 1974). A debate continues among Nigerian professionals whether mother-tongue instruction should be used from six to twelve years of schooling (Bamgbose 1991).

11.2.4 Curriculum

Maintaining the status quo in education has proved to be a disadvantage for Nigeria. That is, it has failed to address the changing conditions of the country socially, culturally, economically, and politically.

Relying on foreign aid as an answer to the educational crisis has not proven to be effective in Nigeria, as well as in other parts of Africa. In fact, it has attracted outsiders who do not have full knowledge of the needs of Africans and, moreover, who do not have their long-term interests at heart. Heavy reliance of African countries on foreign experts has had a serious impact on encouraging and developing local talents.

African governments have spent a fortune importing experts from various countries rather than improving the qualifications of African teachers. Again, such importation of foreign experts has not proven fruitful; rather, it has given the impression among some Africans that "what is good is foreign." Until African communities, parents, teachers, and students make a substantial contribution to their education, it is unlikely that Africa's problems will cease to exist. Such contribution will not occur when Africans are economically, culturally, and socially dependent on foreign experts.

11.2.5 Problems Faced by Nigeria's Intellectuals

The postindependence era in Nigeria has witnessed remarkable changes within the professional community. The country has produced too many specialists in some fields and only a few in others (Mgbejiofor 1977). The large number of Nigerians, who have received Western education outside their country immediately after independence, has not had the final say about areas of specialization. According to Mgbejiofor, scholarships offered by foreign countries determined what people were supposed to study rather than giving them the option to choose what they wanted to study.

Nigerian intellectuals, who studied abroad, found themselves learning about subjects that would neither benefit them nor their country. Later, some realized that they were unable to make solid contributions to Nigeria and that their selected fields were more a result of chance than of planning (Mgbejiofor 1977). According to Mgbejiofor, continuation of such policy means continuation of the wasteful human potential among Nigerian intellectuals.

Because of the lack of sufficient facilities for tertiary education after independence, the most able Nigerians studied abroad; in fact, many were encouraged to reside abroad. Davies (1995) reported that, since independence, Africa has lost hundreds of thousands of highly educated professionals who have emigrated to Western countries in search of job satisfaction. According to Davies, of all the developing regions of the world, Africa has been hit more powerfully by this exodus.

Another dilemma centers on the belief among intellectuals that education is a door to a better life and higher living standards. This notion creates a strong correlation between education and economic and/or material gain, which is not realistic. Associating level of educational attainment with economic wealth is often misleading. Mgbejiofor (1977) stated that the only way to improve the relationship between work and education is to stop seeing education for its economic benefit and to make students and parents understand that it is meant to open the way to thinking and knowing. Education ought to impart to African children a sense of self-reliance that will make them choose to explore the unknown and to discover new domains. True education is aimed at boosting individual performance and productivity for the benefit of society.

Mgbejiofor (1977) described limited access to publishing firms by Nigerian intellectuals as the most pressing problem. Many intellectuals find it difficult to have their academic work published for public use. The limited access to publishing firms, coupled with limited financial resources, ensure that Nigeria continues reliance on its colonial master. For example, most of the textbooks and educational materials used in the schools do not reflect Nigeria' s life and culture. These materials still bear the colonial past, as well as the colonial view of the country and its people.

11.2.6 Research

Developed countries have proven what learning and research are capable of doing for society, whereas developing countries have used university research for academic purposes only rather than solving socioeconomic problems (Woodhall 1995). African governments and policymakers do not seem to understand the association between academic research and national development. Once that connection is drawn, much will change in Africa' s socioeconomic conditions.

Consequently, Africa' s prospects for educational and economic development are dim unless its research base is enhanced. Educational research in Africa must focus on the identification of problems and solutions that Africans perceive to be their own (Eisemon 1989). In turn, research in Africa will accelerate the development of knowledge as a commodity for exchange on the open world market (Woodhouse 1985).

Nigeria, like many African countries, has been slow in research development. Woodhouse (1985) stated that, even in Nigeria, which is solid in terms of the numbers of scientists engaged in research relative to the remainder of the African continent, research is not considered an appropriate, high-status job for an individual with academic credentials such as a PhD. Lack of rewards and/or financial incentives for Nigerian professionals has prompted numerous PhD people to forsake their research positions.

Woodhouse (1985) noted that some doctoral people in Nigeria are forced by family circumstances to look for more lucrative positions in public service and/or private business. More than losing the brain power of the nation, this state of affairs also reduces Nigeria's capacity to use research to benefit the development of the country. Nigerian youth also are denied the opportunity to be trained by the best qualified people. No winner is found in this situation; that is, even professionals may lose by not being able to apply their talents better.

African governments need to offer more rewards and incentives as a way to recognize research projects aimed at solving their social problems. African professionals must place more value on conducting research than on making a fortune. Such practices will benefit a new generation of African professionals and will provide the youth with appropriate role models.

The low priority accorded to university research is not only a Nigerian problem but it affects Africa as a whole. Djangmah (1995) supported the notion:

> Of all the likely national, regional, and international research institutions operating in Africa, only the universities in Africa and other developing countries have the freedom or mandate and the multidisciplinary capability under one umbrella to tackle the more in-depth and wider scope of research required for/by sustainable development. It is conceivable, therefore, that sustainable development and adequate institutional capability can be achieved in Africa as long as universities are inadequately funded and not effectively linked with other institutions in the national research system. (p. 31)

The previous statement is important because, unless Africa views university research more seriously, African countries will continue to be consumers of research findings from foreign experts rather than becoming makers and/or contributors of research findings themselves. Lack of research initiatives by African universities condemns Africa to a state of dependency. Therefore, encouraging research in Nigeria, as well as in other parts of Africa, will automatically offer Africa an opportunity to contribute in world knowledge.

African governments and policymakers should explore a variety of ways to enhance research and development at their universities. For example, practical ways of rewarding and funding research projects in African universities are to be encouraged. Many avenues need to be investigated as a way to influence the perceptions and attitudes of African governments toward university research, but it also is important to consider the financial realities of Africa.

Djangmah (1995) suggested that ways to fund postgraduate training and research in African universities must be investigated, as well as studying the research and development of central governments, specific ministries, public corporations, and science-based institutions. According to Djangmah, the following questions must be asked:

> 1. Has R&D [research and development] a place in the central government budget? What about specific ministries?
> 2. Does the government's R&D budget provide for specific ministries, research institutes, and universities?
> 3. Does the R&D budget of specific ministries and departments include contract research in university departments?
> 4. What provision is made by specific ministries and departments for local capacity building for R&D?
> 5. What provision is made by specific ministries for local postgraduate training of staff and for local continuing education?
> 6. What efforts have been made by universities for sponsorship of their research by government departments?
> 7. What are the sources of funding of current university research? How are university research estimates and budgets compiled?
> 8. What efforts have been made by universities for sponsorship of graduate programs and research from sources other than the Ministry of Education?
> 9. How do universities relate to local nonuniversity research institutes for research, research-related activities, and staff developments?
> 10. What provision is made for staff development and local research by recent donor-funded projects? How much of donor project funding goes into technical assistance from donor countries?
> 11. How do university researchers relate to policymakers in government? How frequent are seminars specially designed to enhance such relationships and to influence policy? (p. 31)

Investigation about funding of research and development for university research that is well-organized and practical provides policymakers and African governments with a wealth of information. Numerous research studies have found that universities throughout the world contribute uniquely to society through research in different fields of studies, in particular, the pure and applied sciences (Djangmah 1995; Woodhall 1995). Most research projects are conducted by graduate students.

Graduate programs, consequently, need to form the cornerstone for intellectual development and knowledge-base foundation in technology and science in Africa, as well as in other developing countries. Solid graduate programs are a necessity in order to provide graduate students at the master's and doctoral levels with the best qualified people. Many African countries have relied heavily on other nations for scholarships and fellowships in training graduate personnel (Davies 1995). Training African intellectuals abroad has resulted in the "African brain drain" in which thousands of highly educated professionals have opted to emigrate to Western countries in search of better opportunities.

Therefore, Africa must look at other alternatives in order to ensure that it invests in its own highly educated professionals for socioeconomic development. Moreover, only a selected few Africans are sent abroad for training. According to Djangmah (1995), the problems that these selected individuals solve generally are more relevant to their host countries than to Africa. Thus, creating a conducive research environment in African universities will help to reduce this problem.

11.2.7 Conclusions

The discussion of challenges in the Nigerian system of education does not mean that there are no successes in this type of education. Since independence in 1960, Nigeria has made dramatic progress in education, given its political and other internal problems. More schools were built after independence; consequently, more children attended school than during colonial times. Nigerian intellectuals have made great contributions through the publication of academic and more popular volumes (Barbour 1984). The status of Nigerian women has improved greatly since independence. Employment opportunities for Nigerian women have improved; currently, more women are employed in clerical or administrative roles than during colonial times (Nyanguru and Peil 1991). Even though Nigerian education has improved tremendously since independence, more changes are expected.

11.3 The Case of Zimbabwe

11.3.1 Introduction

Before independence, education for blacks in Zimbabwe was poor, and the majority of black people was denied access to schooling (Botha 1991). Free and compulsory education was available for whites at government schools but was an option for blacks, with fees charged by mission and government schools (Weiss 1994). Charging blacks for their education meant that full education was available only for those whose parents could afford the full payment of fees.

Educational disparities also were evident in government expenditure for budget and per capita. Weiss (1994) noted that in 1977-78 the budgeted expenditure for education was Z$74.6 million, of which Z$31.7 million was allocated to whites and Z$42.8 million to blacks, giving an average of Z$522 per white student and Z$52 per black student. From 1967 to 1976, the government spent Z$20.7 million of its capital account on white education compared to Z$11.2 million on black education, which is more than twenty times per capita on white than on black children (Weiss 1994).

Education for blacks prior to independence was viewed as insignificant unless it served the interests of the ruling elite. African education was, therefore, left to charity and self-help (Austin 1975). On the other hand, blacks saw education in terms of economic prosperity for the individual and the family. Poor black families preferred to educate boys more than girls, in part, because of economic reasons. Boys were more likely to support their families after acquiring an education, whereas girls married into another family (Weiss 1994). Unfortunately, this belief is still held by many African families.

In Zimbabwe, as well as in Africa, following independence, a vast educational reform occurred that marked the shift from an exclusive system of education to one of inclusive mass education (Dorsey 1989). The rationale for educational expansion in many newly independent African countries was linked to political and economic independence. Policymakers in Zimbabwe perceived education to be the main tool for creating a more egalitarian society, for expanding and modernizing the economy, and as an essential element in the process of nation building (Dorsey 1989).

The colonial period is, in part, responsible for perpetuating the misconception among Africans in their view of education as the most important instrument of social transformation. Dorsey (1989) confirmed this notion. In Zimbabwe, individual demand for greater provision of education was influenced by an instrumental perception of the value of education. This perception was developed during the colonial period in which education was seen to be the only way to salaried employment, providing security, wealth, status, and improved living standards. Even today, many Africans see no other route to social, economic, and political prosperity except through education. Even though other countries in Africa have experienced rapid expansion of their educational systems at independence, none has attempted universal access to primary and secondary education to the same degree or as rapidly as Zimbabwe (Dorsey 1989).

11.3.2 Primary Schools

After independence, Zimbabwe made education the largest item in the budget (Weiss 1994). Education was declared by the government as a basic human right. In September 1980, the government announced free and compulsory primary schooling for all children; consequently, universal primary education was achieved by 1982 (Mundy 1993). Thus, soon after independence, primary schools experienced an increase of the student body. Dorsey (1989) reported that enrollment at the primary level soared from 819,586 at independence to 2,263,947 seven years later, an index increase of 2.76. According to the government's estimates, approximately 97 percent of the children of primary school age were registered in school.

Sudden increase in the number of students in the primary schools created other problems such as insufficient school accommodation and a lack of trained teachers. Salt and Salt (1983) reported that certain measures were taken to improve accommodation problems. For instance, self-help schemes in communal areas were established, including temporary provision of roofing for open-sided classrooms. The new government also planned to provide new schools throughout the country, existing classrooms were to be upgraded, and additional space was to be provided.

According to Salt and Salt (1983), in some areas (in which the demand was greatest), double sessions allowed twice the number of pupils to benefit by using the same facilities. In some areas, the shortage of classrooms was so severe that pupils arrived before any buildings were constructed. According to Dorsey (1989), classes were held in hastily constructed pole-and-mud huts with thatched roofs, and, in some cases, they were held under the open sky. Through government and community initiatives, the number of primary schools nearly doubled from 2,401 in 1979 to 4,291 in 1986 (Dorsey 1989). Teachers' salaries remained the responsibility of the central government, even though the majority of primary schools was owned and operated by local government bodies, missions, firms, and private individuals (Salt and Salt 1983).

11.3.3 Secondary Schools

Primary education is free and compulsory, whereas secondary education is not. It is hoped that secondary education will be free, but, even by 1990, it had not materialized (Botha 1991). Consequently, secondary schooling has become less available to many in Zimbabwe. However, the government has attempted to address this problem by building more secondary schools. Many new secondary schools have been built in rural areas under the management of district councils (Dorsey 1989).

Despite the fact that secondary schooling is not free, its population has soared from 66,215 in 1979 to 537,427 in 1986, an index increase of 8.12 (Dorsey 1989). The number of students entering secondary schools also is expected to increase. Consequently, more amenities and school buildings will be needed to accommodate students. Another crucial issue is providing qualified teachers at the secondary level.

11.3.4 Educational Limitations in Zimbabwe

Even though educational improvements after independence were admirable, government critics pointed out that quantitative increases were not sufficient and that quality of education needed to be the focus if Zimbabwe was to make meaningful changes. Another problem was an increasing number of employment-seeking "school leavers." These school leavers had no skills or possessed limited skills.

11.3.5 Curriculum

Zimbabwe, following independence, rewrote many course syllabi with the hope of adapting the content to the new era. For example, general science was reoriented toward agriculture and health care; physics was redirected toward energy use and telecommunications; and chemistry was reoriented toward mining and industrial-chemical processes such as fertilizer production (Meldrum 1991). According to Meldrum, history was rewritten to be representative of the entire population rather than representing the history of white settlers.

Rewriting curricula, textbooks, syllabi, and teaching materials has been time-consuming and challenging. Certification and Zimbabwe's reliance on the British O-level and A-level examination system continue to reflect its colonial heritage; yet, this is where the problems must be confronted. Many students who fail to pass these examinations are left joblessness.

Perhaps Zimbabwe's problem is providing education that does not lead to employment opportunities. The country suffers from high unemployment rates. Each year more than 200,000 students complete secondary school, but there are only 10,000 jobs available (Meldrum 1991). This situation, if it continues, might affect students' faith in the benefits of education. When people see no economic benefits in acquiring an education, it becomes a problem for the government.

Jansen (1991) found that Zimbabwean curriculum remained largely academic, with rote learning sustained by underprepared teachers and evaluation still largely controlled by the Cambridge examination syndicate. Currently, the curriculum has placed more emphasis on academic achievement in the form of public examinations. Failure to change the curriculum has resulted in unfulfilled expectations for most school leavers because of examination failures, because of the frustration of unemployment, or because of a combination of the two (MacKenzie 1988).

What knowledge base is necessary for the social and economic advancement of the country? This question must be asked by education policymakers and curriculum designers in Zimbabwe. Certainly, educational expansion must be only as fast as the system can maintain teachers and books in the classrooms (Meldrum 1991). The economic reality of the country is to determine the type of education it can afford. Graduates who are not absorbed by the job market add to the problems of the country rather than contributing to its economic growth.

11.3.6 Desegregation Issues

Because the majority of the country is black and whites in Zimbabwe have always had a higher standard of education, this situation has made desegregation more difficult to fulfil. In 1980, desegregation in Zimbabwean schools became effective soon after independence. In urban areas, previously all-white schools quickly became predominantly black (Meldrum 1991). School integration was promoted further by the government, which began busing students from overcrowded township schools to spacious, previously all-white suburban schools.

The Education Act of 1979, at an administrative level, allowed integration of the European and African departments of education, as well as the gradual desegregation of schools (Dorsey 1989). Restructuring government schools consisted of Group A schools (former white schools) and Group B and Group C schools (former African schools). These schools charge different fees. Group A schools are expensive, Group B are moderate, and Group C are free. As a result, the majority schools that are nonfee-paying provide inferior education, whereas fee-paying schools provide schooling for the offspring of elites and whites (Weiss 1994).

Measures also were taken to limit black enrollment in white schools. These measures included strict zoning regulations, allowing the registration of children whose parents owned or leased accommodations in the area (Dorsey 1989). This measure automatically excluded children from poor backgrounds, as well as domestic workers' children. Many whites, fearing a black exodus into their schools, also purchased government schools at a cheaper rate and turned them into community schools (Weiss 1994). In reality, parents now had the right to admit or reject applicants.

More and more private schools became the option for many white parents. Private education also was open to blacks, but it was open to wealthy blacks only. Private and city schools attracted children of affluent blacks. Consequently, educational reform in Zimbabwe tended to enhance elitism in the educational system. Discrimination in this new arrangement was no longer based on race but on class (Baine and Mwamwenda 1994).

School desegregation in Zimbabwe has not benefited the majority of African children who still reside in impoverished townships and rural areas and who still attend poor neighborhood schools. As urban schools became more black, the whites and Indians fled to private schools and even schools abroad. Many parents feared the reduction of standards as a result of increased class sizes (Baine and Mwamwenda 1994). More than a decade after independence, the townships and/or rural schools remain all black, whereas schools in formerly all-white areas have two or three white children per class of thirty-five (Meldrum 1991). Many white students in Zimbabwe receive their education in private schools.

The expansion of schools soon after independence created a problem in which there were more new schools available than qualified teachers to fill them. The teacher shortage, according to Weiss (1994), led to the deployment of unqualified teachers and a lowering of standards. Hundreds of expatriate teachers were recruited, at government expense, from Australia, Britain, and Canada on three-year contracts (MacKenzie 1988). Black teachers and administrators were hired in previously white schools (Baine and Mwamwenda 1994).

11.3.7 Language of Instruction

In Zimbabwe, the pupils' home language is used as the medium of instruction for the first four years of school, with English as a subject. Little importance is accorded to the effective use of local languages for educational purposes because they do not contribute to secondary selection (Williams 1993). The "local language" is Shona or Ndebele.

Several researchers have found that the majority of Africans cannot learn efficiently through English (Baine and Mwamwenda 1994; Kachelhoffer 1995; Williams 1993; Yankah 1995). Williams (1993) stated that an early emphasis on learning English in Africa means that the majority of children forms hazy and indistinct concepts in language, mathematics, science, and social studies. Children whose English is poor are likely to experience an unsuccessful school life.

Williams (1993) explained that the use of English in African schools not only negatively impacts students who must study and learn in a "foreign" language, but it also affects their intellectual development. Moreover, a further result is the enormous waste of time and resources for teachers and pupils. Language instruction in Africa is complicated, with educational views always associated with cultural alienation (Yankah 1995). Unless Africa wakes up and begins to value and develop its own languages, it will continue to be marginalized in the world of knowledge. As the world approaches the twenty-first century, cultures without writings such as Africa will continue to be recipients of intellectual work. Language development in Africa is likely to be slow and gradual, but, nonetheless, it should be pursued. Mother-tongue instruction is crucial in empowering people with basic cognitive skills.

11.3.8 Conclusion

Zimbabwe has spent a lot of money on education since the country's independence in 1980. The following improvements in education were cited by Nyanguru and Peil (1991):

> The number of children in primary school increased from 820,000 in 1979 to 2.2 million in 1986 and the numbers in secondary schools from 66,000 to over 545,000; the university had 7,699 students in 1989 compared to only 1,931 just before independence. (p. 607)

Educational expansion in Zimbabwe has been achieved at a great sacrifice, which has been compounded further by debt repayment plans established by foreign lenders. In new nations such as Zimbabwe, educational improvement has not necessarily satisfied the people's increased expectations as in many other countries (Nyanguru and Peil 1991). School leavers have borne the brunt of unemployment. Even though the government has made great strides in providing formal education, attempts have been limited in furnishing nonformal education, including adult education. Zimbabwe has succeeded in achieving many of its educational goals, but a lot remains to be done.

11.4 The Case of Tanzania

11.4.1 Introduction

Tanzania was granted its independence from Britain in 1961. Soon after independence, educational reform took place. The country's educational policy was twofold: (a) education for self-reliance and (b) adult education, lifelong learning, and education for liberation (Kassam 1983). Education for self-reliance was aimed at increasing access to education, with all members of society having equal opportunity. Tanzania experienced increased enrollment in primary education after independence. Educational expansion, on the other hand, was seen as a quantitative achievement rather than qualitative (Mosha 1988). The problems of quality were due to shortages of teachers, finances, and teaching materials.

Education was considered crucial in achieving equality and participation by a majority of the population in local and national development of a socialist society (Buchert 1994). Tanzania, more than any other newly independent African country, tried to break away from colonial aims and goals of education.

However, implementation of many educational programs did not create the envisaged society in Tanzania (Buchert 1994). Failure in the implementation of education for self-reliance was due to internal and external factors.

11.4.2 Primary Education

Tanzania, unlike other newly independent countries of Africa, first focused on adult education. Adults were seen by the government as people to influence immediately the economic development, whereas children's input was expected in the future. Thus, the country delayed any attempts to make great strides in providing primary education (Mundy 1993). The aim of universal primary education in Tanzania was to enable its recipients to receive basic skills, attitudes, motivation, and knowledge needed for effective participation in national development and individual enhancement (Mosha 1988).

Policymakers in Tanzania were worried about factors affecting the quality of education. No connection seemed to be present between theoretical knowledge gained from school with what was taking place after school. Such education alienated students and the community (Mosha 1988). Primary education was to be comprehensive, with the minimum age of entry raised from five to six years and from seven to eight years. This ruling allowed those who leave school early to do so at a more mature age, ultimately making a greater contribution to rural development (Cameron and Dodd 1970).

11.4.3 Secondary Education

Secondary education was geared towards technical and vocational training. The purpose of secondary education in Tanzania was to prepare individuals to serve their communities. Thus, secondary education was meant to prepare students for life and service in the villages and rural areas of Tanzania (Cameron and Dodd 1970). Soon it was compulsory for students to specialize in a vocational subject of their choice, keeping with Tanzania's philosophy of self-reliance and self-sufficiency in skilled manpower (Urevbu 1988). Tanzania is described as the first country in Africa to link schooling with productive work and to introduce a program of diversified secondary education (Urevbu 1988).

Tanzania's education stressed the importance of rural development. Achieving this goal was encouraged by schools, which contributed to their own maintenance and benefited all (Cameron and Dodd 1970). These recommendations were based on the belief that vocational subjects prepare students for life after schooling.

11.4.4 Curriculum

Attempts were made at the "Africanization" of curriculum content (Foster 1969). Africanization makes the content more appropriate for local needs. For example, European history was replaced by African history, and world geography was replaced by local geography. Political education also was introduced at various levels of schooling. This type of learning made the curriculum more practical and meaningful outside of the school building. Primary education was aimed at rural development; consequently, agricultural education and vocational training became crucial components at this level. However, primary school curriculum changes, after independence, have been less evident. According to Mosha (1988), subjects such as agriculture, handicrafts, and health science were canceled after independence. Ten years later, an attempt was made to reintroduce these subjects, with the country paying for its previous miscalculation. Focus in the curriculum tended to be on academics rather than vocational. Despite obvious changes after independence, limited modifications have been made. The desire to adapt educational systems to African needs and realities has failed to materialize because of Africa's lack of financial means to reach such goals. The option of many African countries, including Tanzania, has been to adhere to the old colonial structure and content of education (Foster 1969).

11.4.5 Foreign Aid

Tanzania received economic aid from Eastern and Western governments at the beginning of independence. As the years continued, such assistance declined in amount and was consumed by the need to repay earlier loans (Cameron and Dodd 1970). According to Cameron and Dodd, private foreign investment did not amount to anything, and there was growing dissatisfaction with economic assistance from the East and West. Dependency on foreign economic aid was seen as unproductive, unpredictable, and a danger to independence.

The slow flow of foreign funds into Tanzania made it difficult for the country to implement new educational policies. Tanzania, on the other hand, focused more on the maximum utilization of the rich local resources such as land and labor rather than seeking foreign assistance (Buchert 1994). Unfortunately, the country suffered from the lack of trained personnel, as well as financial means, to achieve some of the educational policies.

11.4.6 Language of Instruction

Immediately after independence, Kiswahili was selected as the national language. Kiswahili is the medium of instruction for primary and adult education. At the secondary and tertiary levels, English has become the medium of instruction (Rubagumya 1991). English also is used as the medium of instruction at higher levels of education because of its practical economic benefits.

According to Rubagumya (1991), English in Tanzania is the language of the upper courts, diplomacy, and international trade. In higher levels of education, Kiswahili, like many of the African languages, has limited literacy. On the other hand, English is seen as the vehicle for access to world literature and technological information (Rubagumya 1991). Consequently, the preference of English over Kiswahili is more concerned with economic, educational, and political realities.

11.4.7 Conclusion

Tanzania also experienced great educational improvements after independence. Approximately 486,000 children attended primary education before independence (Cowder 1987). However, more than three and one half million children attended primary education in the 1980s. Educational progress in Tanzania also was marked by a tremendous reduction of illiteracy. For example, in 1961, approximately 80% of the adult population were illiterate (Cowder 1987). In 1987, according to Cowder, 85% were able to read and write. Educational improvement has traveled hand-in-hand, with improvement in other areas such as health and living standards.

11.5 Summary of the African Experience

After independence, many African countries were enthusiastic about eliminating their colonial past, hoping that the people would be free to develop their potential. Africans were delighted because, for the first time, they would be able to determine what they wanted to learn and to demand that education be more sensitive to their aspirations and needs. According to Davidson (1994), prior to independence, few Africans were aware of their African surroundings. Instead, British West Africans were taught British history or geography only.

Independence seemed to have opened new horizons to knowledge. An increased demand was made for education, with many independent governments succeeding in making provisions for this demand. However, improving the quality of education seemed to be more difficult for many African countries than increasing the quantity (Davidson 1994). Educational expansion had some benefits because many students were being served by the school system. Research studies conducted in Third World countries found that investing in primary education yields the best return. Studies support the notion that providing instructional materials, especially textbooks, is the most cost-effective way of raising the quality of primary education (Mosha 1988; Samoff 1993).

11.5.1 Curriculum Change

A revolution in education has meant new content of education aimed at decolonizing the minds of African youth. Consequently, syllabi and textbooks have been "Africanized"; that is, they have been rewritten to accommodate African aspirations and needs, not colonizing powers (Davidson 1994). African countries have adopted different approaches in accomplishing this task. For example, more diversity is apparent in what is taught, with postprimary education offering students more choices than during colonial times. A desire exists among Africans for local consumption in terms of content. Nonetheless, the lack of a suitable range of books on the history, geography, or political systems of the African continent, of its major regions, or of specific aspects of African culture has been a severe constraint on the process of decolonization or changing the content for African use (Barbour 1984). After independence, many African countries recognized the importance of subjects such as African history and its impact on African society. African students were taught about African heroes and the ancient kingdoms of precolonial Africa and beyond (Davidson 1994). African art, paintings, artifacts, and folkloric music took on a new look and were included in the curriculum. Science has been accorded high status as a prerequisite for development. The subject has been introduced at the primary and secondary levels.

Various forms of curriculum changes have taken place in African countries. Recently, curriculum centers have been established in countries such as Tanzania, Botswana, Ghana, Guinea, Mali, Somalia, and Malawi. Such centers are aimed at assessing the syllabi, as well as the content and quality of textbooks being used in schools. International experts have assisted in establishing such centers. Research projects also have been introduced in universities and institutions of higher learning for the purpose of testing and assessing these curriculum changes (Jolly 1969).

11.5.2 Textbooks

Curriculum change and the production of textbooks are related and reciprocal; each cannot occur without the other. Empirical evidence shows that providing a sufficient number of textbooks has a substantial effect on pupil performance, particularly on pupils from rural areas, low-income families, or illiterate parents (Mncwabe 1993). Several African countries have responded positively to the need for textbooks with an African background. Writing books by African authors has increased considerably in recent years. Rubagumya (1991) contended that the demand for more reading materials in Tanzania has resulted in the proliferation of the "briefcase publishers" (small, usually one-person publishing "companies").

A wide range of books (fiction and nonfiction) has been published by Nigerians. Barbour (1984) stated that Nigerian lecturers have been the most active in seeking promotion through the publication of academic and more popular volumes; their efforts have benefited not only Africa but other parts of the world. European countries have been instrumental in providing support to Africa for the printing of textbooks. UNESCO has helped with printing, as well as training of technicians, in producing textbooks (Jolly 1969).

11.5.3 Language Issues

The origins of the use of second languages in African education, according to Perren (1969), are historical, ethnographical, and political. English and French were the languages of the colonial powers; they were used when formal education was first introduced in Africa. The importation of foreign languages to Africa was meant to serve the interests of the metropolitan countries more than to benefit Africa. Perren argued that English and French were necessary because a limited number of craftsmen, catechists, teachers, clerks, or minor functionaries was needed for the service of missions or the colonial administration.

In colonial times, foreign languages in Africa were valued and African languages were devalued. In the postindependence stages, English, French, and/or Portuguese remained popular in many African countries. Even though dictated, at times, by practical necessity, the use of foreign languages for educational purposes was detrimental to educational development (Adegbija 1994). Heavy reliance on foreign aid has prevented Africa from finding educational solutions that best suit its conditions. African languages have suffered the same neglect experienced during colonial times. In developing countries, the use of a foreign language is a unifying mechanism; however, this has not been the case in many African countries. A major problem is the assumption that the majority of Africans is able to use English or any other European language. In fact, large sections of the African population are not educated, excluding them from using English or any other foreign language.

The adoption of a foreign language for national unity is based on a false assumption. For example, Rwanda's use of French was not effective in preventing the civil war nor were Ethiopia's, Sudan's, Angola's, and Somalia's. The underlying problems of many conflicts in Africa concern the competition for limited economic and/or material resources rather than ethnicity. In many African countries, foreign languages are regarded as the "languages" of education, not of the home (Perren 1969). Consequently, most Africans speak their indigenous languages more than they speak foreign languages. Language policy in Africa is a complex issue that cannot be addressed in isolation to other issues such as the curriculum, teaching methods, and educational resources available in a given country. One of the problems associated with language, as stated by Perren (1969), is that most African countries have accepted a school curriculum from Europe. Thus, change in the language policy of Africa will be realized with total change of the curriculum only.

The choice of a colonial language in Africa is based on social and economic realities, whereas African languages have not been successful in facilitating the economic development process in nations such as Japan, Korea, and China. The task of developing African languages for scientific works and commerce are yet to be performed.

11.5.4 Foreign Assistance

In designing and implementing educational reform programs, Africans need to take the initiative rather than to rely heavily on foreign expertise. Such reliance not only limits indigenous initiative in solving their own educational problems, but it also encourages dependency. In many instances, foreign assistance programs were not designed to maximize African participation in the process of education or development. Mbaku (1994) maintained that foreign institutions sometimes were established for exploitation, despotism, and degradation. When it became eminent that African countries were gaining their independence, some colonialists hurriedly introduced educational reforms that did not provide for a fundamental transformation in the social, economic, and political domains.

Moreover, for some colonial powers, educational development in their former colonies became a profit-making business (Scheepers 1991). Imported models and materials became the answers in solving some of Africa' s educational problems. Soon after independence, many African countries found themselves lacking economic means to solve some of their local problems. That is, independence was political only, whereas the economic structures remained unchanged. Many African school leavers found themselves unemployed because provisions had not been made for graduates whose aspirations had been raised through educational achievement (Moncada-Davidson 1995).

Another contributing factor to Africa' s educational failure, as explained by Mushi (1991), was the belief that educational innovations are a means of bringing about socioeconomic change. According to Mushi, the introduction of educational innovations should be accompanied by economic innovations because educational innovations are not sufficient to bring about socioeconomic development.

11.5.5 Vocational Training

Vocational training, introduced to many African countries soon after independence, was not a success. Failure occurred because many students regarded such training to be "second best." Therefore, in many African countries, an academic type of education (originally imported by the West) continues to be seen as the only way up and out of a harsh and poverty-stricken environment (Cameron and Dodd 1970). Moreover, vocational training in most African countries did not lead to high income or status. Clearly, such views encouraged many students to favor an academic education over vocational training (Corby 1990). The primary purpose of vocational training in many developing countries has been to combat unemployment and to promote self-reliance. Unfortunately, research studies have suggested that the introduction of vocational training into the schools does little to combat unemployment, promote self-reliance, reduce rural-urban migration, increase self-employment, or improve the quality of life in general (Eshiwani 1989; Urevbu 1988). Vocational training remains an option for students who cannot benefit from academic education. Equality in education is an ideal worth pursuing, even though problems concerning selection and availability of opportunities are unavoidable. Inequalities in all societies tend to perpetuate themselves, allowing differences among people. Jolly (1969) stated that equality of access is an unattainable objective in developed and developing countries. Therefore, the critical issue in educational transformation is the creation of opportunities in which all individuals can benefit. By establishing attainable educational standards, Africa will take its first critical step toward providing a plan that will guarantee quality education for the twenty-first century.

11.5.6 Common Features in Third World Countries

Common features in Third World countries include the following:
1. Poor economies and lack of funds are two features shared by many developing countries. Such economic realities have had a great impact in providing schools in Africa.
2. The rapid population increase in many African countries has made the provision of schooling difficult. There has never been sufficient numbers of schools to accommodate all children. Thus, formal education in Africa remains a privilege made available to the few who can afford it.
3. A shortage of school buildings, coupled with other unfavorable learning conditions such as poorly trained teachers, overcrowdedness, and lack of textbooks, have greatly affected the quality of education.
4. Teachers' qualifications, as well as higher professional status (but not years of teaching experience), are considered to have an influence on school quality when judged on the basis of achievement (Mosha 1988).
5. Language policy has been made difficult by the existence of numerous ethnic groupings with different languages. The use of a single local language in education, which is widely understood and widely spoken, has been compromised for the use of a foreign

language.

6. Lack of textbooks and a shortage of libraries consistently have been associated with poor performance of students in schools. According to Jolly (1969), education in Africa has been deficient in socializing the new societies and has been extremely inadequate in providing technical skills and general knowledge of the world of commerce and business. However, despite all of the economic limitations faced by Africa, sometimes a government' s extravagance and private corruption are partly to blame. For example, Mosha (1988) argued that other African states managed to build stadiums and party buildings that cost many millions of shillings, whereas in some regions children were receiving education in shabby buildings without textbooks or sufficient learning materials.

Another problem facing Africa is a lack of loyalty to the state. According to Bohannan and Curtin (1995), the state' s responsibility to demand taxes and to provide schools, roads, medical care, and jobs is often not the focus of sentiment and support. The state, in many African countries, is the focus of political life. However, the history of the state during colonial times was viewed as a "machine of control," even in postcolonial times.

Developing, nonindustrialized countries find themselves increasingly marginalized, with the gap between the poor and rich widening (Mundy 1993). The prospect for economic improvement in many African countries is not good unless Africa finds a way to solve its internal problems. Civil wars and ethnic conflicts continue to plague many parts of the continent, including Somalia, Yemen, Rwanda, and Angola ("South African Economy Is Key To Future of the Country" 1994).

11.5.7 Political and Economic Realities of Governing

When many African countries were given independence, they became an open field for superpower rivalry. For example, those who followed socialism turned to the Soviet Union for financial and military assistance. The ideological models of these countries were Russia and Eastern Europe. On the other hand, those who followed capitalism turned to the West for support. Therefore, civil wars and political rivalry in many parts of Africa, including Mozambique, Angola, and Rwanda, were between parties supported by the Western or the Eastern Bloc. Wars in many African countries were waged in the name of promoting socialist or capitalist interests. In the process, many African lives were ruined or lost. For example, in Rwanda, the number of dead is estimated from 100,000 to 500,000 ("South African Economy Is Key To Future of the Country" 1994).

Mbaku (1995) argued that after the fall of the Soviet Union and the end of the Cold War, Africa lost most of its importance to the West and the former Soviet Union. The end of the Cold War meant that many political dictatorships in Africa would no longer receive the flow of cash and weapons from their Western and Soviet allies. The result has been the fall of several African Marxist regimes such as in Somalia and Ethiopia (Mbaku 1995).

With limited capital, many African countries have used the state as an instrument for the enrichment of members of the ruling coalition. Zaire's leader is said to be the richest man in Africa and yet the masses in that country are very poor. Zaire is not the only African country whose political leader uses the state as a source of wealth. In Malawi, Banda almost became the lifelong president, until recently when he decided to step down because of old age and failing health. In many parts of Africa, it is common to capture political power and then use it to reward those who hold it with a significant level of economic benefits (Mbaku 1995). According to Mbaku, South Africa, which for many years was regarded by Westerners as a bastion of capitalism and democracy, promoted markets in which the redistributive powers of the state were used on a regular basis to transfer wealth from the black majority to the white minority. Under apartheid, laws were used to limit blacks' participation in economic affairs.

Currently, one of the major crises facing Africa is the repayment of its foreign debt. Ankomah (1996) reported that Third World debt (owed mainly to the International Monetary Fund and the World Bank) is currently 400% higher than it was in 1980. The burden of repayment robs Africa of whatever economy it has. The terms of repayment are said to be a disadvantage to Africa. For example, figures, as reported by Ankomah, show that approximately 400m British pounds in interest and capital repayments were transferred from the Third World to the West each day between 1982 and 1990. Consequently, many African countries spend a great amount of money servicing the multilateral debt than improving their economies. However, foreign debt is not the sole cause of Africa's problems; sometimes more money is spent on defense and grandiose projects, as well as subsidies to inefficient and often corrupt nationalized industries.

11.6 Implications for South Africa

The African experience of political independence is marked with hardships. This experience should be a lesson for South Africa in confirming that the end of an apartheid era, no matter how smooth, marks the beginning of a difficult road to economic independence, which is the true measure of success. Generally, African governments are accused of mismanagement and poor educational conditions.

The legacy of indirect rule by former colonies is often forgotten in this accusation. Indirect rule in Africa means the establishment of the ruling classes, that is, elitists selected by former colonies to share in economic benefits while the balance of the population remains poor (Murphy 1996). As a result of indirect rule, colonial bureaucracies in most African countries remain intact, perpetuating tribalism, corruption, and nepotism. For example, at times, the National Party in South Africa has been able to establish and enforce its far-reaching apartheid program through assistance from tribal chiefs and other greedy Africans. This notion is supported by Christen (1996). He suggested that a more economic populace with a more modern, self-aware institution would never have permitted itself to be exploited and misused in such a fashion. Therefore, the South African scenario is proof that, with no economic base, many African countries become vulnerable to outside manipulation and exploitation.

African countries are not necessarily the same in their local needs, level of development, or historical heritage. Because each African country' s circumstances are different, it would be inappropriate to expect South Africa to adopt its model of educational reform. South Africa' s educational reform must be based on the needs, problems, and economic realities of the country. Therefore, educational reforms for black South Africans will depend on the nature and objectives of the community.

During the apartheid era in South Africa, blacks were never asked to have input in the education process. Attempts to mobilize society to participate in educational reforms will be difficult. Therefore, before black South Africans are asked to participate actively in finding solutions to their educational problems, they must be educated about the process itself. In fact, this participation will help Africans to identify their immediate needs and aspirations as a community. Social awareness of the need for education is necessary if the entire population is to benefit from reforms. Ordinary people need to be well-informed about the educational process before they can participate in making decisions about matters that affect them and their children. Education must be viewed as a lifelong process (Jolly 1969).

Political violence that sometimes interferes with schooling must be minimized. Poor or no education breeds violence and thoughtless criminal activities. Crime, according to Lyman (1996), is harming perceptions of South Africa' s future and its ability to attract foreign investment. Violence threatens the security of society and democracy. Criminal behavior thrives on poverty and ignorance. The root causes of violence must be addressed in order to control it. With regard to political violence in South Africa, Lindsay (1995) stated that documentation has been found that the national government and the Nationalist Party (composed of Afrikaners and conservative English-speaking Europeans) funded the Inkatha Freedom Party and the African National Congress. This support allows these groups to engage in political violence. Political cooperation among Africans is needed in order to insure that such occurrences do not take place again.

Given the fact that politics is regarded by many Africans as an important investment, some will fight and even kill to insure continuation. If South Africa is to avoid the mistakes of other African countries, politics should be used as an instrument to serve its people. Under apartheid, the state used its coercive force to crush its opponents while protecting the interests of the minority. Political violence, including military coups (currently prevalent in many parts of Africa), are a result of greed and the desire to capture the government in order to redistribute wealth (Mbaku 1995). Political rivalry in South Africa can be explained in terms of greed for power and material wealth.

11.7 Legacies of Colonial Education

Under colonial rule, African education was shaped primarily by European settlers and members of the colonial administration (Mbaku 1995). This arrangement helped to explain the position of African interests and aspirations in the colonial scheme. Colonial education excluded and demeaned the cultural and historical experiences of the subject population but celebrated a culture of the dominant population. Thus, Africans were exposed to an educational system designed to benefit the dominant colonial culture but was harmful to its interests and those of its race (Okafor 1992).

The limitations of colonial education deprived Africans of the opportunity to think and work for themselves, thus making them economically dependent on others. The adoption of colonial models, regardless of applicability in the African contexts, has been cited as a weakness that many African states inherited from colonialism (Okafor 1992). For example, it can be argued that Bantu education was not designed to oppress Africans but that the system was constructed to conform with the needs of European settlers. The content and methods of education were in favor of European civilization. Therefore, the challenge is for Africans to change Bantu education, which seemingly does not have a significant impact in their development.

Another shortcoming of colonial education is that it never acknowledged the contributions of Africans to human civilization (Mbaku 1995; Okafor 1992). The negative image of Africa has contributed to making Africans hate and underrate themselves, looking outward rather than inward for solutions to problems (Okafor 1992). The Africans' contempt for themselves also is evident in South Africa. Recently, I was discussing the importance of indigenous languages with a fellow South African, who also was studying in the United States, who showed a low regard of African languages. When I asked her whether or not it was necessary for Africans to record their history in their own languages, she told me that no one was going to look for a job using Zulu or any of the African languages. My colleague's response need not be viewed with shock because it is common for South Africans to believe that they cannot create jobs for themselves or for their race and that they look at Europeans for employment opportunities. The perception is realistic, given the fact that those who hold the keys to economic prosperity are of European descent. However, this perception does not mean that Africans cannot create jobs if they try and also if they have the capital. Self-doubt and lack of confidence in one's possibilities also are dangerous to human development because it discourages one from trying. Okafor (1992) noted that sometimes African scholars tend to doubt the validity of the works of their fellow scholars, even on subjects pertaining to African societies, until their European mentors have approved. According to Okafor, when an African scholar ignores the work of another because it has not met the penchant of the European guardians, then that African needs to reassess.

Many African countries have suffered the consequences of educational careers that did not lead to employment opportunities. Okafor (1992) explained that Africans tend to select disciplines that do not allow self-employment. Given the rising unemployment rates among Africans, they need to emphasize education for self-employment, then they will not have to depend on the benevolence of Europeans or foreign aid (Mbaku 1995; Okafor 1992). In the past, a poor education system for the majority of South Africans has been deficient, leaving many people without the skills necessary for entrepreneurship or employment in technical jobs (Lyman 1996). Land deprivation, plus a myriad of laws, have prevented many Africans from participation in economic affairs. However, with the new dispensation, the situation is likely to improve.

11.8 Conclusion

Over the past few decades, remarkable educational changes have occurred in several African countries. Educational changes in many African countries have, in reality, meant little change in the lives of the poor and those residing in remote rural areas. Many African countries have made remarkable attempts to improve their education, but there are specific patterns that can help explain why noticeable hardships have occurred in providing education.

Importation of educational models designed for other people, without considering an educational system built upon an indigenous foundation, has proven to be problematic for Africans. Limitations in adopting foreign educational models provide lessons for South Africa in its search for postapartheid education. Perhaps, it is more important for South African policymakers to realize that meaningful education has deep roots in the histories and cultures of each nation.

South Africa needs to use local building materials based on local experiences and needs in order to establish a genuine and enduring educational system. When educational models are borrowed from other successful democracies, they must be adapted to local conditions and practices. One must consider that each country, with its special circumstances and unique nature, needs to ponder the educational arrangements that will provide employable skills, as well as lifelong skills, to its populace.

The causes of educational failures in other parts of Africa are external and internal. For example, the majority of educational reforms in Africa has been designed and imposed on the people by foreign agencies with the assistance of each country's urban elite (Mbaku 1994). In addition, poor and disadvantaged groups in rural areas have continued to suffer from inadequate education.

Educational problems in Africa require piecemeal solutions rather than a search for swift or quick fixes to solve all of the existing dilemmas. Even the most developed countries of the world did not reach their current development quickly.

Policymakers and educational planners in South Africa need to be aware of the economic and social realities that contribute to educational inequalities. These realities include, but are not limited to, causes of poverty and population growth.

Jansen (1988) made a convincing statement; that is, in South Africa, a critical moment in black schooling has arrived and an alternative educational system has become morally imperative and politically inevitable. Educational changes are inevitable, but South Africans need to be aware that any changes in black education, as a whole, will require a generation or more before any benefits of such a transformation are realized.

The alternative to Bantu education will not be without problems, given the long history of deprivation during the apartheid era, limited resources, and a shortage of personnel. However, any educational alternative to Bantu education in South Africa that has meaning to black teachers, parents, and students, or their legitimate representatives, must include the following components:
 1. Development of a new language policy for schools
 2. Development of a culturally appropriate curriculum
 3. Development of postapartheid educational aims and objectives
 4. Development of innovative teaching methods

5. Development of reading materials that positively reflect the culture, history, and contributions of the majority
6. Development of alternative ways of raising school funds
7. Development of new programs of nonformal education.

These components will provide a foundation for an alternative education system in a postapartheid era. South Africa needs to look for policy options, as well as for educational changes within itself, and the role of international organizations needs to be acknowledged. For instance, various governments and international organizations have made remarkable contributions to sociopolitical empowerment in South Africa (Lindsay 1995). A large amount of money from major donors has been used to benefit disadvantaged black South Africans educationally. Lindsay cited the following major donors:

1. Foreign governments, including the United States, Scandinavian countries, Australia, Taiwan, Japan, Canada, and the European community
2. Private sector and multinational organizations, including the Anglo-American Chairman's Fund, IBM, Johnson and Johnson, and others
3. A range of foundations such as the Independent Development Trust, the Urban Foundation of South Africa, and most major American foundations such as Ford, Carnegie, Genesis, and Andrew Mellon
4. International organizations such as the World Council of Churches and USAID/South Africa.

In 1992, South Africa received approximately US$343 million in external national donor aid (Lindsay 1995). According to Lindsay, of this amount, approximately US$108 million was donated by the European community, the United States donated US$80 million, and Sweden donated approximately US$57 million (making them the top three donors). The United States provides assistance to black education. For the presidential inauguration, Vice President Al Gore traveled to South Africa in 1994 bearing gifts, including a promise of $600 million in aid, loan guarantees, and other gifts over the next three years ("South African Economy Is Key To Future of the Country" 1994).

11.9 South Africa and the Future

> Out of the experience of an extraordinary human disaster that lasted too long must be born a society of which all humanity will be proud. Never, never and never again shall it be that this beautiful land will again experience the oppression of one by another and suffer the indignity of being the skunk of the world. (Mandela 1994)

South Africa's democratic elections in April 1994 marked an era of hope, coupled with the belief that after years of deprivation under apartheid, changes would emerge in all major social, political, and educational institutions. Since the elections, the new government is making great effort to place its agenda for social and economic improvement through what is known as the Reconstruction and Development Program. According to Brent (1996), the program is being criticized for slow delivery. The creation of better education has remained important to the government of national unity. Brent argued that basic education has the most direct link to future growth and employment and should be favored in allocating scarce government resources. The miseducation of the black population through Bantu education is to be replaced by education for economic development.

The history of Bantu education, with its underlying aims in South Africa and Africa's past, is a necessary component to lay the foundation for the present while preparing for the future. In this book, attempts have been made to provide historical background information while trying to understand the current educational system. In the final chapter, I have tried to highlight educational hardships experienced by other African countries after their independence. These hardships are meant to help South Africa become more realistic in what it can accomplish versus what is available in terms of resources. It is important for those working to improve the quality of black education to work together as new education dispensation is being developed.

Some studies have established that long-term, improved quality of life for the majority of people is consistently associated with the provision and content of education that reflect a society with widespread opportunities for the many rather than for the few (Buchert 1994). In South Africa, where the majority lives in poverty, the widespread existence of quality education will take time to flourish. On the other hand, quality education is crucial in transforming people by replacing hopelessness with a sense of purpose. Postapartheid education will stand the test of replacing Bantu education with quality education, a system of education that will deal with actual problems currently facing South Africa such as joblessness and underemployment.

Change is not easy, and it is always accompanied by fear of the unknown. The postapartheid era brings with it unrealistic expectations, as well as realistic challenges. In the midst of drastic changes currently taking place in South Africa, immense practical problems remain unsolved in black schools. Much work is still to be done in order to meet the educational needs and expectations of the African masses, requiring participation of those committed to the educational reform system. Teachers, parents, students, and professionals from various fields have an important role to play. Major educational transformation requires realistic and financially sound innovative solutions. Nonetheless, diverse opinions on educational transformation will continue to influence the debate. The tolerance of diverse opinions offers the best hope for a liberated South Africa as it attempts to break with its past. Bantu education can be blamed for the current educational inefficiencies, but the responsibility for redressing the past lies squarely on the shoulders of Africans. However, this does not mean that those who hold the best economic cards such as the business community and the white population, in general, are not invited to uplift the disadvantaged. Rather, according to Brent (1996), they, too, must be willing to make contributions proportional to their economic strength.

In fixing the state of black education in South Africa, parents, students, teachers, the business community, ordinary citizens, and other political parties must cooperate. Democracy means free will, not force, even though, under apartheid, other groups have benefited economically and politically through a myriad of laws that generally discriminated against those of African descent. The emergence of a new nation expects more from those who are economically stronger. The proverb says, "Of those to whom much has been given, much will be asked." However, genuine changes will take place through African sacrifice in establishing goals and programs aimed at improved quality and lasting educational betterment.

South Africa's success depends on its economy. The country desperately needs foreign investment to help it accomplish social and political goals. However, foreign investors will be driven away if economic policies look inhospitable or if there is violence and civil turmoil ("South African Economy Is Key To Future of the Country" 1994). If foreign investors do not come, South Africa's new multiracial democracy will be challenged. In order to expect the current political process to eliminate poverty, as well as other social ills, and without considering the economic factors, it is naive and unrealistic. Political change can, however, equip disadvantaged communities with the necessary opportunities to design effective and efficient rules that may give them the opportunity to pursue private objectives in improving their lives.

Chronology

This chronology lists the major changes relating to the South African education that occurred during the period covered in this book.

1652 Jan Van Riebeeck and his merchant colleagues arrived in the Cape peninsula. Their arrival marked the beginning of racial domination in South Africa.

1910 The Act of Union allowed higher education in South Africa to be centrally controlled by the Union or federal government.

1916 One of the largest correspondence universities in South Africa was born University of South Africa (UNISA).

1916 The University of Fort Hare, located in the Eastern Cape, is established for South African nonwhites.

1951 The Eiselen Commission was formulated to provide education for natives as a separate race with a distinctive history.

1953 The Bantu Education Act was passed, making the enforcement of school segregation in South Africa legal.

1959 The Extension of Universities Education Act 45, preventing blacks from attending white universities and vice versa, was introduced. The Act stipulated that each racial group was to attend its designated institution in a separate facility along racial and ethnic lines, except in special circumstances in which ministerial approval was obtained.

1960 The University of the North for the Tsonga, Sotho, Venda, and Tswana people was established.

1960	The University of Durban-Westville for Indian students was established.
1960	The University of the Western Cape was established for colored or people of mixed race, as well as Griqua and Malay students.
1960	The University of Zululand for Zulu and Swazi students was established.
1968	The South African Student Organization, headed by Steve Biko, was formed.
1972	Three important organizations were formed: (a) the South African Student Movement (SASM), (b) the Black People' s Convention (BPC), and (c) the Black Community Project (BCP).
1973	The Black Universities Amendment Act 6 permitted each university to establish branches at other locations within the country. Approval was to be granted by the minister in consultation with the council.
1976	The Medical University of Southern Africa (MEDUNSA) for black students was established.
1976	On June 16th, Soweto students protested against Bantu education and the requirement that they use Afrikaans for school purposes. Many African students were arrested, detained, and killed; others were forced into exile in different parts of the world.
1977	The University of Transkei was established.
1979	The University of Bophuthatswana was established.
1979	The University of Qwa-Qwa was founded.
1979	The University of Venda was founded.
1979	The Universities for Blacks Amendment Act 52 eliminated the admission procedure, permitting persons of a specific black ethnic group to attend any of the black universities. Admissions were to be based on merit, not ethnicity.
1981	The De Lange Committee and its recommendations were made public. The committee recommended equal opportunities in education and unitary control of education.
1981	The government introduced compulsory education for African children living in specific areas, with the clause applying to children who began schooling that year.
1984	The government ended segregation in white universities by banning special permits required to admit nonwhites.

1988	The Union of Democratic University Staff Association (UDUSA) was formed.
1988	Technical colleges were granted permission by the government to desegregate classes.
1989	Universities received permission to integrate their residences, if desired.
1991	The Educational Renewal Strategy document was released, recommending nonracial regional authorities, a unitary system, and compulsory and free education for all South Africans up to Standard Five.
1991	University legislation was passed, giving them full responsibility to determine who to admit.
1993	The National Education and Training Forum (NETF), which served as an open forum for all sectors of society in a combined effort to improve education, was established.
1994	The new country' s constitution recognized all eleven major languages as official.
1995	School integration was passed into law in South Africa, and the feeding program in black schools was reintroduced to assist children from disadvantaged backgrounds.
1995	The White Paper about education and training was drafted, and the New Provincial Education Departments were established.

Clarification Of Terminology

Following is an explanation of key concepts used in this book.

Apartheid: Apartheid is apartness, the state of each race being apart from each other (Williams 1989). Apartheid, in its form and practical terms, is similar to any type of racial segregation. Lipton (1985) cited the following characteristics to define apartheid:

> (a) The economic ordering of the economic, political, and social structures on the basis of race, identified by physical characteristics such as skin color.
> (b) Discrimination against Africans and, to a lesser extent, coloreds (people of mixed races), and Indians, who were excluded from many of the civil, political, and economic rights enjoyed by whites such as the vote, freedom of movement, and the right to do certain jobs or own property in much of the country.
> (c) Segregation of the races in many spheres of life: they lived in separate areas, went to separate schools and universities, used separate buses and trains; there was little social mixing; sexual relations and intermarriage across the color line were illegal.
> (d) The legalization and institutionalization of this hierarchical, discriminatory, and segregated system, which was enshrined in law and enforced by the government. (pp. 14-15)

Apartheid is based on an economic system that has been built on the systematic use of racial discrimination and that has forced the African majority to sell cheap labor for the benefit of the minority. Williams (1989) defined apartheid as a special case of the type of restrictions that are achieved when one class of individuals acquires privilege through the use of state violence to deny another class of individuals the right to engage in voluntary and mutually agreeable exchanges. Therefore, the apartheid system is aimed at discriminating against classes of individuals who are described as low skilled, low educated, latecomers, and politically impotent (Williams 1989).

From the above definitions, there seems to be a consensus as to what apartheid is and what its aim is, that is, to benefit economically those who impose it upon others; it limits the social, economic, and political movements of the intended group of people; and it is a unique form of human subjugation that deprives its victims of any opportunity of economic emancipation while promoting the privileges for the grand designers of the system.

Bantu: According to the South African Bureau of Racial Affairs (1955), the indigenous people of Africa, south of the equator, belonged to a single-language family. These people were classified as a single-language group because of their linguistic use of a noun root similar to -ntu for "person" and a prefix such as ba- for that class of noun (Parsons 1993). As a result, the term "Bantu" was used by the colonists to distinguish these people from Negroes, Hottentot, and Bushmen (South African Bureau of Racial Affairs 1955). The indigenous people of South Africa are the Bantu, which, even today, form the majority of the population.

In the early days, South Africa was inhabited by Bantu groups, as well as other groups, such as the Hottentot and Bushmen. Even though the Bantu people in South Africa have similar physical characteristics, they do not speak the same languages. Languages spoken by the Bantu people of South Africa include, but are not limited to, the Zulu, Xhosa, Sotho, Tswana, Ndebele, Pedi, Shangaan, Swazi, and Venda. However, regardless of their language differences, they form a racial unity.

Even though linguistic differences are evident among the Bantu people, they still share more cultural similarities. With the arrival of white settlers from Europe, ethnic differences among natives was stressed. This fragmentation of Bantus was not an accident; it was a planned form of subjugation. The natives were to be divided into major ethnolinguistic groups for the purpose of economic, social, and political control.

Blacks: The apartheid policy legally separated its 35 million inhabitants into four racial groups: (a) whites (15.5 percent), (b) coloreds or people of mixed race (9.0 percent), (c) Indians (2.8 percent), and (d) Africans (72.7 percent) (Seedat 1984). The term "black" is used in South Africa to refer to all nonwhites. Therefore, the term black is sometimes used to refer to all those not classified as white (Smith 1992). These groups include Africans (natives/indigenous of the country), Indians, and coloreds or people of mixed races. Africans form the majority of the South African population. They have been officially divided into several major ethnic groups, including the Zulus (estimated to number 6.4 million), the Xhosas (estimated to number 2.9 million), the Northern Sothos (estimated to number 2.9 million), the Southern Sothos (estimated to number 1.9 million), the Tswanas (estimated to number 1.4 million), and the Tsongas (estimated to number 1.1 million) (Williams 1989). Most of these groups are homogeneous, with insignificant differences in their languages; however, the apartheid system has exaggerated their differences. The homeland system was designed to divide the Africans and to create fake nations.

The division, which is always overemphasized among Africans, is done for economic and political purposes such as to prevent unity among blacks and to control them with ease. African labor is easily exploited when divided. The division of blacks also has helped in denying them their South African citizenship. Africans under apartheid were not regarded as citizens of a white South Africa.

However, throughout this book, the term black should be understood to be interchangeable with Africans. The primary reason the focus is on Africans is that Bantu education was specifically designed for the African population known officially as Bantu and earlier as natives (Smith 1992).

Ethnicity: Ethnicity in a South African context is the systematic separation of national communities. There are eight major ethnic and/or racial groups of which many are Africans such as the Xhosa, Venda, Zulu, Sotho-Tswana, Tsonga, coloreds, Indians, and whites (Lindsay 1995). Thirteen percent of the land is allocated to the African population, leaving the balance of the rich land available for white settlement. Africans who live in white areas pay rent or pay in the form of labor for living in the land owned by whites. The majority of coloreds is found in the western Cape, with a small percentage of Indians also residing in that part of South Africa. More Indians live in Natal than in any other part of South Africa. Africans are found throughout the country, with large numbers of Zulus in Natal and southern Transvaal, the Sotho-Tswana in the Orange Free State and Transvaal, the Xhosa centered in the eastern and western Cape, and the Venda and Tsonga concentrated in northern Transvaal (Lindsay 1995). According to Lindsay, the largest numbers of English and Afrikaners are in the regions of the Cape, Transvaal, and Natal.

The legal separation of races is justified by the perception that South Africa is a multinational country composed of discrete ethnic groups such as the Zulus, Xhosas, Sothos, and Tswanas, each sharing a common bond and yet different from other racial groups. Under apartheid, differences among African groups were particularly stressed in order to manipulate and control them. On the other hand, people of European descent were treated as a single entity in politics, as well as in the economy. The division of Africans has been promoted in order to help the minority to maintain power, as well as for economic gains. The homelands system, in turn, helped to solidify ethnic differences among Africans.

Homelands: Homelands are specially designated residential areas reserved for Africans. These areas comprise 13 percent of the land (usually the least fertile), providing a pool of cheap labor to the urban and industrial areas of South Africa. This system, based on the notion that separate development breeds good neighborly relationships, fosters ethnic nationalism through the (inherently undemocratic) creation of homogeneous national states (Taylor 1991). Thus, ten homelands came into existence in order to place different African groups in the impoverished rural areas and as a deliberate plan to deprive them of their South African citizenship (Battersby 1994). These homelands include Kwa-Zulu for the Zulus, Transkei and Ciskei for the Xhosas, Kwa-Ndebele for the Ndebeles, Gazankulu for the Shangaans and Tsongas, Lebowa and Qwa-Qwa for the Sothos, Bophuthatswana for the Tswanas, KaNgwane for the Swazis, and Venda for the Vendas.

The designers of this "peculiar institution" used African chiefs as subordinate officials to carry orders and to perform duties, which benefited the colonial government only (Thompson 1990). According to Thompson, the legislative framework, pioneered by Verwoerd, was completed in 1971 when the Bantu Homelands Constitution Act permitted the government to grant independence to any homeland. Government propaganda and monetary rewards promoted through bribery, corruption, and coercion helped legitimize the homeland system. Battersby (1994) estimated that the grand-apartheid plan, which is now defunct, cost South Africa approximately $10 billion in funds and an additional $3 to $4 billion in futile efforts to lure South African industry and the jobs they created from the cities to the homelands. According to Battersby, when looking at the scale of corruption in the name of the homeland system, it is fiscal plundering. The Transkei' s were the first to obtain independence. They became "self-governing" in 1963 and were independent in 1976 (Thompson 1990). The Bophuthatswana' s were granted their independence in 1977, the Venda' s in 1979, and the Ciskei' s in 1981. Citizens of independent nations automatically lost their South African citizenship. African chiefs, whose income came directly from Pretoria, became the sole rulers of the homelands. Economically, the homelands remained poor and depended on white South Africa. These homelands were never recognized by foreign countries.

The homeland system allowed all Africans to be herded to their respective homelands with the exception of a few Africans whose services were needed for the white economy. These Africans were regarded as "temporary" guest workers admitted, as required, by permit (King 1979). The plan was to have all Africans residing in their respective homelands by the year 2000. According to Thompson (1990), in 1967, the Department of Bantu Administration and Development described the homeland policy in a circular:

> It is accepted government policy that the Bantu are only temporarily residents of the Republic for as long as they offer their labor there. As soon as they become, for one reason or another, no longer fit for work or superfluous in the labor market, they are expected to return to their country of origin or the territory of the national unit where they fit ethnically if they were not born and bred in their homeland. (p. 193)

Laws help the government in limiting the number of rural Africans from seeking residence in the urban and industrial areas of South Africa. While homelands became the dumping areas for the urban undesirable such as the sick, the old, and the handicapped, they were, and still are, sources of economic exploitation of Africans. The former government deliberately justified the homeland system in which it had a vested interest. The economic factor can be described as one among many underlying factors that contributed to the development of homelands in South Africa. The homeland population was estimated at 69 percent between 1970 and 1980 (Thompson 1990). Central to the homeland system is the migratory labor system.

Migratory Labor System: Able-bodied Africans living in the homelands are somehow forced to seek employment outside their homelands. Hut taxes, poll taxes, forced removals, and land appropriation are a few examples of impositions that force people to leave impoverished homelands for cities. As a result of the African's limited technological level, they find themselves at the mercy of people who have the economic means in order to provide for their families. Thus, many Africans become easy targets for cheap labor in the economic machinery of South Africa. The African migrant workers toil in unskilled, low-paying, low status jobs such as mining, cleaning offices, working in factories, driving trucks, and making deliveries. Many Africans are forced into single-sexed hostel life, making them vulnerable for political and economic manipulation. Taylor (1991) explained that, under the migrant labor system, African workers live in cold, dark, single-sex hostels, removed from family life and forced to perform the worst type of dirty work in foundries, other heavy industry, and municipalities.

The migratory labor system systematically destroyed black family life. Migrant laborers were forced to live for one year in single-sex hostels without their families. Due to influx control, wives or children of African men were not permitted to visit cities in which their husbands or fathers worked. Political leaders need to reconsider the migratory labor system in order to reduce its negative impact on society.

Nonracialism: Nonracialism is a term commonly used to define racial tolerance or the absence of discrimination based on race. Blacks who, under apartheid, suffered dehumanization and were estranged in their own land will soon enjoy political, social, and economic liberties like all other citizens of the country. Nonracialism does not mean color-blindness; it means allowing all people a fair chance in life; it means not to control the existence of other groups because of their race through unjust laws and/or unfair competition. Privileged and disadvantaged groups in South Africa currently are protected by the country's new constitution. The democratic transition must stand the test to ensure that no one is above the law, rich or poor, black or white, young or old. According to Adam (1995), nonracialism merely holds out the promise that the state will not recognize or tolerate race as a public and legal criterion of exclusion, private racism notwithstanding.

Selected Bibliography

Adam, H. 1995. "The Politics of Ethnic Identity: Comparing South Africa." *Ethnic and Racial Studies* 18(3):457-75.

Adegbija, E. 1994. *Language Attitudes in Sub-Saharan Africa: A Sociological Overview*. Clevedon, England: Multilingual Maters Ltd.

"Affirmative Education." 1994. *In Focus* 2(11):20-26.

Agar, D. 1983. "Curriculum Innovation: The Case of Bophuthatswana." *Perspectives in Education* 7(1):50-59.

Alexander, N. 1992. "Educational Strategies for the New South Africa." *SASPOST* 4(1):1-2.

Ankomah, B. 1996. "For Debt Read Death." *New African* 340:8.

Arnold, M. 1981. "Steve Biko: Black Consciousness in South Africa." *Harvard Educational Review* 51(1):200-01.

Asbury, C. A., V. Maholmes, and S. Walker. 1993. "Is There A Relationship Between Disability and Education?" *The Negro Educational Review* 44(1-2):3-11.

Austin, R. 1975. *Racism and Apartheid in Southern Africa: Rhodesia*. Paris, France: The UNESCO Press.

Avoke, M. K. 1993. "Development of Special Education in Ghana." *The View Finder: Expanding Boundaries and Perspectives in Special Education* 2:38-39.

"Bad School or None." 1987. *The Economist* 302(7481):40.
Badat, S. 1991. "The Expansion of Black Tertiary Education 1977-90: Reform and Contradiction." In *Apartheid Education and Popular Struggle*, edited by E. Unterhalter, H. Wolpe, T. Botha, S. Badat, T. Dlamini, and B. Khotseng, 73-94. London, England: Zed Books Ltd.
Baine, D., and T. Mwamwenda. 1994. "Education in Southern Africa: Current Conditions and Future Directions." *International Review of Education* 40(2):115-36.
Balintulo, M. M. 1981. "The Black Universities in South Africa." In *Apartheid and Social Research*, edited by J. Rex, 141-59. Paris, France: The UNESCO Press.
Bamgbose, A. 1991. *Language and the Nation: The Language Question in Sub-Saharan*. Edinburgh, England: Edinburgh University Press.
Barbour, M. 1984. "The Supply of Books and Articles About African Countries." *African Affairs* 83(330):95-112.
Barnard, D. 1993. "Education and Training: The Way Forward." *Prodder Newsletter: Program for Development Research* 5(3):1.
Barnard, D. 1994. "Southern Africa: The Dawn of a New Era." *Prodder Newsletter: Program for Development Research* 6(2):1-3.
Battersby, J. 1994. "Apartheid's Homelands Haunt Election Campaign." *The Christian Science Monitor* 86(78):6.
Bean, E. 1994. "Computers in South African Schools: Quo Vadis?" *Technology and Teacher Education Annual*:10-13.
Bean, P., and L. Cowley. 1994. "Preparing Educationally Computer Literate Educators for the 'New' South Africa." *Technology and Teacher Education Annual*:7-9.
Behr, A. L. 1978. *New Perspectives in South African Education*. Durban, South Africa: Butterworths.
Bhola, H. S. 1984. "A Policy Analysis of Adult Literacy Promotion in the Third World: An Accounting of Promises Made and Promises Fulfilled." *International Review of Education* 30(3):249-64.
"Black Power in South Africa." 1994. *Newsweek Magazine* (May 9):34-36.
Bohannan, P., and P. Curtin. 1995. *Africa and Africans*. 4th ed. Prospect Heights, Illinois: Waveland Press.

Bor, W. van den, and J. C. M. Shute. 1991. "Higher Education in the Third World: Status Symbol or Instrument for Development?" *Higher Education* 22(1):1-15.

Botha, T. 1991. "Education With Production in Zimbabwe: A Model for Post-Apartheid South Africa?" In *Apartheid Education and Popular Struggle*, edited by E. Unterhalter, H. Wolpe, T. Botha, S. Badat, T. Dlamini, and B. Khotseng, 203-11. London, England: Zed Books Ltd.

Bray, M., P. B. Clarke, and D. Stephens. 1986. *Education and Society in Africa*. London, England: Edward Arnold.

Brent, R. S. 1996. "Tough Road To Prosperity." *Foreign Affairs* 75(2):113-26.

"Bright Ideas To Get Our Schools Buzzing." 1995. *City Press* (September 3):19.

Buchert, L. 1994. *Education in the Development of Tanzania 1919-90*. London, England: Villiers Publications.

"The Business Day: Lack of Qualified Teachers Must Be Addressed." 1994. *This Week in South Africa* 6(1):6-7.

"The Business Day: Warning Lights." 1994. *This Week in South Africa* 5(38):5-6.

Cameron, J., and W. A. Dodd. 1970. *Society, Schools and Progress in Tanzania*. Oxford: Pergamon Press.

Chandler, N. 1995. "The Patterns of Poverty." *Daily News* (June 13):12.

Chatterjee, D. 1995. "Empower Women To Stem World Population Explosion." *The Daily Utah Chronicle* (January 4):2.

Cheater, A. P. 1991. "The University of Zimbabwe: University, National University, State University, or Party University?" *African Affairs* 90(359):189-205.

Chisholm, L., and B. Fine. 1994. "Context and Contest in South African Education Policy: Comment On Curtin." *African Affairs* 93(371):233-48.

Christen, A. 1996. "South Africa After Apartheid." *Swiss Review of World Affairs* 5:6-8.

Christie, P. 1985. *The Right To Learn: The Struggle for Education in South Africa*. Johannesburg, South Africa: Ravan Press.

Christie, P., and M. Gaganakis. 1989. "Farm Schools in South Africa: The Face of Rural Apartheid." *Comparative Education Review* 33(1):77-92.

Cilliers, C., L. Botha, B. Capdevielle, D. Perkins, and D. van der Vyver. 1994. "The Development of a Curriculum for the Thinking Skills for Primary School Pupils in the New South Africa: An International and Multidisciplinary Approach." *International Journal of Special Education* 9(3):257-70.

Clarke, J. H. 1991. *Notes for an African World Revolution: Africans at the Crossroads*. Trenton, New Jersey: Africa World Press.

Cole, M., and J. S. Bruner. 1972. "Preliminaries To a Theory of Cultural Differences." In *Seventy-First Yearbook of the National Society for the Study of Education, Part 11, Early Childhood Education*, edited by I. Gordon, 161-79. Chicago, Illinois: University of Chicago Press.

Collins, C. B., and R. R. Gillespie. 1984. "Moving Education Forward To Keep Society Back: The South African De Lange Report Reevaluated." *Comparative Education Review* 28(4):625-38.

Connell, R. W. 1994. "Poverty and Education." *Harvard Educational Review* 64(2):125-49.

Corby, R. A. 1990. "Focus On the Legacy of British Colonialism in Africa: Educating Africans for Inferiority Under British Rule: Bo School in Sierra Leone." *Comparative Education Review* 34(3):314-49.

Cowder, M. 1987. "Whose Dream Was It Anyway? Twenty-Five Years of African Independence." *African Affairs* 86(342):7-24.

Csapo, M. 1986. "Separate Development: Education and Special Education in South Africa." *International Journal of Special Education* 1:49-91.

"The Daily News: More Turmoil in Schools." 1994. *This Week in South Africa* 5(38):6.

Dakin, J., B. Tiffen, and H. G. Widdowson. 1968. *Language in Education: The Problem in Commonwealth Africa and the Indo-Pakistan Sub-Continent*. London, England: Oxford University Press.

Danaher, K. 1984. "Educational Inequality in South Africa and Its Implications for U.S. Foreign Policy." *Harvard Educational Review* 54(2):166-74.

Davidson, B. 1994. *Modern Africa: A Social and Political History*. 3rd ed. London, England: Longman.

Davidson, J., and M. Kanyuka. 1992. "Girl' s Participation in Basic Education in Southern Malawi." *Comparative Education Review* 36(4):446-66.

Davies, D. 1995. "The African Brain Drain." *West Africa* 4066:1433-35.

Davies, J. 1985. "U.S. Foreign Policy and the Education of Black South Africans." *Comparative Education Review* 29(2):171-88.

De Clercq, F. 1991. "Black Universities As Contested Terrains: The Politics of Progressive Engagement." *Perspectives in Education* 12(2):49-64.

De Lange, J. P. 1981. *Provision of Education in the Republic of South Africa: Report of the National Investigation Into Education*. Pretoria, South Africa: Human Sciences Research Council.

Dempster, C. 1982. "Equal Quality in Education: A Dead Commitment." *The Star* (April 17):12.

Department of Education and Training. 1994-95. *Special Education Information for Schools in the Republic of South Africa*. Pretoria, South Africa: Department of Education and Training.

Desai, Z. 1992. "Democratic Language Planning and the Transformation of Education in Post-Apartheid South Africa." In *Education in a Future South Africa: Policy Issues for Transformation*, edited by E. Unterhalter, H. Wolpe, and T. Botha, 112-22. Trenton, New Jersey: Africa World Press.

Desai, Z., and D. McLean. 1994. "Multilingualism: The New Language Policy." *Mayibuye: Journal of the ANC* 5(3):32-33.

Dillman, C. M., and H. F. Rahmlow. 1972. *Writing Instructional Objectives*. Belmont, California: Fearon Publishers.

Djangmah, J. S. 1995. "Funding of Postgraduate Training and Research in African Universities." *Higher Education Policy* 8(1):30-32.

Donald, D. 1995. "High School Underachievement as a Legacy of Apartheid: Implications for the Development of an Appropriate Education Support Service in South Africa." *IASE Monograph. Empowering Children With Special Needs: Practices Around the World*, 137-42.

Donald, D. R., and M. M. Hlongwane. 1989. "Consultative Psychological Service Delivery in the Context of Black Education in South Africa." *International Journal of Special Education* 4(2):119-40.

Dorsey, B. J. 1989. "Education Development and Reform in Zimbabwe." *Comparative Education Review* 33(1):40-58.
Drew, C. J. 1981, January 7-9. *Research Methods in Teacher Education*. Paper presented at the annual conference, Teacher Education Division, Council for Exceptional Children, Phoenix, Arizona.
Drew, C. J., K. Preator, and M. L. Buchanan. 1982. "Research and Researchers in Special Education." *Exceptional Education Quarterly* 2(4):47-56.
Dreyer, J. M. 1994. "Promoting the Potential of Children: The Teacher' s Role." *Educare* 23(1):69-74.
Dube, E. F. 1985. "The Relationship Between Racism and Education in South Africa." *Harvard Educational Review* 55(1):86-100.
Duminy, P. A. 1967. *Trends and Challenges in the Education of the South African Bantu*. Pretoria, South Africa: J. S. Van Schaik, Ltd.
Eastman, C. M. 1990. "What Is the Role of Language Planning in Post-Apartheid South Africa?" *TESOL Quarterly* 24(1):9-21.
Eckstein, B. 1994. "South Africa' s Young Children: Winning Or Losing?" *International Journal of Early Childhood* 26(1):48-54.
Eisemon, T. O. 1989. "Educational Reconstruction in Africa." *Comparative Education Review* 33(1):110-33.
Eshiwani, G. S. 1989. "The World Bank Document Revisited." *Comparative Education Review* 33(1):116-25.
Evans, I. T. 1992. "Essay Review: Education for an Apartheid-Free South Africa." *Harvard Educational Review* 62(1):66-78.
Everatt, D. 1994. *Creating a Future: Youth Policy for South Africa*. Johannesburg, South Africa: Ravan Press.
Fafunwa, A. B. 1974. *History of Education*. London, England: George Allen and Unwin Ltd.
Fehrenbach, P. A., and M. H. Thelen. 1982. "Behavioral Approaches To the Treatment of Aggressive Disorders." *Behavior Modification* 6(4):465-97.
File, J. 1986. "The Politics of Excellence: University Education in the South African Context." *Social Dynamics* 12(1):26-42.
Foster, P. 1969. "Education for Self-Reliance: A Critical Evaluation." In *Education in Africa*, edited by R. Jolly, 81-101. Nairobi, Kenya, East Africa: East African Publishing House.

Fussell, W. 1996. "The Value of Local Knowledge and the Importance of Shifting Beliefs in the Process of Social Change." *Community Development Journal* 31(1):44-53.
Gardner, C. 1994. "The Role of Women." *The Natal Witness/South Africa* (March 17):8.
Geber, B. A., and S. P. Newman. 1980. *Soweto's Children: The Development of Attitudes.* London, England: Academic Press.
Gelfand, D. M., W. R. Jenson, and C. J. Drew. 1982. *Understanding Children Behavior Disorders.* New York, New York: Holt, Rinehart and Winston.
Gillespie, M. 1993. "Profiles of Adult Learners: Revealing the Multiple Faces of Literacy." *TESOL Quarterly* 27(3):529-41.
Goldemberg, J. 1988. "Financing Education in Developing Countries." *Higher Education Policy* 1(2):37-38.
Goodey, J. S. 1987. "Towards Multicultural Education in Higher Educational Institutions in South Africa." *Journal of Multilingual and Cultural Development* 8(6):553-54.
Gray, B. 1995. "Future Directions in Science Teacher Education." *SAJHE/SATHO* 9(1):47-52.
Green, M. 1991. "The Politics of Education: South Africa's Lost Generation." *The American Enterprise* 2(3):12-15.
Gwalla, N. 1988. "State Control, Student Politics, and the Crisis in Black Universities." In *Popular Struggles in South Africa*, edited by W. Cobbett and R. Cohen, 163-84. Trenton, New Jersey: Africa World Press.
Gwalla-Ogisi, N. 1990. "Special Education in South Africa." In *Pedagogy of Domination: Toward a Democratic Education in South Africa*, edited by M. Nkomo, 271-88. Trenton, New Jersey: Africa World Press.
Hardman, M. L., C. J. Drew, M. W. Egan, and B. Wolf. 1990. *Human Exceptionality.* Boston: Allyn and Bacon.
Hay, M. J., and S. Stichter. 1984. *African Women South of the Sahara.* New York, New York: Longman.
Helge, D. 1989. *Preventing Teenage Pregnancies in Rural America: A Manual.* Washington, DC: National Rural Development Institute.
Herbstein, D. 1992. "Upgrading the Universities." *Africa Report* 37(4):62-65.
Herbstein, D. 1993. "Back To School." *Africa Report* 38(2):36-39.

Hey, P. D. 1961. "The Rural Zulu Teacher in Natal." *Comparative Education Review* 5(1):54-58.
Heyns, R. 1986. *South Africa*. Cape Town: CTP Book Printers.
Heyns, R. 1987-88. *South Africa*. Johannesburg, South Africa: Persko Printers.
Higgs, P., and L. G. Higgs. 1994. "University Education in a Postapartheid South Africa: A Philosophical Response." *Educare* 23(1):40-47.
Hitchens, C., and D. Stephen. 1981. *Inequalities in Zimbabwe: Report No. 8*. London, England: Expedite Graphic Ltd.
Hlatshwayo, T. 1992. "Kwazamokuhle School for the Handicapped." *Southern Africa Today* 9(5):16-17.
"Homework for Parents." 1994. *The Christian Science Monitor* 86(202):18.
Horrell, M. 1968. *Bantu Education To 1968*. Cape Town, South Africa: Cape and Tvl Printers.
Hurwitz, N. 1964. *The Economics of Bantu Education in South Africa*. Johannesburg, South Africa: South African Institute of Race Relations.
Hyslop, J. 1993. "A Destruction Coming In: Bantu Education as Response To Social Crisis." In *Apartheid's Genesis*, edited by P. Bonner, P. Delius, and D. Posel, 393-410. Johannesburg, South Africa: Ravan Press.
Igbalajobi, M. 1984. "Education for the Handicapped Children in Developing Countries: A Review." *International Education* 14(1):44-51.
International Labour Office. 1988. "Special Report of the Director-General on the Application of the Declaration Concerning the Policy of Apartheid in South Africa." Geneva, Switzerland: International Labor Office.
"Investing Cents Will Make Sense for Your Child." 1995. *Education* (August 31):2.
"In Your Language or Mine?" 1994. *The Economist* 332(7881):48.
Jacobs, M. 1991. "A Time for Action: The State of South Africa's Children." *Progress Reports on Health and Development in South Africa* (Spring/Summer):12-13.
Jansen, J. D. 1988. "Curriculum Change and Contextual Realities: An Analysis of Recent Trends in Black South African Education." *International Review of Education* 34(3):378-87.

Jansen, J. D. 1990. "Curriculum Policy in a Post-Apartheid Dispensation." In *Pedagogy of Domination*, edited by M. O. Nkomo, 325-39. Trenton, New Jersey: Africa World Press.

Jansen, J. D. 1991. "The State and Curriculum in the Transition To Socialism: The Zimbabwean Experience." *Comparative Education Review* 35(1):76-91.

Johnson, D. 1992. "Transforming Teacher Provision and Teacher Training for a Post-Apartheid South Africa." In *Education in a Future South Africa: Policy Issues for Transformation*, edited by E. Unterhalter, H. Wolpe, and T. Botha, 186-99. Trenton, New Jersey: Africa World Press.

Johnson, W. R. 1994. *Dismantling Apartheid: A South African Town in Transition*. London, England: Cornell University Press.

Johnson, W. R., and D. E. Devlin-Foltz. 1993. *Forward Together: The United States' Role in Namibian Education and Training. The Namibian Education Program Working Paper No. 2*. New York, New York: Institute of International Education.

Johnston, A. 1990. "Adult Literacy for Development in Mozambique." *African Studies Review* 33(3):83-96.

Jolly, R. 1969. *Education in Africa: Research and Action*. Nairobi, Kenya, East Africa: The English Press.

Jones, R. C. 1986. *Large-Scale Implementation of a Computer-Based Education Program for Disadvantaged High School Pupils at Matriculation Level*. Unpublished M.Ed Thesis, University of the Western Cape, South Africa.

Kabzems, V., and R. Chimedza. 1995, April. *The Use of Paraprofessionals in Educating Children With Special Needs in Zimbabwe*. A paper presented at the International Special Education Congress, Birmingham, England.

Kachelhoffer, P. M. 1995. "Teacher Enrichment Programs in Kwa-Ndebele, South Africa." *Higher Education Policy* 8(2):19-22.

Ka Choeu, C. 1991. "The Right To Education: An Elusive Quest for the Youth in South Africa." *Africa Today* 38(3):72-78.

Karamitas, S. 1994. "Parents Pay Fees To Keep Classes Small." *The Star Newspaper* (September):16.

Kassam, Y. 1983. "Nyerere's Philosophy and Educational Experiment in Tanzania." *Interchange* 14(1):56-68.

Kerfoot, C. 1993. "Participatory in a South African Context: Contradiction and Challenges." *TESOL Quarterly* 27(3):431-47.

"Keys To A Quality Multicultural Curriculum." 1992. *The Good Common School* (Winter):5.
King, E. 1979. "An Educational Way Ahead for South Africa?" *International Review of Education* 25(4):481-500.
Klassen, C., and B. Burnaby. 1993. "Those Who Know: Views On Literacy Among Adult Immigrants in Canada." *TESOL* 27(3):377-97.
Kockott, F. 1994. "Occupational Hazards." *Tribute Magazine* (September):66-103.
Kraak, A. 1991. "Making the Hidden Curriculum the Formal Curriculum: Vocational Training in South Africa." *Comparative Education Review* 35(3):406-29.
Kriegler, S. 1989. "The Learning Disabilities Paradigm: Is It Relevant To the South African Context?" *International Journal of Special Education* 4(2):165-71.
Kriegler, S., and R. Farman. 1994. "Redistribution of Special Education Resources in South Africa: Beyond Mainstreaming Towards Effective Schools for All." *International Journal of Special Education* 9(1):1-12.
Krige, D., S. Cairns, M. Makalima, and D. Scott. 1995. "Mapping Education: The Education Foundation." *Indicator: South Africa* 12(2):76-80.
Kundu, C. L. 1984. *Adult Education*. New Delhi, India: Sterling Publishers.
Kunene, S., and M. Mokae. 1990. "Doing Something About Illiteracy." *True Love Magazine* (June):16.
Kuzwayo, E. 1985. *Call Me Woman*. London, England: Women' s Press.
Lawson, L. 1986. *Working Women in South Africa*. London, England: Pluto Press.
Leming, J. S. 1994. "Character Education and Multicultural Education: Conflicts and Prospects." *Educational Horizons* 72(3):123-30.
Lesage, J. M. 1994. "South Africa: Bridging the Gap." *New African* 321:20-21.
Lewis, L. J. 1961. "Education and Political Independence in Africa." *Comparative Education Review* 5(1):39-49.

Lichtenstein, S. 1993. "Transition From School To Adulthood: Case Studies of Adults With Learning Disabilities Who Dropped Out of School." *Exceptional Children* 59(4):336-47.

Lindsay, B. 1995. "Sociopolitical Realities and Teacher Education in A New South Africa." In *The Political Dimension in Teacher Education: Comparative Perspectives On Policy Formation, Socialization and Society*, edited by M. B. Ginsburg and B. Lindsay, 162-74. London, England: The Falmer Press.

Lipman, B. 1984. *We Make Freedom: Women in South Africa*. London, England: Pandora Press.

Lipton, M. 1985. *Capitalism and Apartheid: South Africa, 1910-1984*. Totowa, New Jersey: Rowman and Allanheld.

"Literacy Education for Community Upliftment." 1995. *The Zululand Observer* (August 25):60.

Lovitt, T. C. 1991. *Preventing School Dropouts: Tactics for At-Risk, Remedial, and Mildly Handicapped Adolescents*. Austin, Texas: Pro-Ed.

Loxton, L. I. 1994. "Fewer Black South Africans Pass Key Examination." *The Chronicle of Higher Education* 11(28):A42.

Lyman, P. N. 1996. "South Africa's Promise." *Foreign Policy* 102:105-19.

Maake, N. P. 1991. "Language and Politics in South Africa With Reference To the Dominance of the Nguni Languages." *English Studies in Africa* 34(2):56-64.

MacKenzie, C. G. 1988. "Zimbabwe's Educational Miracle and the Problems It Has Created." *International Review of Education* 34(3):337-53.

MacKenzie, C. G. 1993. "Academic Standards and Progressive University Provision in a New South Africa: Prospects for Evolution in an African Context." *African Affairs* 92(368):403-16.

Malherbe, G., K. Naidoo, M. Meintjies, C. Nagoor, and J. Brown. 1995. "Principals Optimistic: Schools Face Mammoth Changes." *The Daily News/South Africa* (January 9):3.

Maliyamkono, T. L. 1980. "The School as a Force for Community Change in Tanzania." *International Review of Education* 26(3):335-47.

Mandela, N. 1994, May 10. *Presidential Inaugural Address*. Pretoria, South Africa.

Marcum, J. A. 1982. *Education, Race, and Social Change in South Africa*. Berkeley, California: University of California Press.

Martin, S. O. 1981. *A Study of Utah Secondary Education Dropout Rates Before and After Public Law 94-142*. Unpublished thesis, University of Utah, Salt Lake City, Utah.

Matabane, S. M. 1990. "Developing a Campaign To Eliminate Illiteracy." In *Pedagogy of Domination: Toward a Democratic Education in South Africa*, edited by M. Nkomo, 341-64. Trenton, New Jersey: Africa World Press.

Matloff, J. 1996. "South African Schools Struggle To Make Grade." *The Christian Science Monitor* 88(30):10-11.

Mbaku, J. M. 1994. "Africa After More Than Thirty Years of Independence: Still Poor and Deprived." *Journal of Third World Studies* 11(2):13-58.

Mbaku, J. M. 1995. "Post-Independence Opportunism and Democratization in Africa." *The Journal of Social, Political and Economic Studies* 20(4):405-22.

McClellan, G. S. 1979. *The Reference Shelf: Southern Africa*. New York, New York: The H. W. Wilson Co.

McDowell, D. W. 1980. "The Impact of the National Policy on Education on Indigenous Education in Nigeria." *International Review of Education* 26(1):49-64.

McFadden, P. 1990. "Youth Transformation Education: Observations at the Solomon Mahlangu Freedom College." In *Pedagogy of Domination: Toward a Democratic Education in South Africa*, edited by M. Nkomo, 217-29. Trenton, New Jersey: Africa World Press.

Meldrum, A. 1991. "Lessons from Zimbabwe." *Africa Report* 36(3):16-17.

Mgbejiofor, S. E. 1977. "The Dilemmas of the Nigerian Intellectuals." *Africa Quarterly* 17(1):37-48.

Miller, S. 1995. Big Influx Expected: Schooling Fees a Problem. *The Daily News* (January 23):3

"Millions Lack Basic Facilities." 1994. *This Week in South Africa* 5(10):6-7.

Mingat, A., and J. P. Tan. 1986. "Financing Public Higher Education in Developing Countries." *Higher Education* 15(3-4):283-97.

Minnery, T. 1994. "Values in Education: Goals Should Be the Best." *Educational Horizons* 72(3):136-40.

Mkhize, L. 1993. "Schools: Make the Right Choice." *Thandi Magazine* (August):21-23.
Mncwabe, M. P. 1993. *Post-Apartheid Education:Towards Non-Racial, Unitary and Democratic Socialization in the New South Africa.* Lanham, Maryland: University Press of America.
Molobi, E. 1988. "From Bantu Education To People's Education." In *Popular Struggles in South Africa,* edited by W. Cobbett and R. Cohen, 155-62. Trenton, New Jersey: Africa World Press.
Molobi, E. 1991, November 8-11. *Education in the Present South African Context.* Paper presented at the Third Annual CDI Reentry Conference, Washington, DC.
Moncada-Davidson, L. 1995. "Education and Its Limitations in the Maintenance of Peace in El Salvador." *Comparative Education Review* 39(1):54-75.
Moodie, G. C. 1994. "The State and the Liberal Universities in South Africa: 1948-1990." *Higher Education* 27(1):1-40.
Morris, A. 1986. "Social Class and Matric Results." *Perspectives in Education* 9(1):23-33.
Mosha, H. J. 1988. "A Reassessment of the Indicators of Primary Education Quality in Developing Countries: Emerging Evidence From Tanzania." *International Review of Education* 34(1):17-45.
Mundy, K. 1993. "Focus on Southern Africa: Toward a Critical Analysis of Literacy in Southern Africa." *Comparative Education Review* 37(4):389-411.
Murphy, J. T. 1996. "Don't Blame Africans for Bad Rulers." *The New York Times* (January 31):A12.
Mushi, P. A. K. 1991. "Origins and Development of Adult Education Innovations in Tanzania." *International Review of Education* 37(3):351-63.
Mwamwenda, T. 1994. "Educational Expansion in Africa, With Special Reference to Southern Africa." *Research in Education* 51:59-65.
Mwiria, K. 1990. "Kenya's Harambee Secondary School Movement: The Contradictions of Public Policy." *Comparative Education Review* 34(3):350-68.
Natriello, G. 1987. *School Dropouts: Patterns and Policies.* New York, New York: Teachers College Press.
"New Schools Scheme a Clean Break With Past." 1992. *Focus on South Africa* (March):10.

Ngugi, T. 1993. *Decolonizing the Mind: The Politics of Language in African Literature*. London, England: James Currey.

Nkabinde, Z. 1993a. "Special Education for Black South Africans." *SASPOST* 4(3):4.

Nkabinde, Z. 1993b. "Special Education in a Changing South Africa." *The Journal of Special Education* 27(1):107-14.

Nkabinde, Z. 1993c. "The Relevance and Applicability of Special Education in the New South Africa." *Paidonomia, Journal of the Faculty of Education, University of Zululand* 18(1):17-25.

Nkomo, M. O. 1981. "The Contradictions of Bantu Education." *Harvard Educational Review* 51(1):126-38.

Nkomo, M. O. 1984. *Student Culture and Activism in Black South African Universities*. Westport, Connecticut: Greenwood Press.

Nkomo, M. O. 1990. *Pedagogy of Domination: Toward a Democratic Education in South Africa*. Trenton, New Jersey: Africa World Press.

Nkomo, M. O. 1991. "The Current Crisis in Education and the Challenge of the Future." *SASPOST* 2(2):1-5.

Nkomo, M. O. 1992. "Democratizing Higher Education: Imperatives of Quality and Equality for Development." In *Quality and Equality in Higher Education: Proceedings of the 1992 SAARHE Congress*, edited by E. Bitzer and A. Beylefeld, 68-85. Bloemfontein, South Africa: University of the Orange Free State.

Nordkvelle, Y. 1990. "The Academic Boycott of South Africa Debate: Science and Practice." *Studies in Higher Education* 15(3):253-75.

Norward, J. N. 1994. "The Efficacy of Prevention: Improving the Status of Children in South Africa." *Journal of Multicultural Social Work* 3(3):75-86.

Nyanguru, A., and M. Peil. 1991. "Zimbabwe Since Independence: A People' s Assessment." *African Affairs* 90(361):607-20.

Nyerere, J. 1985. "Education in Tanzania." *Harvard Educational Review* 55(1):45-58.

Nxumalo, O. E. H. M. 1990. "Teacher Education and Social Change." *Paidonomia* 16(2):27-38.

OAU. 1992, November 25-27. *Africa' s Children, Africa' s Future: Human Investment Priorities for the 1990s*. Background Sectoral Paper presented at the International Conference on Assistance to African Children, Dakar, Senegal.

Obiakor, F. E. 1992. "Education in Nigeria: A Critical Analysis." *International Education* 21(2):55-66.

"Occupational Hazards." 1994. *Tribute Magazine* (September):66-103.

Ogbu, J. U. 1992. "Understanding Cultural Diversity and Learning." *Educational Researcher* 21(8):5-14.

Okafor, V. O. 1992. "A Reevaluation of African Education." *Journal of Black Studies* 22(4):579-92.

"One, 6-M Black Children Not in School." 1994. *This Week in South Africa* 5(27):3-4.

"Operation Date for Education Departments Set." 1994. *This Week in South Africa* 5(31):6.

Oyiborhoro, J. M. A. 1984. "The Concept of Special Education and Implications for Teacher Education in Nigeria." *International Education* 14(1):38-43.

Pampallis, J. 1991. *Foundations of the New South Africa*. London, England: Zed Books Ltd.

Parsons, N. 1993. *A New History of Southern Africa*. 2nd ed. London, England: Macmillan.

Peirce, B. N. 1989. "Toward a Pedagogy of Possibility in the Teaching of English Internationally: People's English in South Africa." *TESOL Quarterly* 23(3):401-20.

Penny, A., S. Appel, J. Gultig, K. Harley, and R. Muir. 1993. "Just Sort of Fumbling in the Dark: A Case Study of the Advent of Racial Integration in South African Schools." *Comparative Education Review* 37(4):412-33.

Peresuh, M. 1994. "The Role of African Universities in Promoting Special Education Programs in Higher Institutions." *International Journal of Special Education* 9(3):224-31.

Perren, G. E. 1969. "Education Through a Second Language: An African Dilemma." In *Education in Africa: Research and Action*, edited by R. Jolly, 197-207. Nairobi, Kenya, East Africa: English Press Ltd.

Phillipson, R. 1992. *Linguistic Imperialism*. Oxford, England: Oxford University Press.

Pillay, P. 1992. "Financing Educational Transformation in South Africa." In *Education in a Future South Africa: Policy Issues for Transformation*, edited by E. Unterhalter, H. Wolpe, and T. Botha, 98-111. Trenton, New Jersey: Africa World Press.

"Plan for Nonracial Education Unveiled." 1993. *Focus on South Africa* (February):6.

Possi, M. K. 1994. "Special Education in Tanzania: A Critical Analysis of Special Education Services." *International Journal of Special Education* 9(1):41-52.

Poth, J. 1980. *National Languages and Teacher Training: A Methodological Guide for the Use of Teacher Institute.* Paris, France: The UNESCO Press.

Powell, A. D. 1994. "Race and Class." *The Progressive* 58(7):5.

Qirbi, A. 1993. "Poverty and Handicap in the Republic of Yemen." *The View Finder: Division of International Special Education and Services* 2:12-16.

"R30bn in Reserves Needed Before Exchange Controls Can Be Scrapped." 1994. *This Week in South Africa* 5(38):5.

Ralekhetho, M. 1991. "The Black University in South Africa: Ideological Captive or Transformative Agent?" In *Knowledge and Power in South Africa: Critical Perspectives Across the Disciplines*, edited by J. D. Jansen, 101-10. Johannesburg, South Africa: Skottaville Publishers.

Ramphele, M. 1990. "Women and Rural Development: The Debate About Appropriate Strategies." *SAGE* 7(1):9-12.

Redding, S. 1993. "Legal Minors and Social Children: Rural African Women and Taxation in the Transkei, South Africa." *African Studies Review* 36(3):49-74.

Regehr, E. 1979. *Perceptions of Apartheid: Churches and Political Change in South Africa.* Scottdale, Pennsylvania: Herald Press.

Riley, D. 1995. "Cultural Diversity: What Is Its Meaning Today?" *The Utah Special Educator* 15(4):4.

Roberts, C. 1956. *An English-Zulu Dictionary.* London, England: Routledge and Kegan Paul LTD.

Rubagumya, C. M. 1990. *Language in Education in Africa: A Tanzanian Perspective.* Clevedon, England: Multilingual Matters LTD.

Rubagumya, C. M. 1991. "Language Promotion for Educational Purposes: The Example of Tanzania." *International Review of Education* 37(1):67-85.

Rugemalira, J. M., C. M. Rubagumya, M. K. Kapinga, A. F. Lwaitama, and J. G. Tetlow. 1990. "Reflections On Recent Developments in Language Policy in Tanzania." In *Language in Africa*, edited by C. M. Rubagumya, 25-35. Philadelphia, Pennsylvania: Multilingual Matters LTD.
Sachs, A. 1990. "Judges and Gender." *Tribute Magazine* (August):36-42.
Saleh, L. 1992. "UNESCO and Special Education: New Initiatives To Match New Thinking." *The Viewfinder: Expanding Boundaries and Perspectives in Special Education DISES* 1:4-7.
Salt, J., and M. H. B. Salt. 1983. *Zimbabwe: A Handbook*. Harare, Zimbabwe, South Africa: Mercury Press Ltd.
Samoff, J. 1993. "The Reconstruction of Schooling in Africa." *Comparative Education Review* 37(2):181-222.
Sandoval, A. 1995. "The Changing Faces of Education." *The Utah Special Educator* 15(4):3.
Satyo, S. C. 1988, August 24. *The Apartheid Context of African Language Studies* (Inaugural Lecture), University of Cape Town, South Africa.
Schadeberg, J. 1990. *Nelson Mandela and the Rise of ANC*. Johannesburg, South Africa: The Penrose Press.
Scheepers, J. 1991. "Stop Pointing Fingers." *Tribute Magazine* (May):6-7.
Schoeman, H. S. 1981. "Education and Training in Multicultural Societies." *Africa Insight* 11(2):128-32.
"School Lessons Remain Unlearned." 1995. *Sunday Times* (September 3):26.
Schrire, R. 1991. *Adapt or Die: The End of White Politics in South Africa* (South Africa Update Series). Washington, DC: Ford Foundation, Foreign Policy Association.
Sebidi, L. 1992. "Towards the En-Enfleshment of a Dynamic Idea: People' s Education." *Focus on Education* 1(1):32-41.
Seedat, A. 1984. *Crippling a Nation: Health in Apartheid South Africa*. London, England: IDAF.
Seipel, M. M. O. 1994. "Disability: An Emerging Global Challenge." *International Social Work* 37(2):165-78.
September, R. T. 1990. "How Does It Work and Who Benefits? The Distribution of Scientific Knowledge in South Africa." *International Review of Education* 34(4):469-84.

Sherman, M. A. B. 1990. "The University in Modern Africa: Toward the Twenty-First Century." *Journal of Higher Education* 61(4):363-85.

Simon, A. 1991. "Reasons Provided by Black Pupils in the Rural Mahlabatini Area in Natal Province, South Africa, for Poor Academic Performance in Black Secondary Schools." *Journal of Negro Education* 60(4):581-92.

Sithole, E. 1991. "Education in the New South Africa." *SASPOST* 2(4):1-7.

Skuy, M., and H. Partington. 1990. "Special Education in South Africa." *International Journal of Disability* 37(2):149-57.

Slammert, L. 1991. "Rethinking Mathematical Knowledge: The Quest for People' s Mathematics in South Africa." In *Knowledge and Power in South Africa: Critical Perspectives Across the Disciplines*, edited by J. D. Jansen, 203-12. Johannesburg, South Africa: Skottaville Publishers.

Smith, D. E. 1991. "Understanding Some Behaviors of Culturally Different Children." *International Education* 21(1):31-40.

Smith, D. M. 1992. *The Apartheid City and Beyond: Urbanization and Social Change in South Africa*. London, England: Routledge.

Sonn, R. A. 1994. "The Teacher' s Role: A Sociological Analysis." *Educamus* 40(1):21-23.

"South Africa: Between Two Worlds." 1993. *The Economist* 326(7803):1-25.

"South Africa Unschooled." 1990. *The Economist* 314(7638):45-46.

South African Bureau of Racial Affairs. 1955. *Bantu Education: Oppression or Opportunity*? Stellenbosch, South Africa: South African Bureau of Racial Affairs.

"South African Economy Is Key To Future of the Country." 1994. *Deseret News* (May 10-11):A12.

South African Institute of Race Relations. 1994. *1990 Race Relations Survey*. Johannesburg, South Africa: South African Institute of Race Relations.

"Soweto Schools Chaos." 1994. *This Week in South Africa* (September 6-12):6.

Stairs, A. 1994. "Indigenous Ways To Go To School: Exploring Many Visions." *Journal of Multilingual and Multicultural Development* 15(1):63-76.

Strenski, J. B. 1994. "Stress Diversity in Employee Communications." *Public Relations Journal* 50(7):32-35.
Stromquist, N. P. 1990. Women and Illiteracy: The Interplay of Gender Subordination and Poverty. *Comparative Education Review* 34(1):95-111.
Sure, K. 1991-92. "Language, Law and Pluralism in Kenya." *Africa Quarterly* 31(3-4):60-72.
Swarts, M. 1994. "African Solutions for African Problems." *In Focus, HSRC/RGN* 2(11):55-56.
Taylor, E. W. 1994. "The Need To Rethink Adult Education for Women in Tanzania." *International Higher Education* 23(2):30-45.
Taylor, R. 1991. "The Myth of Ethnic Division: Township Conflict On the Reef." *Race and Class* 33(2):1-14.
Terry, R. 1995. "Cultural Diversity: A Perspective From Rural Utah." *The Utah Special Educator* 15(4):9-10.
Texas Dropout Information Clearinghouse. 1989. *Successful Schooling for Economically Disadvantaged At-Risk Youth*. Austin, Texas: Texas Education Agency.
Thembela, A. J. 1993. "Effective Educational Models." *Paidonomia, Journal of the Faculty of Education, University of Zululand* 18(1):39-50.
Thompson, L. 1990. *A History of South Africa*. New Haven, Connecticut: Yale University Press.
Thompson, M. J. 1990. "Something More Than Color." *Tribute Magazine, South Africa*:58-62.
"Too Many Infants Die in South Africa-UNICEF." 1994. *This Week in South Africa* 5(27):7.
Trappes-Lomax, H. R. 1990. "Can a Foreign Language Be a National Medium?" In *Language in Education in Africa*, edited by C. M. Rubagumya, 94-104. Philadelphia, Pennsylvania: Multilingual Matters LTD.
Twala, C. 1994. "South Africans Should Mind Their Language." *Mayibuye: Journal of the ANC* 5(3):30-31.
Tygesen, P. 1991. "The ABCs of Apartheid." *Africa Report* 36(3):13-22.
Unterhalter, E., H. Wolpe, and T. Botha. 1992. *Education in a Future South Africa: Policy Issues for Transformation*. Trenton, New Jersey: Africa World Press.

Unterhalter, E., H. Wolpe, T. Botha, S. Badat, T. Dlamini, and B. Khotseng. 1991. *Apartheid Education and Popular Struggles*. London, England: Zed Books Ltd.

Urevbu, A. O. 1988. "Vocationalizing, the Secondary School Curriculum: The African Experience." *International Review of Education* 34(2):258-70.

Van Dyken, J. R. 1990. "The Role of Minority Groups for Literacy and Education in Africa." *African Studies Review* 33(3):39-52.

Van Hook, M. P. 1994. "Educational Challenges in Southern Africa: Implications for Social Work." *International Social Work* 37(4):319-31.

Van Vuuren, D. J., N. E. Wiehahn, J. A. Lombard, and N. J. Rhoodie. 1985. *South Africa: A Plural Society in Transition*. Durban, South Africa: Butterworth Publishers.

Van Zyl, C. 1995. "Mobilizing Research for a Just Education." *In Focus* 3(2):5-7.

Vergnani, L. 1993a. "Black Enrollment in South Africa Falls as Universities Exhaust Scholarship Funds." *The Chronicle of Higher Education* 39(30):A32-A33.

Vergnani, L. 1993b. "South Africa Boosts University Support, But Financial Crisis Continues." *The Chronicle of Higher Education* 39(30):A39.

Waldman, A. 1993. "Suffer Disabled Children." *Tribute Magazine* (October):86-91.

Walker, C. 1990. *Women and Gender in South Africa to 1945*. Cape Town, South Africa: Clyson Printers.

Walker, M. 1992. "Transforming Teaching in Primary Education: A Project for Development and Democracy." In *Education in a Future South Africa*, edited by E. Unterhalter, H. Wolpe, and T. Botha, 200-20. Trenton, New Jersey: Africa World Press.

Warner, R., Jr. 1974. "Research in Counseling: Consulting Parents." *Personnel and Guidance Journal* 53(1):68-70.

Watkins, W. H. 1990. "Teaching and Learning in the Black Colleges: A 130-Year Retrospective." *Teaching Education* 3(1):10-25.

Watson, R., J. Contreras, and J. Hammer. 1994. "Black Power." *Newsweek Magazine* (May 9):34-39.

Weiss, R. 1994. *Zimbabwe and the New Elite*. London, England: British Academic Press.

West, L. L. 1991. *Effective Strategies for Dropout Prevention of At-Risk Youth*. Gaithersburg, Maryland: An Aspen Publication.
"What National Language Should We Speak?" 1994. *Bona Magazine* (July):90-92.
Wheeler, D. L. 1994. "The Death of Any Language Diminishes the Store of Ideas of a Different Way of Looking at the World." *The Chronicle of Higher Education* (April 20):A8.
White, J. 1982. *The Aims of Education Restated*. London, England: Routledge and Kegan Paul.
Whittaker, S. 1991. "A Critical Historical Perspective on Psychology in Tanzania/South Africa." In *Knowledge and Power in South Africa*, edited by J. D. Jansen (Ed.), 55-68. Johannesburg, South Africa: Skottaville Publishers.
Williams, E. 1993. "First and Second Language Reading Proficiency of Year 3, 4 and 6 Children in Malawi and Zambia." *Reading in a Foreign Language* 10(1):915-29.
Williams, P. 1995. "Teen Mix." *Bona Magazine* (January):40-41.
Williams, W. E. 1989. *South Africa's War Against Capitalism*. New York: Praeger.
Wilson, F., and M. Ramphele. 1989. *Uprooting Poverty: The South African Challenge*. New York, New York: W. W. Norton and Company.
Woodhall, M. 1995. "Financial Diversification in Higher Education: A Review of International Experience and Implications for African Universities." *Higher Education Policy* 8(1):16-23.
Woodhouse, H. R. 1985. "Knowledge and Educational Dependency." *Interchange* 16(2):1-16.
Wren, C. S. 1992. "For Black Students in South Africa, Dismal Scores." *SASPOST* 4(1):9.
Yankah, K. 1995. "Displaced Academies and the Quest for a New World Academic Order." *Africa Today* 42(3):7-25.
Yoloye, E. A. 1986. "The Relevance of Educational Content to National Needs in Africa." *International Review of Education* 32(2):149-72.

Index

Absenteeism 30, 52, 53, 166
Academic .... xiii, xv, 17, 20-22, 26,
28, 29, 31-33, 35, 39, 55, 68,
108, 110, 119, 127, 128-130,
132, 151-153, 157, 162, 166,
176, 188, 191, 195, 204, 206,
207
Academics 21, 58, 70, 83, 201
Accountability 169
Act 5, 8, 29, 144, 196, 219, 220,
226
Admission 10, 14, 17, 119, 220
Adult .... xvii, 21, 60, 63, 65-74, 80,
129, 143, 155, 166, 169, 198,
199, 201, 202
Africa .... x, xi, xii, xiii, xiv, xv, xvi, xvii,
xviii, xix, 2-5, 8-15, 18-30,
32-34, 36-39, 41, 42-58, 61,
62, 65-69, 71-73, 75, 76,
77-97, 99-113, 115-123, 125,
126, 132, 133, 135-139, 141,
142, 144, 145, 147-153, 155,
157-162, 165-168, 170, 173,
175, 176, 177-180, 183-193,
197-201, 203, 204-221,
224-228

African .... x, xi, xii, xiii, xiv, xvi, xvii,
xviii, 3-6, 8, 9-11, 14-20,
22-44, 46, 47, 49-55, 58, 60,
61, 67, 69-71, 76-80, 82-86,
89-93, 95, 96, 99-113,
115-118, 120-123, 125-131,
133, 135-144, 149-152, 154,
159-161, 167-170, 173-180,
183, 184, 186, 188-192, 196,
197, 199, 200-213, 215-217,
219, 220, 223, 224-228
Africanization 200
Africans .... x, xi, xii, xiii, xiv, xvi, xvii,
xviii, xix, 2, 3-6, 10, 12, 15,
17-19, 21-28, 32, 35, 38, 44,
46, 49-52, 55, 58, 62, 66, 67,
75-83, 86, 88, 91-97, 99, 101,
102, 103, 105, 107-112, 115,
116, 118, 119, 122-126, 128,
131, 133, 139, 150-152, 155,
158, 159, 161, 162, 165, 167,
169, 170, 173-178, 180, 184,
186-188, 191, 193, 197, 202,
203, 205, 210-215, 217, 221,
223-228
Afrikaans 19, 91, 99-101, 103, 106,
110, 120, 124, 151, 220
Afrikaners 120, 211, 226
Albinism 77
American 5, 103, 215
Andrew Mellon 215
Angola 205, 208
Apartheid .... x, xi, xii, xiii, xiv, 8, 15,
18, 20, 23, 24, 34, 36, 41, 45,
48, 67, 70, 110, 118, 119,
122, 124, 128, 130, 136, 137,
138, 151, 159, 161, 162, 177,
209, 210, 211, 214, 216, 217,
223, 224, 225, 226, 228
Australia 197, 215

Index 253

Autism 76, 88
Backwardness 123
Banda 209
Bantu .... xi, xii, xiii, xiv, xvi, xvii, xviii,
2, 4-9, 12, 18, 22, 32, 33, 35,
48, 50, 57, 118-120, 122, 124,
147, 148, 150, 151, 165, 169,
170, 174, 175, 183, 212, 214,
216, 217, 219, 220, 224,
225-227
Bantus 224
Basketry 67
Berlin 5
Black .... xi, xii, xiii, xiv, xvi, xvii, xviii,
xix, 2-15, 18-21, 23-32, 34-60,
62, 63, 75, 76, 79-86, 89-91,
93-97, 99, 101-110, 112,
116-133, 135-145, 147,
148-157, 159, 160, 162, 165,
166, 167, 168, 170, 173-176,
178, 180, 181, 185, 192, 196,
197, 209, 210, 214-217, 220,
221, 224, 225, 228
Black teachers 19, 27-30, 34-43,
46-48, 53, 58, 62, 89, 95, 109,
121, 153, 154, 167, 170, 197,
214
Black universities .... xvii, 86, 117-133,
220
Blacks .... xii, xiii, xix, 2-10, 12, 14, 18,
26-29, 34, 36, 41, 43, 44, 46,
50-52, 56, 57, 60, 61, 65, 75,
76, 78, 79, 80, 81, 84, 90,
101, 103, 104, 109, 110, 118,
121-123, 125, 133, 136, 139,
143, 148-152, 155, 159, 160,
161, 166, 168, 170, 175, 181,
192, 196, 209, 210, 219, 220,
224, 225, 228
Blindness 77, 79, 228

Bophuthatswana 119, 120, 220,
                                           226, 227
Bosele 83
Botswana 178, 203
Boycotts 4, 28, 31
Britain 197, 199
Bursaries 176
Canada 197, 215
Capitalism 208, 209
Carnegie 215
Catholic 77
Cerebral palsy 76, 77, 88
China 205
Christian civilization 123
Ciskei 226, 227
Cities 19, 72, 83, 94, 227, 228
Citizenship 123, 149, 225-227
Colleges .... xiii, xviii, 7, 26, 30, 35-37,
                              42, 43, 47, 86, 133, 136, 221
Colonialism 4, 123, 138, 184, 212
Coloreds .... xi, 10, 14, 27, 44, 51, 52,
                                67, 80, 88, 120, 122, 181,
                                                 223-225
Communal 3, 7, 193
Community .... xvii, 3, 5-7, 13, 22,
                              24-26, 32, 35, 37, 45, 47, 55,
                              57-61, 67, 70-72, 74, 76, 79,
                              81, 84, 90, 95, 96, 106, 114,
                              115, 125, 128-130, 133, 138,
                              139, 141, 142, 144, 155-157,
                              161, 166, 175, 176, 178, 179,
                              187, 194, 196, 200, 210, 211,
                                               215, 217, 220
Comprehensive .... xvi, 2, 168, 200
Compulsory 9, 11, 14, 40, 43, 44,
                              49-51, 56, 58, 78, 96, 128,
                              168, 175, 176, 192-194, 200,
                                                  220, 221
Congress 11, 122, 211

Conservative 78, 122, 124, 170, 211
Constitution 43, 221, 226, 228
Creativity 12, 28, 37, 38, 46, 102, 124, 130, 154
Crisis 5, 47, 53, 133, 186
Culture .... xi, xvii, 3, 10, 12, 13, 23, 31, 38, 39, 65, 73, 89, 92, 103, 106, 109, 111, 113, 116, 123, 131, 150, 152, 156, 158, 160-162, 165, 188, 203, 212, 214
Curricula 9, 18-20, 25, 47, 121-123, 132, 147, 152, 153, 168, 195
Curriculum .... xvii, 2, 5-8, 11, 12, 18-26, 32, 33, 35, 36, 37, 39, 42, 45-47, 52, 60, 61, 66, 68, 89, 115, 119, 121, 124, 128, 130, 131, 150-154, 156, 160-162, 167, 186, 195, 200, 201, 203, 204, 205, 214
Deafness 77
Democracy 105, 115, 126, 137, 209, 211, 217, 218
Democratic .... x, xi, 10, 30, 31, 47, 61, 63, 96, 128, 138, 150, 169, 216, 221, 228
Demographic xix
Departments 10, 14, 15, 18, 152, 165, 190, 196, 221
Desegregation 11, 170, 196, 197
Disabilities 55, 75-97, 125, 169
Discipline 30, 52-54, 155, 158, 162
Discrimination .... x, xvii, 10, 11, 23, 28, 75, 100, 138, 139, 140, 143, 158, 160-162, 169, 196, 223, 228
Diseases 61, 93, 94, 133

Diversity .... xviii, 10, 32, 115, 127,
157-162, 203
Dominican 76, 77, 85
Dropout rate 20, 49-51, 57-59, 62,
143
Durban 119, 120, 220
Dutch Reformed churches 77
Economy 2, 5, 6, 8, 9, 11, 50, 57,
65, 101, 118, 123, 150, 177,
180, 192, 208, 209, 215, 217,
226, 227
Education .... x, xi, xii, xiii, xiv, xv, xvi,
xvii, xviii, xix, 2-16, 18-27,
29-37, 39-53, 55-63, 65-83,
85-97, 99, 101-103, 107-109,
113, 117-120, 122, 123-126,
128-131, 133, 135, 136, 137,
138, 140-145, 147-153,
155-162, 165-170, 173-181,
183-188, 190-208, 210-217,
219-221, 225
Elitism 196
Employment 6, 7, 21, 22, 41, 42,
80, 82, 95, 116, 139, 179,
191, 193-195, 207, 212, 213,
216, 228
Empowerment 47, 70, 140, 144,
215
English 7, 19, 28, 38, 67, 69, 91,
99-110, 112, 113, 115, 120,
124, 126, 151, 186, 197, 201,
202, 204, 205, 211, 226
Enrollment 11, 43, 50, 120, 133,
176, 193, 196, 199
Entrepreneurship 213
Epilepsy 76, 88
Equal 9, 12, 45, 58, 96, 97, 102,
104, 110, 128, 136, 167, 168,
199, 220

Equality	xvii, 102, 103, 122, 137, 145, 168, 199, 207
Ethembeni	86, 87
Ethiopia	205, 209
Ethnicism	205
Ethnolinguistic	224
Europe	20, 150, 160, 205, 208, 224
European	4, 7, 105, 110, 121, 123, 160, 184, 196, 200, 204, 205, 212, 213, 215, 226
Examinations	2, 16, 17, 20-22, 26-30, 42, 124, 186, 195
Expenditure	14, 43, 44, 81, 174, 177, 192
Ezibeleni	87
Faculty	59, 126, 127, 133
Family	xv, 3, 28, 31, 32, 52, 55, 56, 59, 61, 68, 138, 139, 141, 142, 188, 192, 224, 228
Farms	139
Film	72-74
Finances	68, 156, 167, 168, 173, 199
Ford	215
Foreign	23, 26, 38, 45, 50, 69, 94, 101, 103, 104, 106, 108, 109, 111, 112, 116, 129, 177, 180, 184, 186, 187, 189, 198, 201, 204-207, 209, 211, 213, 214, 215, 217, 218, 227
Formal	4, 14, 19, 20, 22-24, 29, 63, 81, 83, 85, 95, 142, 149, 169, 198, 204, 207
Fort Hare	118, 120, 219
Foundation	18, 19, 45, 58, 66-68, 74, 105, 113, 131, 133, 165, 169, 190, 213, 215, 216
Freedom	6, 55, 109, 119, 126, 127, 132, 168, 169, 189, 211, 223

French 104, 204, 205
Future .... x, xvii, xviii, 9, 10, 12, 19,
21-24, 33, 41, 45, 49, 57, 60,
61, 63, 75, 78, 93, 96, 97,
104-106, 108, 110, 111, 112,
113, 117, 128, 130, 132, 142,
145, 147, 148, 152, 153, 161,
162, 167, 177, 199, 208, 209,
211, 215, 216, 217
Gazankulu 226
Gender .... x, xvii, 21, 135-140,
142-144
Genesis 215
Geography 20, 52, 123, 126, 153,
200, 202, 203
Ghana 203
Girls 4, 51, 55, 56, 136, 138, 142,
143, 155, 192
Glasgow 5
Government .... xiii, xvi, xvii, 4-6, 9,
12-15, 33, 34, 43, 44-46, 56,
57, 59, 61, 73, 76, 91, 94, 96,
101, 113, 114, 118, 120, 121,
126, 127, 128, 130, 132, 139,
145, 166, 169, 170, 173, 174,
176, 177, 179, 180, 181, 186,
190, 192-199, 208, 211, 216,
219-221, 223, 226, 227
Guinea 203
Harambee 178
Harding 87
History .... x, xiii, xvi, xvii, 18, 20, 22,
23, 57, 70, 71, 76-78, 102,
103, 106, 107, 110, 116, 117,
123, 150, 152, 153, 157,
160-162, 195, 200, 202, 203,
208, 212, 214, 216, 219
Homelands 34, 84, 139, 226-228
Housing 113, 176

Index 259

Illiteracy 9, 37, 65-67, 71, 72, 101,
129, 136, 143, 155, 169, 202
Incentives 58, 143, 181, 188, 189
Indaleni 85
Independence .... xviii, 6, 8, 24, 103,
108, 178, 180, 183, 184, 185,
187, 191-203, 206, 208, 210,
216, 226, 227
Indians .... xi, 10, 14, 27, 44, 51, 67,
80, 88, 120, 122, 197,
223-225
Indigenous 2, 3, 33, 93, 101-103,
105, 109, 111, 112, 114-116,
152, 169, 178, 205, 212, 213,
224, 225
Industrial 45, 195, 226, 227
Industries 210
Influx 175, 228
Informal 2, 4, 79, 155
Inkatha 211
Innovative .... xii, xviii, 2, 19, 21, 32,
36-38, 41, 42, 47, 58, 75, 115,
117, 126, 131, 154, 169, 214,
217
Institute 14, 120
Integration 11-13, 18, 44, 45, 115,
128, 154, 161, 165, 196, 221
Intellectuals 6, 118, 125, 133, 187,
188, 191
International 27, 45, 47, 67, 103,
117, 152, 153, 189, 201, 203,
209, 215
Japan 205, 215
Jobs 6, 7, 20, 42, 71, 81, 121,
124, 129, 131, 140, 151, 166,
195, 208, 212, 213, 223, 227,
228
Johannesburg 41, 44, 120
Joint 2, 131

Junior 15-17, 26, 34, 35, 43, 51,
121, 138
Kenya 178
Khanyisa 86
Kingdoms 203
Kiswahili 201, 202
Korea 205
KwaDingane 85
KwaThintwa 85
Kwazamokuhle 87
Land 52, 123, 130, 137, 139, 142,
201, 213, 216, 225, 226, 228
Languages .... xvii, 5, 10, 19, 20, 24,
70, 73, 89, 91, 93, 99-116,
121, 125, 150-152, 158, 160,
167, 169, 197, 198, 202, 204,
205, 207, 212, 221, 224, 225
Laws .... xvii, 49, 94, 135-138, 140,
144, 149, 166, 209, 213, 217,
227, 228
Lebowa 226
Legislation 13, 60, 81, 82, 92, 94,
143, 165, 221
Libraries 23, 26, 29, 57, 72, 73,
109, 112, 126, 157, 208
Literacy 20, 33, 49, 51, 65-67, 69,
71-74, 105, 108, 142, 143,
151, 185, 202
Loans 73, 176, 177, 201
London 5, 122
Lonwabo 87
Lutheran 77
Malawi 203, 209
Malay 119, 220
Mali 203
Mandela .... x, 18, 216
Marxist 209
Matriculants 9

Medium	7, 19, 33, 101-103, 105, 108, 112, 113, 120, 186, 197, 201
Medunsa	119, 120, 220
Middleburg	84
Migrant	139, 228
Missionaries	5, 76
Models	13, 37, 58, 66, 138, 143, 156, 184, 189, 206, 208, 212-214
Moravian	5
Mother tongue	7, 19, 28, 38, 69, 70, 99, 101-103, 112, 186
Mozambique	208
Multilingualism	99
Multiracial	218
Natal	15, 81, 119, 225, 226
National	xix, 8, 10, 15, 24, 25, 45, 56, 57, 59, 62, 79, 83, 88, 104-107, 109, 113, 115, 117, 119-121, 137, 152, 153, 160, 170, 177, 180, 188, 189, 199, 201, 205, 210, 211, 215, 216, 221, 225-227
Native	5, 7, 109, 175
Ndebele	5, 41, 99, 100, 197, 224, 226
New South	xviii, 39, 44, 58, 97, 101, 104, 113, 141, 173
Newspaper	73, 157, 161
Nguni	5
Nigeria	33, 178, 185-189, 191
Noluthando	85
Nonracialism	228
Nyerere	130, 132
Oppression	135, 140, 158, 216
Oral	3, 23, 112
Orange Free State	15, 122, 225
Organizations	11, 14, 68, 76, 77, 175, 215, 220

Paralysis 79
Parents 11, 13, 14, 19, 21, 25, 28,
31, 32, 40, 45, 46, 48, 49, 51,
53-56, 58-61, 77, 78, 81-83,
90, 92-97, 101, 114, 136, 141,
143, 148, 149, 155, 156, 158,
162, 166, 168, 170, 174, 175,
177, 186, 187, 192, 196, 197,
204, 214, 217
Paris 5
Pedi 224
Philanthropic 76, 77
Philip Kushlick 87
Physicians 80, 94, 157
Pietermaritzburg 84
Policy .... xi, xvii, 7, 30, 41, 43, 45, 46,
63, 67, 69, 91, 99, 101, 102,
104-107, 113-116, 124, 128,
139, 169, 170, 178, 187, 190,
199, 205, 207, 214, 215, 224,
227
Polio 93
Population .... x, xiii, xvi, xviii, 2, 6, 9,
10, 14, 37, 41, 44, 52, 61, 65,
66, 72, 74, 78, 81, 83, 89, 92,
96, 99-101, 111, 123, 128,
152, 159, 162, 175, 180, 181,
194, 195, 199, 202, 205, 207,
210, 211, 212, 214, 216, 217,
224, 225, 227
Postapartheid .... xii, xiii, xiv, xvi, xvii,
xviii, xix, 9, 10, 18, 19, 22, 25,
32, 47, 54, 66, 99, 100, 108,
113, 116, 125, 147, 148, 150,
151, 152, 155, 159, 166, 167,
170, 174, 213-217
Poverty 18, 28, 31, 33, 37, 52, 55,
56, 61, 62, 65, 78-80, 130,
133, 138, 143, 149, 165, 173,
180, 206, 211, 214, 216, 218

Index 263

Presbyterian 77
Preschool 112
Pretoria 15, 85-88, 227
Primary 9, 14-17, 19, 20, 26, 34,
35, 42, 43, 51, 61, 66, 93,
102, 103, 105, 109, 113, 131,
136, 152, 158, 162, 167, 174,
175, 176, 178, 180, 185, 186,
193, 194, 198-203, 206, 225
Private 10, 12-14, 33, 58, 60, 71,
91, 96, 128, 132, 168,
175-177, 179, 180, 186, 189,
194, 196, 197, 201, 208, 215,
218, 228
Productivity 29, 66, 72, 111, 114,
126, 142, 188
Professional 39, 40, 73, 81, 129,
131, 132, 148, 151, 157, 187,
207
Propaganda 226
Provincialization 15, 168
Qualifications 5
Quality . . . . xii, xiii, xviii, 9-14, 32, 34,
36-38, 40, 41, 42, 44-47, 57,
65, 66, 72, 74, 92, 96, 97,
117, 119, 122, 127-132, 147,
148, 149, 150, 154, 155, 160,
165-170, 173, 176, 179, 180,
184, 194, 199, 202, 203, 207,
216, 217
Quantity 167, 184, 202
Qwa-qwa 220, 226
Race . . . . x, 2, 5, 10, 13, 14, 21, 27,
51, 57, 105, 119, 120, 123,
135, 137, 140, 149, 161, 165,
169, 196, 212, 219, 220, 223,
224, 228

Racial .... x, 3, 4, 6, 8, 10, 13, 14, 23,
26, 34, 35, 44, 51, 57, 60, 61,
63, 76, 78, 82, 86, 92, 123,
128, 133, 136, 140, 149, 151,
157-161, 170, 180, 219, 223,
224-226, 228
Radio 71-74, 154, 157, 161
Reform .... xviii, 33, 46, 59, 96, 133,
142, 192, 196, 199, 205, 210,
217
Religion .... xvii, 3, 10, 57, 109, 123,
169
Research .... xi, 25, 36, 40, 49, 55, 59,
61, 62, 78, 87, 88, 92, 93, 96,
97, 114, 116, 121, 122,
124-127, 129, 131-133, 140,
152, 156, 188-191, 202, 203,
206
Resources .... xi, xii, xv, 8, 14, 24, 27,
45, 54, 69, 75, 82, 84, 92, 96,
101, 112, 114, 115, 126, 128,
131, 133, 147, 166, 167, 168,
169, 173, 174, 178, 180, 188,
198, 201, 205, 214, 216
Responsibility .... xiii, xix, 18, 19, 25,
30, 33, 34, 48, 55, 60, 70, 81,
115, 128, 144, 149, 158, 162,
169, 174, 180, 185, 194, 208,
217, 221
Reuben Birin 85
Reunion 87
Rhenish 5
Rural 19, 22, 26, 42, 43, 56, 57,
72, 73, 79, 94, 105, 130, 139,
165, 173, 179, 194, 197, 200,
204, 207, 213, 214, 226, 227
Rwanda 205, 208, 209
Scandinavian 215

Schools .... xii, xiii, xvii, 3-15, 18-26,
28-32, 34, 35, 36-47, 49, 50,
52-61, 76-78, 82, 83, 84-87,
92, 93, 95, 101-103, 105, 106,
108, 109, 112, 114, 115, 127,
129, 133, 144, 147, 148,
150-155, 158, 159, 161, 162,
166, 167, 168, 170, 173-180,
184-186, 188, 191-194,
196-198, 200, 203, 207, 208,
214, 217, 221, 223
Self-employment 22, 207, 213
Self-reliant 71, 83, 89
Shangaan 99, 224
Shona 197
Sibonile 86
Siloe 86
Sizanani 85
Sizwile 85
Somalia 203, 205, 208, 209
Sotho 99, 100, 119, 219, 224, 225
South Africa .... x, xi, xii, xiii, xiv, xv,
xvi, xvii, xviii, xix, 2-5, 8-15,
18-30, 32-34, 36-39, 41-58,
61, 62, 65-67, 69, 71, 72, 73,
75-97, 99-113, 115-123, 125,
132, 133, 135-139, 141, 142,
144, 145, 147-153, 155,
157-162, 165, 166, 167, 168,
170, 173, 175-180, 183,
209-219, 221, 224-228
Soweto 14, 30, 175, 220
Specialists 26, 71, 84, 90, 92, 187
St. Martins 85

Students .... xiii, xviii, 4, 8, 11-13, 15,
17, 19-24, 26-34, 36-40, 42,
45, 46, 48, 49, 50, 53-63, 70,
71, 76, 77, 82, 84, 85, 86, 87,
89-92, 96, 101, 104, 106, 108,
109, 112-115, 117, 119, 123,
124, 125-133, 148-159, 161,
162, 165, 166, 169, 170, 176,
177, 179, 185, 186, 187, 190,
191, 193-198, 200, 202, 203,
206-208, 214, 217, 220
Sudan 205
Superstitious 87, 90, 94, 95
Swazis 226
Sweden 215
Taiwan 215
Tanzania 178, 199-204
Taxation 174-176
Taxes 174, 177, 208, 228
Teachers 2, 6, 7, 9, 16, 18-22, 24,
25, 27-30, 32, 33-48, 50, 53,
54, 56-60, 62, 68, 70, 71, 73,
78, 81, 82, 85, 86, 89, 90, 92,
95, 101, 102, 106, 108, 109,
111, 112, 114, 115, 119, 121,
124, 127, 128, 131, 136, 139,
141, 143, 144, 147, 148,
153-157, 161, 162, 166, 167,
169, 170, 173, 174, 178, 179,
185-187, 193-195, 197-199,
204, 207, 214, 217
Teaching .... xii, xvii, xviii, 6, 11, 12,
17, 19, 20, 22, 25-29, 32-42,
45-48, 50, 53, 57, 58, 66, 70,
71, 89, 91, 92, 102, 112, 117,
118, 119, 121, 124-133, 136,
138, 139, 147, 150, 153-159,
162, 165, 167, 168, 170, 175,
178, 180, 184, 195, 199, 205,
207, 214

Index

Television 71-73, 105, 154, 157, 161
Tembalethu 87
Textbooks 9, 18, 24, 25, 29, 32, 33, 37, 42, 60, 83, 91, 110, 112, 113, 131, 160, 161, 162, 175, 179, 180, 184, 188, 195, 203, 204, 207, 208
Third World 101, 107, 184, 202, 207, 209
Townships 13, 50, 119, 166, 197
Traditional 3-5, 7, 23, 82, 91, 92, 127, 136, 138, 143, 144, 156, 184
Training .... xviii, 3, 6-8, 13, 15-17, 19, 21, 22, 24, 25, 26, 29, 34-38, 40, 42, 43, 47, 51, 58, 62, 63, 70-72, 75, 82, 84-87, 89, 90, 92, 95, 96, 101, 120, 123, 124, 125, 131-133, 136, 142, 151, 152, 153, 166, 167, 169, 190, 191, 200, 204, 206, 207, 221
Transkei 34, 42, 43, 119, 120, 220, 226, 227
Transvaal 15, 77, 119, 225, 226
Tribalism 159, 210
Trichardt 84
Tshilidzini 84
Tsongas 225, 226
Tswanas 225, 226
Tswellang 87
Umlazi 119
Umtata 83
Unemployment 18, 21, 37, 80, 149, 166, 195, 198, 206, 207, 213
Unhygienic 80
Unitary 165, 167-169, 220, 221
United States 90, 212, 215

Universities .... xiii, xvii, 7, 15, 17, 30,
35, 86, 89, 92, 97, 117-133,
136, 151, 152, 189, 190, 191,
203, 219-221, 223
University .... xv, 14, 21, 52, 53, 71,
86, 88, 97, 114, 118-123, 126,
127, 130-133, 136, 157, 173,
179, 185, 188, 189, 190, 198,
219-221
Urbanization 79
Van Riebeeck 219
Venda 99, 100, 119, 219, 220,
224-227
Vereeniging 15
Vernacular 101, 107-110, 112-115,
125, 152, 169
Verwoerd 5, 226
Victimization 31, 125, 129, 130,
160
Violence 25, 31, 53, 54, 62, 79,
130, 133, 148, 155, 158, 166,
211, 217, 223
Vista 119
Vocational 3, 15, 21, 22, 60, 82,
84, 89, 151, 166, 200, 201,
206, 207
Wars 123, 208
Wesleyan 5
Western 4, 15, 22, 38, 52, 76, 94,
103, 114, 119, 120, 150, 159,
162, 187, 191, 201, 208, 209,
220, 225, 226
Western Cape 15, 52, 119, 120,
220, 225, 226
Western missionaries 76
Whites 7, 8, 10, 14, 27, 43, 44, 51,
52, 67, 79, 80, 88, 121-123,
133, 181, 192, 196, 197,
223-225
Witchcraft 95

Index

Women .... xvii, 68, 80, 135-145, 167, 180, 191
Workers 6, 8, 9, 33, 68, 71, 72, 90, 94, 114, 118, 142, 148, 161, 196, 227, 228
World .... x, xix, 2, 12, 20, 22, 24, 39, 41, 45, 48, 70, 74, 101, 103, 105, 107, 108, 110, 111-113, 122, 123, 126, 132, 137, 140, 141, 149-154, 170, 184, 187, 188-190, 198, 200, 202, 204, 207, 208, 209, 214-216, 220
Writers 101, 109, 112, 115, 116
Xhosa 5, 99, 100, 224, 225
Xhosas 225, 226
Yemen 208
Youth 41, 49, 50, 53-55, 57, 58, 60-63, 108, 149, 156, 158, 162, 166, 167, 189, 203
Youths 3, 8
Zaire 209
Zimbabwe 192-198
Zulu 5, 99, 100, 107, 119, 212, 220, 224, 225, 226
Zululand 119, 120, 220
Zulus 225, 226

About The Author

Zandile Nkabinde was born and raised in the Republic of South Africa. Currently, she is completing graduate studies in the Department of Special Education at the University of Utah. A graduate of Harvard University, she also has had experience as a high school teacher and a university lecturer. She is married and has two sons and one daughter. Writing educational articles and experimenting with writing children' s books in Zulu are Zandile' s life greatest pleasure.